Gardening with Prairie Plants

The prairie itself, though it once covered vast areas, is in many respects a small-featured, fine-textured community, so that it is possible to reproduce many—though certainly not all—of the attributes of a prairie in an area as small as an acre or even less.

WILLIAM R. JORDAN III

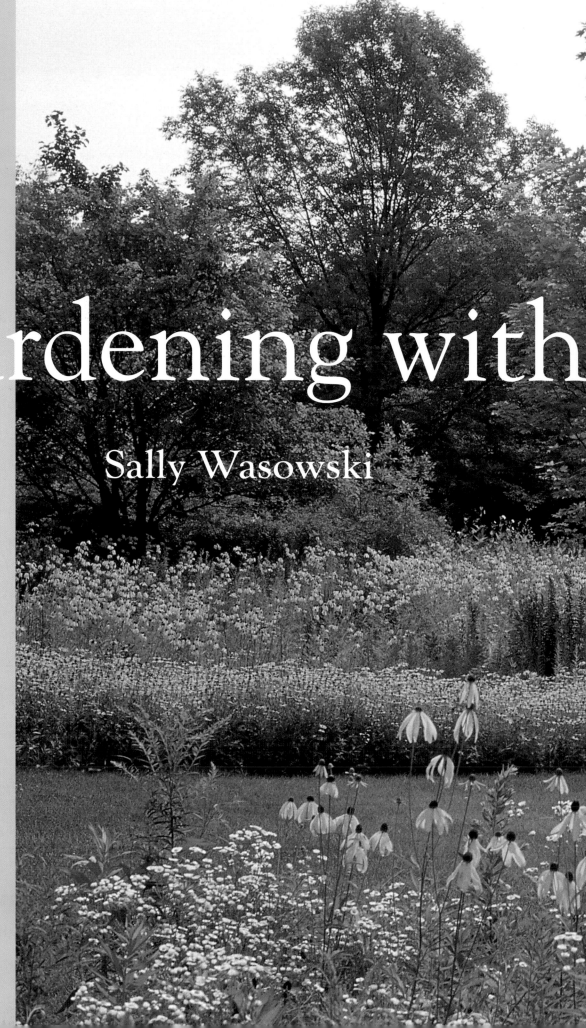

Gardening with

Sally Wasowski

HOW TO

CREATE

BEAULLIFUL

NATIVE

LANDSCAPES

Photography by

Andy Wasowski

UNIVERSITY OF
MINNESOTA PRESS

Minneapolis ■ London

Prairie Plants

The University of Minnesota Press gratefully acknowledges the generous assistance provided for the publication of this book by the Hamilton P. Traub University Press Fund.

Cover photograph: The Krueger prairie garden at this moment in midsummer is over five feet tall and dominated by many easy-care flowers in yellow and white. In the foreground, seeds of prairie flowers and grasses were broadcast over bare dirt twenty years ago by designer and restorationist Bob Ahrenhoerster. In the background, plugs were planted into an old field. What looks like a low border of blackeyed Susans is a new first-year planting from seed. Marsha and Dick Krueger. Mequon, Wisconsin. August 2, 1994.

Photograph on page iii: The slantface grasshopper has evolved to camouflage itself on the red and green stems of big bluestem in late summer. It is estimated that crickets and grasshoppers ate almost as much plant material as bison and elk. The grasshoppers, in turn, were eaten by prairie chickens and meadowlarks. Konza Prairie, Kansas. September 10.

Dedication photograph: Lorrie Otto, native garden advocate and founder of Wild Ones, pioneer in grassroots ecological protest, and recipient of the National Wildlife Federation's coveted Conservation Achievement Award for 1998, stands in her prairie garden amid pale purple coneflower, Ohio spiderwort, and white wild indigo. Milwaukee, Wisconsin. July 4, 1997.

Landscape drawings in the book are by Michael Parkey. Used with permission.

The photograph of J. E. Weaver and of his root drawing on page 68 are reproduced courtesy of James Stubbendieck, director, Center for Great Plains Studies.

The photographs by Benny Simpson on pages 237 and 238 are used with the permission of the Texas Agricultural Experiment Station. Copyright Texas Agricultural Experiment Station.

The maps in Part III are reproduced from the *Synthesis of North American Flora,* copyright 1999 by John T. Kartesz and Christopher A. Meacham, and are used with the permission of the Biota of North America Program of the North Carolina Botanical Garden.

Chapter 7 includes an excerpt from John T. Curtis, *The Vegetation of Wisconsin* (Madison: University of Wisconsin Press, 1959); reprinted by permission of the University of Wisconsin Press.

Printed in China by HK Scanner Arts International Ltd

LIBRARY OF CONGRESS CATALOGING-IN-PUBLICATION DATA

Wasowski, Sally, 1946–
    Gardening with prairie plants : how to create beautiful native landscapes / Sally Wasowski ;
    photography by Andy Wasowski.
        p. cm.
Includes bibliographical references (p.   ).
    ISBN 0-8166-3087-9 (pb : alk. paper)
    1. Prairie gardening. 2. Prairie plants. 3. Native plants for cultivation. I. Title.
SB434.3 .W37 2001
635.9'5177—dc21   00-013004

Published by the University of Minnesota Press
111 Third Avenue South, Suite 290
Minneapolis, MN 55401-2520
http://www.upress.umn.edu

Design and composition by Diane Gleba Hall

The University of Minnesota is an equal-opportunity educator and employer.

11 10 09 08 07 06 05 04 03   10 9 8 7 6 5 4 3 2

For Lorrie Otto, with love and admiration

Who made this prairie which man can't replicate? Was it a creator, a God who knit together such dizzying diversity and such awe inspiring beauty? Or did it all just evolve over millions and millions of years as fossil records seem to indicate? Either way! No matter! It is greater than a library, a school, a museum, a church. These small patches of old prairie are truly temples for all time for all of us. They are not to be traded for condos or money or for anything else. Never! Never!

LORRIE OTTO

Contents

Part III
PLANT PROFILES

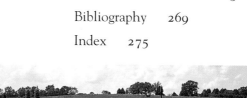

Acknowledgments

If you have never written a book, then you will probably not understand when we say that the acknowledgments are one of the hardest parts to write. You see, we began work on this book in 1994, and from that time until we finally mailed off the manuscript four and one-half years later, we have relied heavily on an army of people—from academics to homeowners—who were extremely generous with their time, knowledge, and encouragement. Imagine how terrible it would be if even one of those individuals somehow slipped through the proverbial crack and did not get listed here. It happens. And it keeps authors awake at night.

If somehow your name belongs here but was omitted, please know that this does not in any way reflect our gratitude, but means only that our filing system needs a lot of work. To you and all the others listed here, know that you have our sincere thanks. This book could not have happened without you.

Charlotte Adelman, Bob Ahrenhoerster, Steve Apfelbaum, Patricia Armstrong, Joel Asp, J. David and Margaret Bamberger, Richard Barloga, Keith and Gladys Barr, Martha Barrett, Char Bezanson, Devon Blean, C. Colston Burrell, Theresa Carter, Anne Charlton, Patricia Cooper, Chase Cornelius, Bill Davit, Neil Diboll, Richard Edlich, Bill Eisle, Milt Engelke, Amy Farstad, Al and Pat Fedkenheuer, Jim French, Shirley Froelich, Denise Gehring, Robin Gillispie, Nancy Goodman, Susan Gossman, Joe and Carol Harcarik, Lorna Harder, Nancy and Michael Hartrup, Deb Harwell, Mary and Dave Hendricks, Eileen and Don Herring, Carol Hesselton, Cindy Hildebrand, David Hillary, Jim Hodgins, and Nels Holmberg.

Pete Jensen, Lorraine Johnson, Marilyn Jordan, John Kartesz, Doris and Jim Kimball, Leah and Andy Knapp, Brent Knazan, Marsha Krueger, Dave Kropp, David Kun, Larry Lamb, Mollie and Garland Lasater, Mark Leach, Camille LeFevre, Rick Lehman, Susie Lehnhardt, Elizabeth Lofgren, Eileen Long, Pete Longbrake, Bob Lootens, Kenneth

McCarty, Roger Maddux, Karen Mathany, Helen McKean, John Morgan, Vincent Neglia, Bill Neiman, Dianne O'Connell, Paul Olsen, Lorrie Otto, Ken and Linda Parker, Randy and Janet Penner, Carol Piller, Mandy Ploch, Patricia Ploegsma, Glenn Pollack, Nancy Powell, Joyce Powers, Randy Powers, and Paul Pratt.

And Connie Ramthun, Bret Rappaport, Laura Rericha, Terry Riordan, Eileen Robb, Herbert and Eva Rosenberg, Gregg Ross, Ernie Rousek, Mike Rues, Ray Schulenberg, Shirley Shirley, Howard and Michele Snyder, David Sollenberger, Mary and Dick Stanley, Angie Stanton, James Stubbendieck, Andy Sudbrock, Kathy Taylor, Jeff Thompson, Gene Towne, Kim Tyson, John Ubelaker, Bob van Abel, Helen Vandenburg, William Volkert, Don Vorphal, Alan Wade, Dorothy Wade, Ann Wakeman, Wendy Walcott, Scott Weber, Rochelle Whiteman, Gerald Wilhelm, Mike Williams, Patty and Mike Wilson, Dave and Roselee Wondra, Scott Woodberry, Bob Zeremba, and Zile Zichmanis.

Special thanks to Constance Taylor of Durant, Oklahoma, and Floyd Swink of Wheaton, Illinois, for reading the manuscript and checking the slides for errors. Any errors that remain are ours.

This roster would not be complete without mentioning our hard-working and ever optimistic agent, Jeanne Fredericks, and our friend Beryl Schwartz, who typed the index. At the University of Minnesota Press, we would like to thank our editor Todd Orjala for his patience and good advice, and Laura Westlund, Amy Unger, Mary Keirstead, and Diane Hall for their dedication to painstaking detail. Without them, this book could not have been simultaneously beautiful and easy to use.

Introduction to a Prairie Garden

WHEN WE FIRST BEGAN working on this book, we contacted one of the many people on our list of experts to set up a research and photography visit. This person worked at a restored prairie and was extremely knowledgeable. His input would be invaluable. His first question was, "So, what's the purpose of this book?"

We replied that our book would not be another homage to the prairie. Many excellent books had already done that: *Grassland* by Richard Manning, *Where the Sky Began* by John Madson, and *Tallgrass Prairie* by John Madson and Frank Oberle, to name a few of the best. Instead, we wanted to go beyond merely exposing the general public to the beauty of prairie plants—we wanted to encourage them to actually *use* these plants in their home landscapes.

There was a five-second pause on the other end of the line. Then, "You want people to *landscape* with prairie plants?" he asked. "Why would anyone want to do that?"

Perhaps this question has crossed your mind as well. The first objection you might voice is that you do not live on a 100-acre estate. Prairies, after all, are vast, once reaching from horizon to horizon. In these pages, you will see homesites where more modest lot sizes were not an obstacle. And you will discover the many benefits of adopting a more natural landscape look and rejecting the conventional, well-manicured lawn-box hedge look that has turned America's neighborhoods into boring clones of one another.

If you live where prairie once existed, converting to a prairie garden makes sense for many reasons. It is perfectly suited to your locale and is easy to maintain. After all, the prairie existed for millennia without benefit of landscape crews and garden centers. A prairie landscape is also ecologically sound, requiring none of the water needed for

PATRICIA ARMSTRONG has successfully maintained a native habitat garden in suburbia since 1983. Tallgrass prairie shields her front door from a busy street. In early July, a hot dry time of the year, this area is vibrant with pale purple coneflower, Ohio spiderwort, and orange butterfly milkweed. In late July, the cool refreshing whites of Culver's root and rattlesnake master give a quiet, reflective quality. By late September, when this photo was taken, traditional autumn colors are provided by the gold of stiff goldenrod, the purple of asters, and the bright red fruits and leaves on the smooth sumac. The feeling of fall on the prairie is completed by the waving heads of Indiangrass and big bluestem. *View A.*

conventional, thirsty lawns. And the need for declaring chemical warfare on weeds and insect pests is virtually eliminated.

A natural prairie around your home is also a great learning experience. A prairie landscape will attract and sustain meadowlarks, butterflies, grasshoppers, toads, voles, and a host of other small animals—and in observing them you will learn and appreciate how they contribute to making all of nature work together in harmony. What a wonderful way to educate your children, renew your spirit after a hard day's work, and bring joy to all who take the time to observe its changes throughout the seasons.

A prairie landscape can also be eye-poppingly gorgeous!

Still, the idea of a prairie landscape is a radically new notion for most people, and you will have many questions. What exactly does one look like? How do you maintain it? And perhaps the concern that many of you will raise: how would a prairie garden fit into your conventionally landscaped neighborhood?

A prairie landscape defies that old rule—well over five generations old—that says a good neighbor must have a "perfect" lawn. It violates many weed ordinances, restrictions imposed by municipalities or neighborhood associations that mandate conformity and the perpetuation of the lawn-centered landscape. Happily, when challenged, these weed laws are usually overturned or revised to allow natural landscapes.

Here is a portrait of a successful prairie garden that uses native prairie plants in authentic combinations, and yet has peacefully existed in a typical Chicago suburb for more than fifteen years.

Patricia K. Armstrong, principal of Prairie Sun Consultants, is an ecologist, landscape designer, and popular lecturer on native plants. Practicing what she preaches, she has one of the finest and oldest home prairie gardens. She planted it on October 1, 1983, and it is now composed of approximately three hundred species, almost all local genotypes. A genotype is an individual plant that has evolved certain characteristics that make it especially well suited for its area. It may have traits such as exceptional cold hardiness or tolerance for drought or inundation, or it may develop distinctive coloring or markings that are especially attractive to local butterflies.

To get local genotypes, Patricia collected local seed by hand. While this method is still necessary for gardeners in most parts of the prairie regions, in southern Wisconsin,

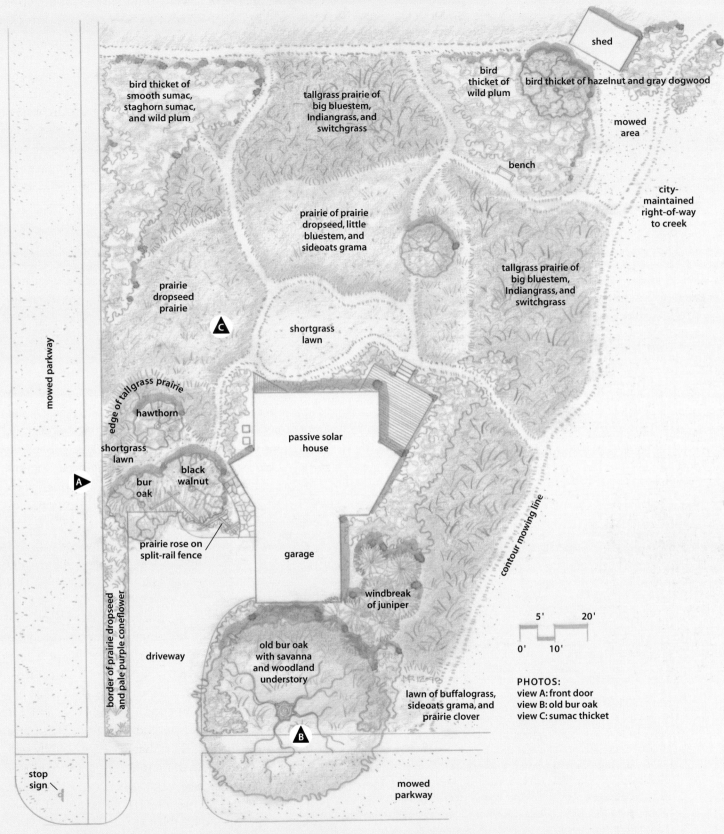

bird thicket of smooth sumac, staghorn sumac, and wild plum

tallgrass prairie of big bluestem, Indiangrass, and switchgrass

shed

bird thicket of wild plum

bird thicket of hazelnut and gray dogwood

mowed area

bench

city-maintained right-of-way to creek

prairie of prairie dropseed, little bluestem, and sideoats grama

tallgrass prairie of big bluestem, Indiangrass, and switchgrass

prairie dropseed prairie

C

shortgrass lawn

mowed parkway

edge of tallgrass prairie

hawthorn

shortgrass lawn

passive solar house

A

bur oak

black walnut

prairie rose on split-rail fence

garage

contour mowing line

windbreak of juniper

border of prairie dropseed and pale purple coneflower

driveway

old bur oak with savanna and woodland understory

lawn of buffalograss, sideoats grama, and prairie clover

5'   20'

0'   10'

PHOTOS:
view A: front door
view B: old bur oak
view C: sumac thicket

B

stop sign

mowed parkway

A PLAN OF PATRICIA'S GARDEN shows how she uses native species in natural combinations. Screening consists of bird thickets. Flower beds are tallgrass and prairie dropseed prairies. Shady ground covers are savanna and woodland flowers. The lawn areas are composed of shortgrass prairie. The color lasts for months.

Introduction to a Prairie Garden   XV

THE RESTORED AREA under the bur oak contains nearly one hundred indigenous savanna and woodland species. Yellow false sunflower and blue Drummond's aster (*Symphyotrichum drummondii* var. *drummondii*) are in bloom now, but earlier there were Virginia Bluebells (*Mertensia virginica*), blue phacelia (*Phacelia bipinnatifida*), yellow celandine poppy (*Stylophorum diphyllum*), white false rue anemone (*Enemion biternatum*), and bloodroot (*Sanguinaria canadensis*). The shrubs and small trees that screen this area from the driveway bloom to provide nectar and include witch hazel, arrowwood viburnum, and hazelnut. *September 23. View B.*

northeastern Illinois, southeastern Minnesota, Manitoba near Winnipeg, Iowa near Ames, and central Texas, nurseries exist that carry fifty to one hundred or more species of local seed and local seed-grown plants. And as interest in landscaping with native plants continues to grow, more such nurseries will open their doors to meet the market's needs.

The Armstrong garden occupies an average-sized corner lot in Naperville, a western Chicago suburb. When Patricia bought the lot, it was a farm field adorned with a venerable bur oak. In the early 1800s, savanna flowers and shrubs grew in the shade of that bur oak and gently blended into those prairie species growing in full sunshine. Patricia restored what she surmised might have originally been growing on her land, creating a shady savanna garden under the tree, and prairie everywhere else. She mows the parkway for safety and uses this space to play with a few non-native flowers.

Maintenance consists primarily of a burn around March 15 each year; she picks that time because the killdeers choose their nest sites in April. Before setting her fire, Patricia gets a permit from the Environmental Protection Agency and the local fire department; she invites the neighbors to watch, wanting to educate them as well as inspire them to try their own prairie landscapes. Next, she mows and rakes next to the house and around all the shrubs that grow there, getting rid of as much dry grass and dead twigs as possible. Then she lights a backfire where she mowed and raked, eliminating the remaining combustibles. This forms a fuel-free buffer zone that the main fire cannot cross.

Then she lights the main fire next to the thicket shrubs at the far end of the property. It takes a wind of 3 to 15 miles per hour to move the fire across the area to be burned. Ample water is always close at hand to take care of any unexpected and unwanted flare-ups.

A LARGE THICKET composed of smooth sumac and staghorn sumac hides the compost pile, a vegetable garden, and experimental beds. The lovely soft prairie in the foreground is dominated by knee-high prairie dropseed. *July 31. View C.*

Besides burning, there is a day or two of maintenance, usually in July, when Patricia cuts root sprouts to control prairie shrubs such as sumac, gray dogwood, and wild plum. A few transplants and seeds are added each year to keep diversity high. Patricia's two worst weeds—black medic and Kentucky bluegrass—are hand-weeded whenever they dare appear. In the fall, she mows to maintain contour lines, paths, and a firebreak, and to keep big bluestem from spreading into her buffalograss meadow.

Establishing the garden took three years. The site was originally covered with quackgrass and smooth brome, two perennial alien farm grasses deadly to prairie. Patricia plowed these under, exposing their roots to an Illinois winter. Luckily, it was cold enough that year to kill off most of these weeds. The same day she plowed, Patricia planted her prairie seed and let two short-lived non-natives—red clover and Queen Anne's lace—act as a cover crop to shade the ground and keep other weeds from germinating. Their seed was already present in the soil, and because they live only a season or two, they do not hurt a prairie. As the prairie seedlings began to appear, Patricia would stake them and weed around them. Where seedlings were far apart, she mowed.

By 1985, the garden was becoming very attractive. Patricia weeded periodically during the year and mowed nowhere, as desirable seedlings were thick. In 1986 she had her first burn. By 1988, when there was a severe drought in Chicago and lawns were dying left and right, her prairie garden was green and healthy.

PART ONE

Prairies and Prairie

I started with surprise and delight.
I was in the midst of a prairie!
A world of grass and flowers
stretched around me, rising and
falling in gentle undulations, as if
an enchanter had struck the ocean
swell, and it was at rest forever....
We passed whole acres of blossoms
all bearing one hue, as purple, perhaps, or masses of yellow or rose;
and then again a carpet of every
color intermixed, or narrow bands,
as if a rainbow had fallen upon
the verdant slopes. When the sun
flooded this Mosaic floor with light,
and the summer breeze stirred
among their leaves the iridescent
glow was as beautiful and won-
drous beyond anything I had ever
conceived.

ELIZA STEELE, near
Joliet, Illinois, in 1840, from
Summer Journey in the West

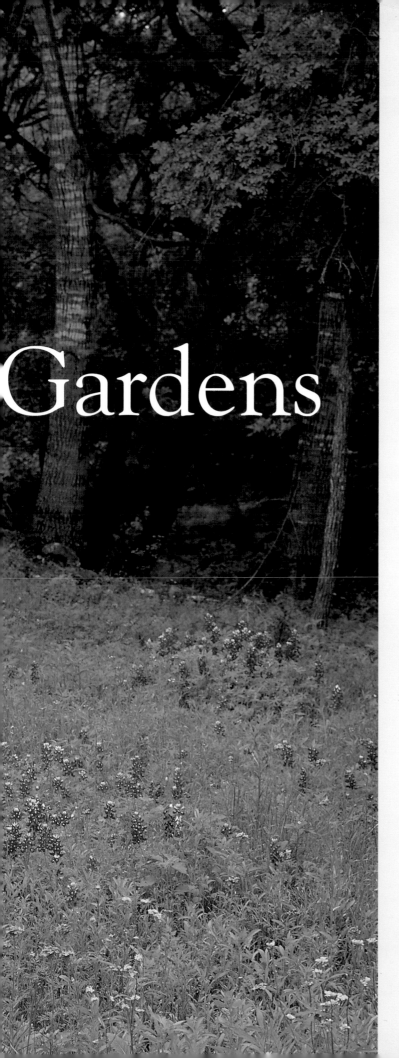

Gardens

THIS BOOK IS ABOUT HOW TO REPLICATE A PRAIRIE around your home, or business, or school. But before we can begin to do that, we need to understand what a prairie is. We may have a mental image of a prairie based on some old cowboy movie, or something we read in a book. Say "prairie," and we see vast expanses of grasses waving in the breeze.

But this is a simplistic image, not unlike trying to define an ocean as being just a lot of water—ignoring the currents, the varying degrees of salinity, and the countless forms of animal and vegetable life that are integral components.

A true prairie has many elements and aspects, and some understanding of how they fit together is necessary before you embark on creating one for yourself. For that matter, you cannot set out to make a prairie without realizing that there are many kinds. Which one is right for where you live?

As you read through this book, you may notice that most of the photography and helpful hints are derived from Wisconsin, Minnesota, and northeastern Illinois. That is because this is where prairie gardens and prairie restorations have been done successfully for two generations. But equally good work can be done everywhere prairie is indigenous. We hope that the examples here will inspire homeowners and professional landscapers alike to create prairie plantings all over North America.

THE PRAIRIES of North America are divided roughly into four quadrants. The east-west division is the 100th meridian. To the east are tallgrass prairies dominated by big bluestem, or upland prairies dominated by little bluestem or prairie dropseed. These prairies are bordered by oak savannas. To the west, where average rainfall is insufficient to sustain trees, there are vast stretches of plains dominated by knee-high little bluestem, needlegrasses, and grama grasses. The few trees that do exist are found only along creeks and rivers or on rocky breaks. The north-south division at the 39th parallel marks a line where the northern prairie and savanna species meet the southern ones. For example, prairie dropseed and prairie dock live north of this line, and eastern gamagrass and pitcher sage are south of it. The savannas bordering the western plains are aspen parklands in the north, ponderosa savannas on the edges of the Rockies, and juniper or mesquite savannas in the Southwest. Close to Mexico's uplands, oak and pine savannas again appear. Of course, nature did not use a straightedge to define these lines. Drought-tolerant plains species are nudged farther east of this line going south, because longer, hotter summers cause drier growing conditions. Likewise, Minnesota forbs are found in the mountain pastures of New Mexico.

Chapter 1

I will never forget my first visit to the prairies in Windsor, Ontario. Virtually every species was new to me. What intrigued me most was that little could be seen from the road, but once into the tall grasses, myriad colourful forbs were encountered. The prairie does not give up all of its secrets easily. Each year, with every change of season, the prairie is different—unpredictable—yet it never fails to impress.

LARRY LAMB, *University of Waterloo, Waterloo, Ontario*

Getting Acquainted with Prairies

PRAIRIE IS A TERM used to describe grasslands all over North America. Similar grasslands on other continents are called *llanos*, *pampas*, or *steppes*. *Prairie* was given to us by the French explorers of the Mississippi-Missouri River system. The word means "meadow," which seems a little inadequate to describe the vast stretches of grasslands that swept from the Mississippi River to the Rocky Mountains, covering one-fifth of the North American land mass north of Mexico.

Using the term *prairie* is something like using the term *automobile*. You get the general idea, but you miss those all-important specifics. Is it foreign or domestic? Is it a gas-hog or an economy model? In the same sense, saying "prairie" leaves an awful lot unsaid.

Here we will cover the basic types of prairies, and how they differ. You will use this information when you begin to create your own prairie landscape. For it to be successful, it will have to match as closely as possible the type of prairie that once existed where you live, or if conditions have changed, is now appropriate for your soil, water table, slope, and climate.

■ KEEPING IT SIMPLE

For the purposes of this book, *a prairie is a native grassland*. Where the native grasses are ankle-high to waist-high, the grassland is called a shortgrass prairie. A tallgrass prairie is where the native grasses are knee-high to head-high or more and are dominated by big bluestem, Indiangrass, switchgrass, or cordgrass.

Prairies and Prairie Gardens

Both tallgrass and shortgrass prairies have flowers throughout the warm season, and in the winter have ornamental seed heads with richly colored gold and copper grasses.

The most dramatic prairie on our continent was tallgrass prairie. Its original range was so vast that if you live north of Florida and east of the Rocky Mountains, you can probably landscape with some form of tallgrass prairie, as long as you have full sun.

Closer to the Rockies, where rainfall is scarce, tallgrass prairie is found in swales and places where moisture collects, but the vast majority of prairie is shortgrass or midgrass prairie.

Other kinds of prairies were also bountiful in North America; many of these were dotted with widely spaced, fire-resistant trees. These tree-grasslands are called savannas.

The North American Prairies Province is defined as lying between the Appalachians and the Rocky Mountains, bounded by the Canadian coniferous forests to the north and the arid semideserts to the southwest. The Edwards Plateau in central Texas is considered by the Flora of North America Editorial Committee to be its southern toe. The Blackland Prairie of Texas, which extends from Oklahoma to the eastern boundary of the Edwards Plateau, is considered by most botanists to be the southernmost extension of the tallgrass prairies.

Nowhere are these boundaries well defined, as fingers of prairie interlace with fingers of forest. And, of course, there are prairies outside of the basic province, such as eastern prairies, coastal prairies, California prairies, and the Palouse Prairie of Idaho and southeastern Washington. But the bulk of North American prairies lies in the Missouri River–Mississippi River drainage system between the Rocky Mountains and the Mississippi River. The Red River that runs north from the Dakotas into Manitoba is also part of this system.

All these prairies look very different, as they range from tallgrass to shortgrass prairies according to whether they are wet or dry, and whether the fiercest season is a cold winter or a hot summer. In fact, some ecologists

A PIONEER'S VIEW of prairie was of rolling limitless vistas of grassland with trees in the creek bottoms. The sumac in the foreground, often a problem in home prairie gardens, is stunted and exists only in a small patch. This scene is of the Flint Hills in Kansas, where southern tallgrass species meet northern tallgrass species, and where western shortgrass species meet eastern tallgrass species. *Konza Prairie, Manhattan, Kansas. August 9.*

decided that only tallgrass prairies could be called "true" prairie, and that shortgrass prairie should be called plains or steppe. However, all the wet or dry or tall or short native grasslands in this book are referred to as prairie.

■ PRAIRIES FROM EAST TO WEST

In the main, tallgrass prairies grow in the East and shortgrass prairies are found in the West. Where the two meet, there is confusion over definitions. Some ecologists consider shortgrass prairie to be only ankle-high grama grasses and buffalograss, and refer to knee-high grasses, such as sideoats grama, little bluestem, prairie dropseed, western wheatgrass, needlegrasses, and fescues, as midgrasses. However, I have always found midgrasses growing in conjunction with the grama grasses and buffalograss, so I consider them part of the shortgrass palette.

Some people say that it is not *mid*grass but *mixed*grass prairies that are significant, and that they are a mixture of tallgrass and shortgrass species. There is indeed a broad swath from Manitoba through the Dakotas, Nebraska, and Kansas where the shortgrass and tallgrass prairie palettes mingle. Here, the shortgrasses grow taller than they do in the Far West, and the tallgrasses grow shorter than they do in the Northeast, so they are all more of a midheight.

■ PRAIRIES FROM NORTH TO SOUTH

Because of the tremendous differences in geography between Canada and Texas, there is a pronounced north-south split in tallgrass and shortgrass prairies. These two prairies do not even look alike. Average annual rainfall may be similar, but heat, evaporation, and the length of the growing season make even the same plant species behave differently. Northern prairies normally green up in early June, become colorful by mid-June, reach climax from mid-July to mid-August, and then quickly go to seed before the snows arrive in October.

Southern prairies, on the other hand, start blooming in March (sometimes as early as February), have a big burst of color in late May to June, and take a rest during the hottest times until late August. Then there is another peak in late September, or whenever rain occurs. Blooms continue until November, with a few scattered flowers occurring after Christmas. Because the bloom periods for various plants are scattered, the effect is not as dramatic as in northern prairies.

■ THE RIGHT PRAIRIE FOR YOU

The prairie plants that were originally native to the soil and drainage found on your site will thrive in your landscape with the least maintenance.

In the eastern half of the continent, tallgrass prairie will do best. But on dry hilltops or fast-draining rocky or sandy soils, eastern shortgrass species can be used.

Those of you who live west of the 100th meridian will find it easier to landscape with short- or midgrass prairie plants. If you choose the shorter species, you can have a flowery lawn. But even in the driest prairies, swales were originally filled with tallgrass prairie species. A gardener who lives as far west as Denver or as far south as Austin can create the right conditions for a lush tallgrass prairie garden by channeling rainwater from roof and driveway into a shallow depression or swale.

As for those of you who live somewhere else and still wish to landscape with prairie, the truth is that you will not find the specific plants in this book helpful. But once upon a time there were probably prairie sites indigenous to your area. If you can find a local remnant, you can gather seed there if you obtain permission from the landowner. Then, following the guidelines in this book about how to design a home or corporate landscape using prairie, how to replicate a local prairie, how to plant a prairie, and how to maintain it, you too can have a prairie garden.

◼ REMNANT PRAIRIES

The best model for creating a prairie garden is a local prairie remnant, although unplowed prairies are now extremely rare. Tallgrass prairies used to be the dominant vegetation from southeastern Saskatchewan to central Texas east to the middle Mississippi River. Now less than 1 percent remain. East of the Mississippi River, there are remnants of tallgrass prairies in Ohio, on Long Island, and in Kentucky. At some time in the past, small prairies and savannas must have been present throughout eastern North America, as dominant tallgrass prairie species such as big bluestem are native from Florida to New Brunswick.

As recently as 1800, the Midwest was still unsettled by Europeans and consisted of a rich mosaic of prairie and woodland maintained by various tribes of Native Americans. After Thomas Jefferson sent Meriwether Lewis and William Clark to explore the West in 1803, opening the door to western migration, these areas were soon cleared, plowed, and farmed. Native tallgrass prairies were sometimes on sandy soil, and sometimes on heavy clay, but all represented rich, irresistible soil to farmers fresh from Europe. Huge areas of the northern tallgrass prairies flooded every spring, but farmers figured out how to lay tiles under the soil—an enormous network of French drains—to dry the land so they could plow it and plant crops.

In contrast, the shortgrass prairies on the Great Plains were naturally dry. Ranching rather than farming made more sense on this land of uncertain rainfall. But the official policy of the United States was to support and encourage farmers, so this land too was plowed and fenced. This policy resulted in the disaster of the dust bowl during the depression of the 1930s. Farm topsoil blew away, and rangeland was grazed down to dirt.

But the destruction did not stop there. After World War II farmers learned to pump water from the Ogallala and other aquifers to water their farmland. They plowed up more prairies to plant crops that needed to be watered to survive. Then ranchers compounded the problem by seeding alien grasses from other continents onto the worn-out rangeland. Many of these aliens were invasive and crowded out the remaining native grasses. It is estimated that barely 1 percent of shortgrass prairies still exist.

In a real sense, when you decide to re-create even a small prairie garden around your home or business, you are helping preserve a rapidly vanishing but vital piece of our natural heritage. Suburban prairie gardens may turn out to be zoos for endangered plant species. Maybe we could call them "bots."

◼ LATIN NAMES

Latin names tend to intimidate most lay gardeners and exasperate not a few professionals because the names always seem to be changing. All Latin names in this book follow the *Digital Floristic Synthesis of North America North of Mexico* (Kartesz and Meacham 1999). I know many native-plant people will be unhappy to find me using names that are different from what they had learned, but I made this decision because the *Synthesis* is the most up-to-date science, and I believe it will be the standard of the future. Also, it is the only source that carries Latin names for *all* the species covered in this book, and I had no other way of resolving the disagreement on Latin names of the various botanical tomes I was using.

Because most field guides reflect Latin names other than those in Kartesz and Meacham, the older names also will be given. When a species has been split up, or varieties have been lumped (*splitting* and *lumping* are how botanists term this reshuffling), it sometimes gets confusing and several Latin names get involved. I have tried to be as clear and helpful as possible.

All plants native to North America mentioned in this book are identified by their Latin names. If not profiled in part III, the Latin name is given directly after the common name in the text. Non-native plants are consistently identified as non-native, alien, or exotic, but their Latin names are usually not provided.

Why Latin Names Are Necessary

Some prairie gardeners create magnificent gardens without knowing any Latin names. If you hand-collect all local seed and know how to avoid all non-native weeds, you can get away with this. But if you want to do restoration work and plan to buy seed, you have to learn Latin names because they are more specific than common names.

For example, the common name "wild indigo" usually refers to one of the tropical indigos (*Indigofera*), famous for producing indigo blue dye. But "wild indigo" can also refer to *Baptisias* in general or to *Amorpha fruticosa*. Indigos, *Baptisias*, and *Amorphas* are all in the bean family and have pealike flowers, but they are far from being the same plant. *Indigofera suffruticosa* is a tropical shrub. The *Baptisias* are prairie or woodland herbs in eastern North America that have blue, yellow, or white flowers. *Amorpha fruticosa* is a tall North American creekside shrub with purple flowers. So some guidebooks tried to differentiate the common names by calling *Baptisia* "false indigo" and *Amorpha* "bastard indigo," but, unfortunately, there is no real consistency.

And even if you are talking only about *Baptisias*, you need Latin names to indicate which *Baptisia* you mean. *Baptisia australis* has blue flowers, *Baptisia bracteata* variety *leucophaea* has creamy white flowers, and *Baptisia lactea* has pure white flowers.

Why Latin Names Change

The Latin names are not etched in steel. They change periodically when ongoing genetic or ecological studies show relationships between plants that we were not able to determine by just looking at them. There is also the matter of differing opinions. At what point have two plants evolved far enough apart that they deserve different Latin names?

Pronouncing Latin Names

If you pronounce a Latin name out loud, it does not seem as scary, and it is tons easier to remember. The pronunciations that I have provided are somewhat arbitrary, as they are simply the ones that I have heard most often. We in North America combine classic Roman pronunciations with English vowels and consonants to make a mongrel mess, and every botanist and nursery person and amateur pronounces these names differently. Just try to pronounce every vowel separately, and you cannot go far wrong. The capitalized syllable is the one accented or emphasized. The family names, like Liliaceae, are pronounced with an *ee* at the end, like lill-ee-A-see-ee.

How Latin Names Are Broken into Categories

A *family* is a big group of related plants. For example, grasses are one family, called Poaceae, and asters, sunflowers, and silphiums are another family, called Asteraceae.

A *genus* is a smaller group within a family that is tightly related genetically. For example, grama grasses (*Bouteloua*) are a genus within the grass family. Sunflowers (*Helianthus*) are just one genus within the Asteraceae. The plural of genus is genera.

A *species* is a specific plant within a genus. For example, species in the grama genus are blue grama, black grama, hairy grama, sideoats grama, and so on. Sunflowers are divided into Maximilian sunflower, prairie sunflower, paleleaf sunflower, and so forth. Species have double names, the genus name plus a specific name. For example, blue grama is *Bouteloua gracilis* and Maximilian sunflower is *Helianthus maximiliani*.

A *variety* is a division within a species. Sideoats grama is divided into two varieties: *Bouteloua curtipendula* var. *curtipendula* and *Bouteloua curtipendula* var. *caespitosa* (*variety* is usually abbreviated as *var.*). Sometimes varieties are called *subspecies*. Some species have such a wide range with so many isolated pockets of evolution that there are marked genetic differences in leaf size or flower color or downiness or winter hardiness. Because they interbreed, most botanists agree they are not really enough different to be called a separate species, but this is a gray area, and many plants go back and forth between being called a separate species and a variety.

Chapter 2

Is natural landscaping an exercise in habitat restoration or a form of gardening? If the latter, then a natural landscape may be regarded as a work of art, since essentially this is what gardening is. Gardening, like any art form, is an expression of self and every natural landscape that I saw while in the Midwest had its creator's thumbprint clearly emblazoned across it.

HELEN SHAW, *garden designer from Great Britain,* Wild Ones Journal

A Gallery of Home Prairie Gardens

A PRAIRIE LANDSCAPE can be a simple residential garden as small as a few hundred square feet, or it can be the primary vegetational expression for a whole subdivision. It can be a totally natural replication or restoration of a prairie (such as Patricia Armstrong's landscape). Or it can look more like a classic flower garden that substitutes prairie forbs and grasses for standard exotic nursery stock, all arranged according to their soil and moisture preferences (like Wendy Walcott's garden). Each prairie garden has a special story to tell in how it was designed, installed, and maintained.

■ PRESERVED PRAIRIE GARDENS

By far the easiest way to have a prairie landscape is to preserve, not destroy, the prairie when you build. Unfortunately, each year, many acres of natural prairie are bulldozed to make way for hospitals, parking lots, shopping malls, and neighborhoods. Yet, with a little creative planning, and at no great cost, these developments could be built so that the existing prairie *becomes* the landscape.

Preserving the natural landscape while building on it is a technique called Building Inside Nature's Envelope. All the materials and equipment and the building itself are confined within a fenced area (the envelope); the natural area itself is sacrosanct. When construction is completed, the house (or office building) looks as if it had been gently set down into an undisturbed landscape. The envelope method is already used all over the country in deserts, woodlands, and coastal areas.

When Howard and Michele Snyder built their home in 1972 in the midst of virgin

THE SNYDERS built their home with as little intrusion as possible on 25 acres of prairie within view of the Canadian Rockies. On the day we visited, the prominent flowers in bloom were arrowleaf balsamroot, sticky purple geranium, and silvery lupine, along with seven other forbs in white, cream, yellow, and pink. *Cardston, Alberta. June 21.*

prairie, they used a modified form of the envelope. Except for the house and driveway, there are only four disturbed areas on the Snyder property. The first disturbance happened when Howard decided to create a play area for his children by filling in a natural hollow with soil trucked in from town. As often happens with trucked-in soil, this load contained smooth brome and Canada thistle, noxious weeds that he has been laboring to keep out of his prairie ever since. Ironically, the Snyder kids prefer to play in the prairie. Moreover, Howard later discovered that these hollows are home to many prairie species that prefer the lower, wetter habitat. To this day, Howard has not forgiven himself for this decision.

The second disturbance happened because the Snyders needed a windbreak. They have a terrific view of the Canadian Rockies, but the wind coming off the glaciers is unrelenting. It was blowing about 30 miles per hour during our visit, and we were told that 40 miles per hour is not unusual. At first, the Snyders planted a wall of conifers native to their area. The conifers stayed alive, but they refused to grow because they themselves need wind protection. Eventually the Snyders planted an enclosure of non-native shrubs.

The third and fourth disturbed spots are the result of a neighbor's horse, who deposited his domestic breakfast (and an assortment of weed seeds) on the Snyders' pristine prairie. In the future, Howard vows he will use a pooper-scooper after any visiting farm animal.

When we asked Howard to describe what it felt like to live on a natural prairie, he wrote this:

What don't we have here in our "little house on the prairie"? For starters, we don't have a lawn. We have a front yard of wild flowers—over a hundred species that bloom from March to September in a beautiful tangle of native fescue grasses. So we have goldfinches (five nesting pairs last season) who dine on the balsamroot seeds and nest in the caragana hedge, vesper sparrows who live in the dense ground cover, and meadowlarks who sing us awake in the morning.

We don't have poison sprays for insects. As a result, we have barn swallows and cliff swallows who nest under the eaves of the house, and whose children perch on our open windows as they learn to fly.

We don't have a fear of snakes, spiders, or insects, and we don't pass such an irrational fear on to our children. Instead, we have garter snakes that teach our children the wonders of nature and spiders that weave lessons in geometry.

So much of the world has been "improved," altered, and exploited until the natural wonder has been driven out of it. Our unimproved piece of the world provides us with endless pleasure, and glimpses of a prairie Eden that has all but disappeared.

ARROWLEAF BALSAM-ROOT (*Balsamorhiza sagittata*) is a key species in cold, mountainous prairies from the Dakotas to the Pacific.

■ THE TRANSPLANTED PRAIRIE GARDEN

Another way to get a complex mix of indigenous prairie is to transplant it. Anne Charlton, a landscape architect with the city of Calgary, was aware of a subdivision

LANDSCAPE ARCHITECT Anne Charlton rescued blocks of prairie sod and transplanted them to her front yard. As you can see, Anne's front yard is tiny, only about 500 square feet. Shown here are mouse ear chickweed (*Cerastium fontanum* ssp. *vulgare*), yellow paintbrush (*Castilleja lutescens*), and northern bedstraw. The silvery leaves are Louisiana sage. "I am supremely happy with the low maintenance and no watering. It also supplies my home with bunches of wildflowers all summer." *Calgary, Alberta. June 21.*

being built that would destroy part of a prairie. In May 1993, Anne rescued as much of the prairie as she could by transplanting it to her own front yard. Using the techniques she first tried out on her own front yard, Anne is now able to transplant prairie to small, high-profile public installations, where the location matches the prairie in need of rescuing.

With a sod cutter and the help of a friend, she cut blocks of sod approximately 30 inches by 16 inches. Anne ripped out the shale driveway covering her front yard, brought in 6 inches of loam, and laid the sod on top. She now wishes she had brought in "browns," a mixture of topsoil and subsoil that is less organically rich and better suited to this particular kind of prairie.

Maintenance is easy. The only burn to date was in the spring of 1994. Anne usually mows without a bag in March. She picks up the straw and shakes off any remaining seeds back into the prairie.

Sun-loving, drought-tolerant plants used to dominate, because her prairie came from a hot, dry site. Now the shade-tolerant plants are gaining ascendancy. What is interesting is that all these plants originally coexisted naturally in the prairie sod.

Shade-tolerant species in the garden that have gained dominance, besides those visible in the photograph, are blanketflower, velvety goldenrod, prairie goldenbean, western smooth blue aster, and large, golden yellow-flowered false dandelion. Those flowers that are declining are wild blue flax, mountain blue-eyed grass, and native yarrow.

Dominant grasses in the sod are Parry oatgrass (*Danthonia parryi*) and Hall's fescue (*Festuca hallii*). Other grasses are blue grama, slender wheatgrass (*Elymus trachycaulus* ssp. *trachycaulus*), northern wheatgrass (*Agropyron fragile*), and Junegrass.

■ THE RE-CREATED PRAIRIE GARDEN

Because prairie has become so rare, it is unlikely that you will be able to purchase an undisturbed prairie, or even have the chance to rescue one. Most prairie gardeners begin with what was once a cornfield, a hay meadow, or an existing lawn. If you are lucky, the old hay meadow will still possess a fair number of prairie species; these plants are then the basis for a process called restoration. If, however, there are no native species left, you can use a process called replication; in other words, by using locally acquired native seed, you re-create as nearly as possible a replica of the prairie that used to exist on your land. If you use prairie plants that are native somewhere else in North America, you will not have a replicated prairie, although your garden may still have many of the same advantages of drought tolerance, minimal maintenance, and wildlife habitat.

In 1971, Joyce Powers replaced most of the lawn around her country home with a prairie garden that mimics as closely as possible the clay-soiled prairies that were once native to her site. Over one hundred indigenous species, planted from locally harvested seeds, are grouped by habitat according to moisture preferences. In 1974, she founded Prairie Ridge Nursery in Mount Horeb, Wisconsin, and started planting prairies and showing others how to do the same.

Joyce thinks that the natural balance between grasses and flowers was maintained by bison eating the grasses and deer eating the forbs. Deer still eat the forbs, but since bison no longer roam across her land, big bluestem now outcompetes the forbs. To keep big bluestem from crowding out the prairie flowers, she uses a weed whacker a couple of times in early summer, and every other year, she burns in midsummer or fall.

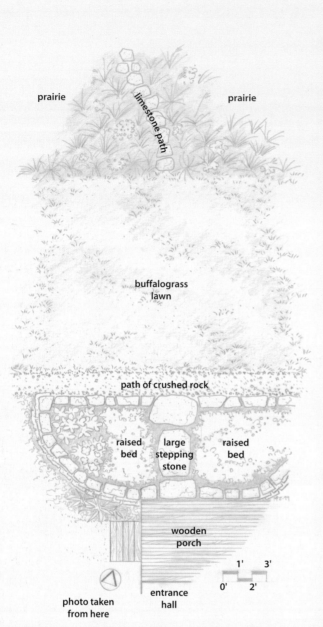

prairie   prairie

limestone path

buffalograss
lawn

path of crushed rock

raised
bed

large
stepping
stone

raised
bed

wooden
porch

1'   3'

0'   2'

photo taken
from here

entrance
hall

LANDSCAPE ARCHITECT David Kropp designed this transition from house to prairie. The entrance hall doorway opens onto
a wooden porch, and from there large stepping stones bisect a
raised bed filled with non-native alyssum and white petunias. The
stepping stones come to a T at a path of crushed rock, which runs
east to a large patio and the river, and west around the house.
Parallel to the path is an ultrasoft swath of rarely mown buffalograss lawn. On the far side of the lawn is a limestone path that
leads out into the prairie. *Plainfield, Illinois. September 23.*

THE DAVID KROPP PRAIRIE, hand-planted by Ray Schulenberg, is dominated by prairie dropseed, but in autumn the really noticeable grass is Indiangrass with its narrow golden plumes. A path of limestone flagstones meanders through the prairie toward the house. *Plainfield, Illinois. September 23.*

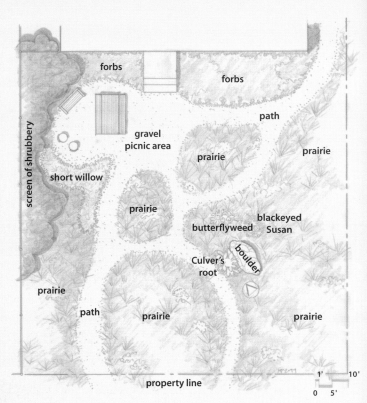

forbs

forbs

path

gravel
picnic area

prairie

prairie

screen of shrubbery

short willow

prairie

prairie

butterflyweed

blackeyed
Susan

Culver's
root

boulder

prairie

path

prairie

prairie

prairie

property line

1' 10'

0 5'

A BOULDER, a gravel picnic area, and a screen of shrubbery give
structure to this backyard prairie garden planted by Larry Lamb
and now owned by Nancy Hartrup. *Kitchener, Ontario. July 14.*

— Ray Schulenberg, who planted the exquisite Schulenberg Prairie at Morton Arboretum, near Chicago, started installing a home prairie garden in 1968 for David Kropp. There are seventy indigenous species in this prairie, which is dominated by knee-high prairie dropseed. The original wet prairie was plowed, tiled, and drained in the 1850s, so the site is now mesic. Ray burns the prairie every spring, usually in late March or early April. He is a perfectionist, so he weeds out smooth brome, box elder, green ash, red twig dogwood, and reed canary grass several times a year.

— Larry Lamb, adjunct lecturer and director of the Environmental Studies Ecology Lab at the University of Waterloo in Ontario, installed his prairie garden in 1979–80. It is neither a replication nor a restoration, for two reasons: it is on woodland, not prairie soil, and not all the species are indigenous to the local prairies. The species he obtained from Walpole Island and nursery stock are not local genotypes. This makes the garden no less attractive to humans or wildlife, and it recently won a landscape award from the North American Prairie Conference. Bed preparation was done for Larry by the builder. Usually a third of the prairie is burned each year, but no burning had been done for four years at the time the photo of the prairie was taken.

— Deb Harwell, with the help of Donald Vorpahl of Landscape Environmental Planners, Hilbert, Wisconsin, designed the entire area around her home with native prairie and woodland plants, using remnants of the existing lawns as paths and open vistas. She did the whole conversion in less than two years. Some of the plants came from nurseries and may not be local genotypes. Others were dug from local sites on a "rescue" with the Wild Ones. When prime native landscapes are going to be destroyed by development, many native plant organizations alert their members, who rescue as many plants as possible.

— Sometimes people like to start small. They try a bit of prairie in a spot that is too difficult to mow on a regular basis. Nancy Powell in Minnetonka, Minnesota, has such a spot—a steep slope behind her house. In 1985 she asked Prairie Restorations to design and install a prairie garden, which they still maintain for her. The seed was collected within 200 miles of Minneapolis. Nancy loves the wildlife that came in with the prairie. She had no fireflies until the

FROM THE PATIO, a broad swath of lawn gives shape and contrast to Deb Harwell's tall-grass prairie garden. Smoke rises from a back portion being cleaned up with a burn. To the left is a garden of shade-loving native plants. *Milwaukee, Wisconsin. August 4.*

prairie was planted, and when we visited, we saw scads of white butterflies, dragonflies, and bluebottles.

— Ann Wakeman of Fulton, Missouri, started a prairie restoration on a hill above her house. Finding more pleasure in the prairie landscape than in her formal flower gardens, she then started moving prairie plants into the flower beds. Now, long curving borders of forbs and bunchgrasses, with a backdrop of prairie shrubs and trees, line the ravine that runs the length of her property. Even her vegetable garden is made pretty by a border of prairie forbs, many of which are edible or have medicinal properties.

■ PRAIRIELIKE GARDENS

Helen McKean turned half her backyard into a prairie garden and is gradually extending a curving bed into the front. Helen did not intend to do a prairie replication; she simply wanted "something pretty." This design and installation were by Donald Vorpahl, who put in a larger proportion of forbs to grasses for lots of color. He used woody plants, such as the elderberry at the fence and a serviceberry tree at the deck, to give structure to the design. Grasses, such as a local little bluestem, saved on a rescue, and a few bunches of Indiangrass and big bluestem, are kept well in check so that the forbs predominate.

— Neil Diboll, a partner of Prairie Nursery in Westfield, Wisconsin, is excited about creating both replications and showy prairie gardens. He sells his wildflower mixes over a large area, so they cannot be strictly indigenous everywhere. He picks the showiest and easiest to germinate.

ROSINWEED, cup plant, and grayhead coneflower towered over my head, making this mowed path seem like an adventure. *Deb Harwell, Milwaukee, Wisconsin. August 4.*

THE PRAIRIE-STYLE GARDEN of Mollie and Garland Lasater was designed and installed by Rosa Finsley of Kings Creek Gardens in 1994. It is by no means a replica of a prairie, because the grasses and forbs come from all parts of Texas, and some come from other continents. However, the design is stunning and so is the pink Gulf muhly grass (*Muhlenbergia capillaris*). Native trees and prairie thicket shrubs, such as prairie flameleaf sumac (*Rhus lanceolata*), screen the driveway. The rocks are part of a water feature, around which are grouped the less drought-tolerant plants. *Fort Worth, Texas. October 14.*

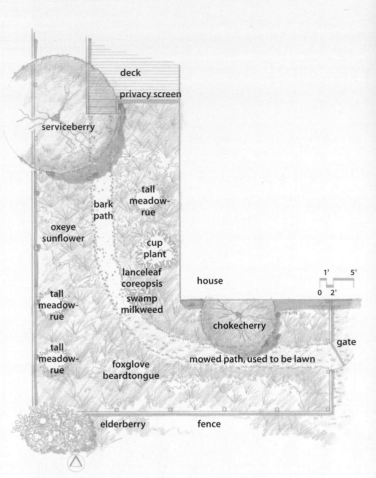

deck

privacy screen

serviceberry

tall meadow-rue

bark path

oxeye sunflower

cup plant

lanceleaf coreopsis

swamp milkweed

house

tall meadow-rue

chokecherry

tall meadow-rue

gate

foxglove beardtongue

mowed path, used to be lawn

0 1' 2' 5'

elderberry

fence

THE WHITE FLOWERS of elderberry (*Sambucus canadensis*)
are on one side of a fence, while in the prairie garden are the
white of foxglove beardtongue and the gold and yellow of oxeye
sunflower and lanceleaf coreopsis (*Coreopsis lanceolata*) with
a pink accent of swamp milkweed. *Helen McKean, Appleton,
Wisconsin. July 2.*

NEIL DIBOLL AND REEN DURNING, always experimenting, planted the clay mix from Neil's Prairie Nursery catalog on a sandy slope near their house. Blooms out of season are often an indicator of nonlocal stock or a new planting, and Neil's pale purple coneflowers, usually an early summer flower, were a beautiful part of his fall garden in its second year. The two goldenrods, showy and stiff, are indigenous, as is the skyblue aster. Sideoats grama and little bluestem are the primary grasses. Cream indigos are hidden down among the grasses—a treat for those who take the time to walk through the prairie. The main weed is sweet clover, which Neil controls with a weed whacker. *Pardeeville, Wisconsin. September 16.*

A SMALL FLOWER BED either side of a short front walk contains an amazing number of native prairie forbs and grasses, including big bluestem, bottle gentian, four kinds of asters, sweet blackeyed Susan, and common mountain mint. *Wendy Walcott, Milwaukee, Wisconsin. September 20.*

PRAIRIE FORBS encircled by a lawn combine a traditional landscape with food for butterflies. *Jeff and Mary Lou Thompson, Kitchener, Ontario. July 14.*

■ THE PRAIRIE FLOWER GARDEN

You can use prairie plants in formal beds. The steps for installation and maintenance are the same as for prairie restorations. It is the design and the large proportion of forbs to grasses that make the difference.

Wendy Walcott laid out English-style flower beds around openings and pathways of lawn to create a large, sophisticated perennial garden. What makes it unique is that almost every one of the flowers and ornamental grasses is native to Wendy's part of Wisconsin. Native wildlife such as bees, butterflies, and hummingbirds love the intense color and abundance of nectar.

— Jeff Thompson, formerly a student of Larry Lamb, designs, installs, and maintains prairie landscapes. Naturally, he wanted a prairie front yard. His wife, Mary Lou, on the other hand, wanted a traditional landscape. They compromised with a conventional-looking perennial border surrounded by lawn. But as in Wendy Walcott's garden, all but a couple of the flowers are native, butterfly-attracting prairie forbs.

■ PRAIRIE NEIGHBORHOODS

If you think a single private home landscaped with prairie is an exciting idea, imagine an entire neighborhood devoted to prairie. Subdivision developers are beginning to see the advantages of using prairie instead of high-maintenance, high water-use lawns. Even established neighborhoods can adopt this concept. You and your neighbors can convert your block to native habitat yard by yard.

Rochelle Whiteman of Glendale, Wisconsin, got excited about native plants and habitat gardening in 1979. She gradually replaced the exotic trees around her house with natives. She dug up turf and planted prairie and woodland flowers. Today, not one scrap of lawn remains, and her whole garden is a delight to walk through. Rochelle says she does not know a single Latin name, and yet she has developed a native garden with as much sensitivity and authenticity as any ecologically trained botanist.

Moreover, through her example and enthusiasm, Rochelle is gradually converting her neighborhood. She shares her garden, her plants, and her knowledge with all interested parties. Those with shade get starts of woodland native plants, and those with sun dig up their lawns and start beds of shrubs and prairie flowers. Participating neighbors can be found all around Rochelle's home—seven so far have converted—and one couple told us that they bought in this neighborhood because of the environmentally friendly look of the landscapes.

IT IS HARD TO TELL where Rochelle Whiteman's garden starts and stops, because on one side her neighbors have extended her woodland garden onto their own property, and on the other side, her mix of prairie flowers continues as far as her neighbor has sun enough to grow them. *Glendale, Wisconsin. July 16.*

— Often, two neighbors go in together to install and maintain a prairie landscape. In 1992 Dave and Roselee Wondra of Chanhassen, Minnesota, bought 3 acres of subdivided alfalfa field. House, driveway, and lawn occupy 1 acre, but the other 2 acres are devoted to natural landscapes. They inspired their next door neighbor to use 2 acres of his own land to create an enlarged prairie and to share maintenance costs.

The basic design was done by C. Colston Burrell of Native Landscape Design and Restoration, who created a mini-forest, lovely sweeps of prairie, and natural-looking thickets. Seeds and plants were chosen and installed by Prairie Restorations.

Between the back lawn and the tallgrass prairie is a curving flower bed, where Dave and Roselee set aside a couple of square feet for every kind of seed they use, so that they can identify the forbs and grasses at each stage of development, from seedling to rosette to full flower. This way they do not accidentally weed out something they had planted—or leave a thuggish weed, thinking it was a desirable plant.

In spring and early summer, the shortgrass prairie is the most colorful area in the Wondras' landscape. This area covers the hilltop in front of their house. Bluebottles and butterflies hover over yarrow, fleabane, blackeyed Susan, and northern bedstraw. In 1997, when we saw the property, the backlit coppery stems of little bluestem were almost as bright as the orange flowers on the butterfly milkweed. The Wondras had left last year's grass uncut to build up a fuel load for a spring burn in 1998, which would kill dandelions and cool season grasses. Dave takes a sensible approach to maintenance; he fights the most obnoxious weeds for about two hours a month whenever he is in the mood, and lets nature take care of the rest.

"You can't just look at a prairie. You've got to be inside it," says Dave. "I'll come home from work all wound up, and all it takes is a walk down the path and I'm better." Roselee notes, "There may be one or two fireflies over the lawn, but there are zillions over the prairie every year." Their two daughters, grade-school age, build "forts" out of the tall grasses and help during a burn by transporting mice and baby rabbits to safety.

— A 40-acre neighbor-to-neighbor project is in Wisconsin. Patricia and Michael Wilson used to live in Madison, overlooking the Greene Prairie. They loved it so much that when they moved out to the country, they decided to plant a prairie and persuaded their neighbors Ron and Sheila Andrews to form a joint conservancy. Neil Diboll of Prairie Nursery designed and planted the old farm fields.

The acreage contained smooth brome, farm weeds, and no prairie plants. In 1992 a master plan was developed, and 8 acres were planted. Up to 13.5 acres at a time have been planted each year since, and the Andrewses are anxious to add more land to the conservancy.

The first year of planting costs as much, acre per acre, as having a crew plant and maintain a lawn. That includes discing (turning the soil), controlling noxious weeds, buying and applying seed, and two mowings. Not included in

BIG BLUESTEM and Indiangrass, when backlit, display magnificent fall color. At the same time, tallgrass species of asters and goldenrods bloom purple, white, and yellow, while the remains of summer flowers are still colorful. *Wondra prairie garden, Chanhassen, Minnesota. September 14.*

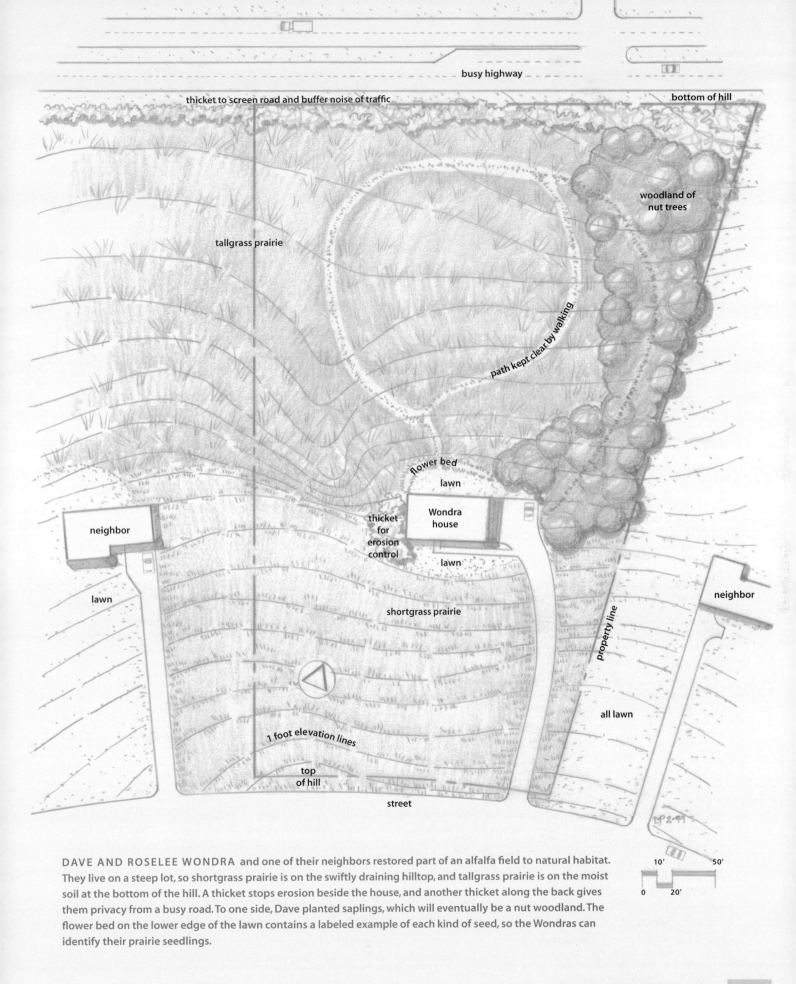

busy highway

thicket to screen road and buffer noise of traffic

bottom of hill

woodland of nut trees

tallgrass prairie

path kept clear by walking

flower bed

lawn

thicket for erosion control

Wondra house

lawn

neighbor

shortgrass prairie

property line

neighbor

lawn

all lawn

1 foot elevation lines

top of hill

street

10'   50'

0   20'

DAVE AND ROSELEE WONDRA and one of their neighbors restored part of an alfalfa field to natural habitat. They live on a steep lot, so shortgrass prairie is on the swiftly draining hilltop, and tallgrass prairie is on the moist soil at the bottom of the hill. A thicket stops erosion beside the house, and another thicket along the back gives them privacy from a busy road. To one side, Dave planted saplings, which will eventually be a nut woodland. The flower bed on the lower edge of the lawn contains a labeled example of each kind of seed, so the Wondras can identify their prairie seedlings.

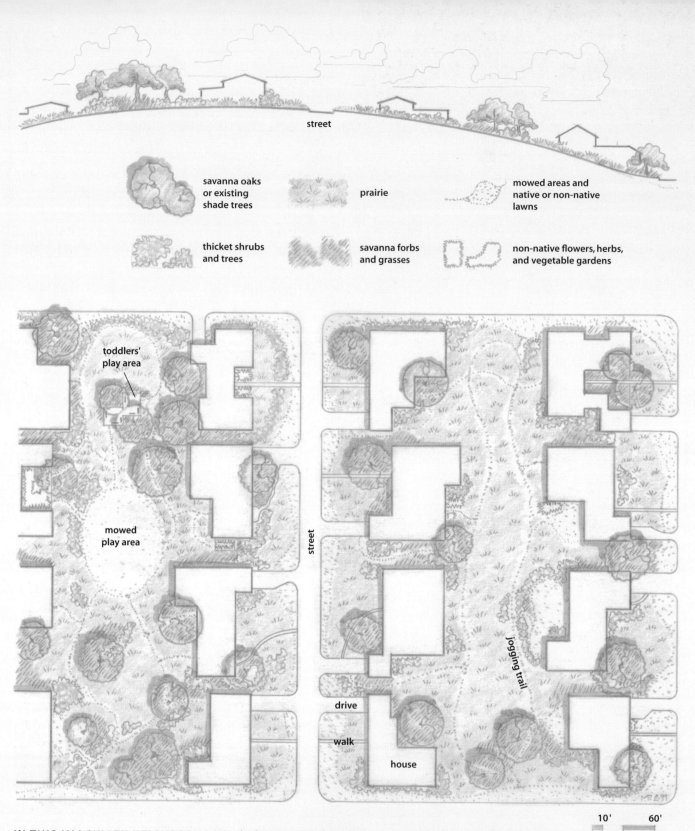

street

savanna oaks or existing shade trees

prairie

mowed areas and native or non-native lawns

thicket shrubs and trees

savanna forbs and grasses

non-native flowers, herbs, and vegetable gardens

toddlers' play area

mowed play area

street

jogging trail

drive

walk

house

10'   60'
0   30'

IN THIS IMAGINARY NEIGHBORHOOD, the homeowners have banded together to convert their typical American landscapes into a connected wildlife-friendly habitat. Lawns have been replaced by prairie, ground covers have been replaced by savanna species, birds and butterflies are being nurtured, and many hours of mowing, watering, and spraying are being saved. The trees are newly planted savanna oaks, or existing shade trees that are healthy and not invasive. Native thicket shrubs and trees have replaced existing sterile hedges. Arranged in nonlinear clumps, they enhance the appearance of the houses, provide privacy, block views of traffic, and buffer noise. There is a mowed edge along the streets and driveways for traffic safety, while the communal play areas and paths are mowed as needed. Note that individuality is not dead; each home landscape still reflects the owners' personal tastes and styles; a few homeowners have even opted to retain private lawns.

this cost are the countless hours Patricia spends weeding out thistles and sweet clover. But by the second year it gets easier; only cleanup weeding and an annual mow are needed. And once she has a newly planted area under control, Patricia says that the psychological benefits are beyond any price.

— Long Grove, Illinois, is a 95-percent residential village on the north side of the greater Chicago area. In 1979, the village developed a conservancy ordinance to decide which lands and soils should be protected and left undeveloped. As new subdivisions went in, significant portions of the land were preserved as natural landscapes. In one development, composed of 3-acre lots, 2 of every 3 acres were left natural.

In many of these subdivisions, the homes are surrounded by soft colorful waves of prairie. Curving walkways and road margins are mowed strips of buffalograss lawn, which, like the prairie, receive no supplemental water or fertilizer and no herbicides or pesticides. The sewage is specially treated to create safe, healthy wetlands for native wildlife.

Permission is needed to restore a conservancy area, and the plan must be reviewed for accuracy. It takes authentic prairie awhile to develop, so non-native weeds, such as

DESPITE AGGRESSIVELY WEEDY ROADSIDES, many homeowners, like Joe and Carol Harcarik, have planted lovely prairie gardens in accordance with the covenants of Noll Valley. Here are orange butterfly milkweed, pale purple coneflower, Indiangrass, big bluestem, blackeyed Susan, roundhead bushclover, and leadplant. *Verona, Wisconsin. July 5.*

Queen Anne's lace, are allowed, making a graceful transition in the early stages while the longer-lived native prairie forbs get established.

— Noll Valley, Wisconsin, south of Madison, is another prairie subdivision. Oak savanna and prairie remnants made this acreage particularly worth preserving, and local naturalists fought hard to save this area from being bulldozed. Their story is instructive but also heartbreaking.

The developers decided to add color to the roadsides. The cost of planting good-quality indigenous prairie plants was higher than purchasing non-native, but well-adapted highway flowers. So they planted birdfoot trefoil and crown vetch, two of prairie's worst invasives. Smooth brome, reed canary grass, and orchard grass also turned out to be part of the mix. All the preserved savannas and newly planted native prairies in this development are now being overrun by these weeds. At the edge of Joe and Carol Harcarik's garden, for example, is an invasive monoculture of ravenous, non-native smooth brome. It spread from the shoulder of the roadside, where it should never have been planted, and it has now taken over much of the area reserved for prairie.

— Green Meadows in Johnstown, Iowa, was founded as a prairie residential community. The developer planted annual wildflowers from a big glossy catalog. They came up and were pretty for one year. But they did not reseed, as they were native either to Europe, California, or Texas—but not Iowa. Weeds sprang up everywhere.

Most of the homeowners were ready to give up and mow down the mess, until one of them, Dr. Eileen Robb, explained that they had not given prairie a chance because no prairie plants had been sown. The homeowners persuaded the developer to purchase appropriate seed and plant again. A common area of big and little bluestem is now getting started. A team of residents led by Eileen gather seed and raise plants to add to the common areas. They also publish a newsletter to inform residents about the names, appearance, and uses of individual prairie plants and to tell them what to look for at each season, how they can see the prairie developing, and what they can do to help.

EACH YEAR the homeowners add more species to the common areas of this residential prairie community. Dr. Eileen Robb and another volunteer homeowner, Rick Lehman, are planting native grasses that Eileen grew from seed in her backyard. *Green Meadows, Johnston, Iowa. September 13.*

Chapter 3

About 150 years ago, the harmony of nature and all its natural processes came to an abrupt halt. A great transformation occurred, although it went unnoticed at the time. We shifted from accruing species richness and ecosystem diversity over millennia, to shedding them in a geologic instant.

   PAUL NELSON, *Missouri Resource Review*

Beyond Home Landscapes

A THANK-YOU NOTE from a schoolchild who learned a little more about the natural world after visiting the native gardens at Ojibway Park. *Windsor, Ontario.*

NOT ALL PRAIRIE GARDENS are home landscapes. Many are found at elementary schools, churches, libraries, and museums, where the plants are often supplied by lay gardeners. When towns put native landscapes around municipal buildings and parkways, officials soon discover that they save money on irrigation and maintenance. They also set a good example in environmental landscaping for the community. Corporations are also discovering the economic and ecological benefits of native landscapes, especially on the large acreages that surround their headquarters.

When tended native gardens blend into public parks and drainage easements, wild plants and animals can travel from one habitat to another via these natural corridors, and all habitats benefit. The more habitats we restore or replicate, the better chance we have of saving our natural world for our grandkids.

Some people claim that restoring our native landscapes is a futile task; the world, after all, is always changing. Evolution is action, not stasis. Full ice ages, for the last million years, have recurred in rhythms of approximately 100,000 years, making forests run down mountains and deserts retreat south. Human-caused global warming will undoubtedly meddle with the natural rhythms of our earth. Exotic weeds, exotic diseases, and exotic predators such as fire ants are already changing our natural ecosystems. We cannot set the clock back.

But one thing is clear: the more diversity there is, the greater the chance our ecosystem has to adjust itself to new conditions. A landscape of a hundred species is more flexible than a landscape of only ten. Nature needs hundreds of thousands of years to evolve a species or an ecosystem. At our present accelerated rate of extermination, the next twenty to thirty years will determine whether we are smart enough to protect our diversity.

Native plant gardens that reach out to educate our children, both future power moguls and average citizens, help to bring this enormous issue to public awareness. It is time to teach people how to save rather than destroy, to work for genetic diversity rather than species simplicity.

This is the aim of the Kauffman Museum in Newton, Kansas. When Ukrainian Mennonites first came to farm in central Kansas, prairie was the only landscape they saw. So, it is fitting that prairie surround the museum that was founded by their descendants. Museum curator Lorna Harder told us that when her grandmother went out to play in the tallgrass prairie, she was warned: "Keep the house in sight. If you get lost in the grass you'll never be found."

Prairie is often perceived as scary, or puzzling, or messy to people who are first introduced to it. Lorna told us about an eighty-two-year-old lady who frequently visits the museum. She would occasionally stop to examine a flower, and Lorna would tell her the name and something about it. One day she said to Lorna, "When I first started seeing the prairie, it was like seeing a crowd of strangers. But now I know a few faces in the crowd, and it has changed my whole experience and perception of the prairie."

The Kauffman Museum prairie garden was begun in 1984 by Lorna and her botany professor Dr. Dwight Platt. Composed of 60 percent grasses and 40 percent forbs, seed was collected wherever possible from hay meadows and roadsides in a 50-mile radius. The species list was based on a one-hundred-year-old herbarium collection originally gathered in the area.

Half the grounds are still a conventionally mowed lawn, but each year Lorna changes the contour mow line to let the prairie expand. Her long-term plan is to convert the entire grounds of the museum to prairie and native riparian woodland.

THE ENTRANCE to the Kauffman Museum is landscaped with 1.5 acres of replicated tallgrass prairie. Lorna Harder, curator of natural history, is passionate about her bit of prairie: "In low winter light, the stems glow like sunshine coming from the ground. It has all-year color, not just spring, summer, and fall." *Newton, Kansas. September 10.*

— The Provincial Royal Saskatchewan Museum is part of a larger park in Regina, Saskatchewan. The lawn area directly in front of the museum was converted into a prairie garden by a group of volunteers. Earl Wiltse, Nora Stewart, Keith and Gladys Barr, and Al Bodnarchuk gathered seed from prairie remnants in a radius of 150 kilometers, germinated the more precious and rare of the seed in the Barrs' greenhouse, and set out both plugs and seed in 1994.

Maintenance is done by the original group of volunteers. They cut down dead stalks sometime between late fall and early spring. During the growing season, they weed out invasives, thin out aggressive native plants, and add new species.

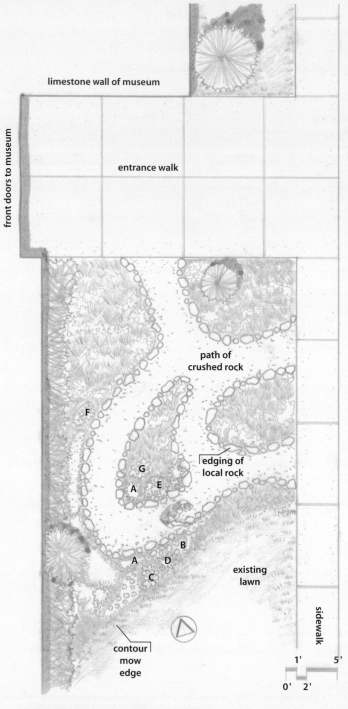

limestone wall of museum

front doors to museum

entrance walk

path of
crushed rock

F

edging of
local rock

G

A   E

B

A   D

C

existing
lawn

sidewalk

contour
mow
edge

1'   5'

0'   2'

A   harebell
B   yarrow
C   prairie alumroot
D   lilac beardtongue
E   blanketflower
F   Canadian milkvetch
G   northern bedstraw

LINDSEY WILKINSON and her dad examine the tiny flowers in the head of a native yarrow in the prairie garden at the Provincial Royal Saskatchewan Museum. Because the garden is on the south side of the building, it blooms about two weeks earlier than the local remnant prairies. *Regina, Saskatchewan. June 22.*

— The Prairie School in Racine, Wisconsin, is a K-12 private school built by Frank Lloyd Wright and Associates. In 1974, the principal and the science department decided that The Prairie School should have a prairie landscape. Richard Barloga, a prairie restorationist from Hales Corners, Wisconsin, collected local seed to make a pure restoration. In July, it is glorious with prairie dock, rosinweed, and bergamot. Big bluestem is the dominant grass, but many species are present in this fine replication.

— When putting in a school prairie, it is best to get the whole school involved— parents, students, faculty, and, very important, the maintenance staff. Otherwise, in their zeal to keep things lawnlike, they are apt to mow the native gardens down. Before Patricia Armstrong designed the Lincoln Elementary School prairie garden in 1994, she gave a slide show to a full school assembly. Then she took every class in the school on a field trip to a real prairie.

After preparing the site, she supplied forbs in nursery pots. Teachers supervised while the children planted. After the forbs were in, grass seed was mixed with sand, and the children sprinkled it around. Everything came up and did well. The forbs, already a year old, bloomed the first year, which gave everyone a feeling of success.

— A number of school prairie gardens have been planted in the Milwaukee area, thanks to the influence of Lorrie Otto and the Wild Ones. The oldest landscape in the area was at the Bayside Middle School. Lorrie planted it under existing apple trees in 1974 and called it a meadow garden. Strictly indigenous prairie and woodland gardens were added in 1993 with the help of the science teacher and his students. For twenty years, Lorrie did the maintenance herself.

PRAIRIE RESTORATIONIST Richard Barloga designed and installed a prairie garden at The Prairie School for $700. Between 1974 and 1994 he maintained it with annual burns. The maintenance cost? The price of one match a year. Compare that to the many thousands of dollars spent on maintaining the lawn area. *Racine, Wisconsin. July 30.*

THE ORIGINAL PRAIRIE GARDEN at Bayside Middle School, consisting of plants gathered by science students from local prairies, was a favorite bicycling stop for Abby Freedman. *Bayside, Wisconsin. August 2.*

In 1997, the gardens were destroyed and sodded over by the school's superintendent. The school board quickly learned how much the gardens meant to the students and parents. Protests were so vociferous that the destruction of the garden made front-page news in the *Milwaukee Journal*. This unleashed further letters that were so impassioned that the school board made amends by planting a new native plant garden on the school grounds.

THE LIBRARY at Hales Corners, Wisconsin, was situated next to the historic Ben Hunt Cabin. Ben Hunt was an early conservationist, and the cabin was originally surrounded by prairie. In 1985, Richard Barloga, a prairie restorationist who lives in the neighborhood, talked the library into letting him landscape both cabin and library with prairie. An area at the entrance to the library is contour-mowed to give standing room for lectures on the prairie. *Hales Corners, Wisconsin. August 1.*

— Lorrie also planted a prairie at the Mequon Unitarian Church on Port Washington Road north of Milwaukee. It was a seeded project managed by Lorrie for several years. There is no lawn; the sanctuary is completely surrounded by prairie. Several young trees, native bur oaks and hawthorns, were also planted, so this landscape will gradually evolve into a bur oak savanna.

— Union Gas in Brantford, Ontario, has a 4.5-acre prairie that is seen by the many customers who come here to pay their gas bills. The garden was laid out by MacKinnon, Hensel, and Associates of Waterloo, Ontario. A natural wetland of sedges and cattails was extended. The environmental design, installation, and organic maintenance are by Jeff Thompson of Kitchener, Ontario.

The garden was planted in June 1995, replacing an overworked cornfield. The soil is 3 feet of sand over clay

pan. The first plant to bloom was partridge pea, which had not been seen in the area for sixty years; the seeds had been lying dormant. For the first two years, 150 hours of weeding were required each summer. Jeff estimates that the construction-installation costs were 60 percent that of a lawn, and the maintenance is 100 percent for the first four years. Then it drops to 15 percent—a big savings for the long term.

— The national headquarters for Sears, located in the Prairie Stone Business Park, Hoffman Estates, west of Chicago, is a fine example of enlightened corporate landscaping. The 200-acre perimeter to the Sears compound was designed as a low-maintenance naturalistic prairie meadow that would blend in harmoniously with the surrounding area. Botanist Patricia Armstrong was hired by the village of Hoffman Estates as a plant consultant. The project was begun in 1992 and also includes woodlands, restored wetlands, and nature trails.

— The Fermi National Accelerator Laboratory (FermiLab)—where scientists seek to understand the very composition of the universe—is also a showcase for sophisticated prairie plantings. The facility sits on 6,800 acres of old farm land, 1,030 of which have been planted in prairie. Dr. Robert Betz, retired professor from Northeastern Illinois University, is the consulting biologist. At first, maintenance engineer Bob Lootens and the other groundsmen were highly skeptical. As Lootens put it, "He was asking us to plant *weeds* on a good corn crop!"

But Dr. Betz had people skills as well as technical know-how, and now Lootens is a prairie advocate. "These forbs and grasses are as long-lived and impressive as an oak tree," he says. "Everyone knows it's a crime to cut down an oak. It's as big a crime to plow a prairie."

The original seed source for the Fermi Prairie was from the Gensberg-Markham Prairie. Now the Fermi Prairie exchanges seed with local forest preserves (which include prairies and savannas) to increase diversity. They also donate seed to forty local middle schools. Seven thousand students visit the prairie each year to do bug sweeps, pond nets, and other prairie learning activities.

— Thistle Hill Bed and Breakfast is a working farm in Wakeeney, Kansas. The U.S. government, in recognition of the need to take marginal, eroding farmland out of cultivation, created the Restoration Conservation Program (RCP) to pay farmers to replant worn-out fields with native grasses. The owners, Mary and Dave Hendricks, took the RCP payment, obtained grass seed from a Kansas grower, and planted two fields in Indiangrass, switchgrass, big bluestem, prairie dropseed, and little bluestem.

THIS COLORFUL DISPLAY of prairie grasses, common golden-rod, New England aster, and heath aster flanks one of the entrance roads to Sears National Headquarters. *Hoffman Estates, Illinois. September 22.*

Unfortunately, not enough expertise came along with the grant money to make a true restoration possible. The Hendrickses bought wildflower seeds from two out-of-state sources. None of the seeds were local genotypes, and most of the seeds were not even native to North America. One crown vetch seed, accidentally planted, germinated and in just six years formed a 300-square-foot monoculture.

According to the Hendrickses, RCP is not likely to have long-term environmental benefits for two reasons. First, the program requires farmers to keep the land out of production for only ten years. When ten years are up, most farmers will plow the tallgrasses under again, because they make more money on subsidized wheat than they do from the RCP stipend. Second, the government still pays farmers to plow up their hay meadows. Naturally, local farmers return eroding fields to RCP and then turn ancient hay meadows into cropland. The net result: we are using tax money to replace real prairies with poorly restored ones that are only temporary. *Our farm-use laws are in serious need of revision.*

— Twenty-eight years ago J. David Bamberger bought Selah, an old worn-out Texas Hill Country ranch of 5,500

A WAIST-HIGH STAND of native Indiangrass, bushy bluestem, little bluestem, Lindheimer's muhly, and silver bluestem, plus the African klein grass, supports more than twice as many cattle per acre as typical overgrazed land. In back are escarpment live oaks with an understory of cedar sedge (*Salvia roemeriana*), little bluestem, sideoats grama, twistleaf yucca (*Yucca rupicola*), frostweed (*Verbesina virginica*), zexmenia (*Wedelia texana*), and several shrubs and vines. *Selah Ranch. Johnson City, Texas. October 15.*

Prairies and Prairie Gardens

acres. Overgrazing had ruined the grasses, and the topsoil had washed away, exposing the limestone bedrock. The native "cedar," *Juniperus asheii*, originally found only in creek bottoms and on unburned escarpments, had invaded what used to be grassy slopes.

David experimented with unorthodox techniques. He cut cedar, even on the soil-bare hilltops. Then he went against local practice and refused to burn the cedar in bonfires, which scorch the earth and produce nothing but horehound. He learned to leave the cut cedar where it fell to provide shelter for wildlife and to capture soil and moisture for seedlings. Where there were gullies, he hand-built 2-by-3-feet dams of stones. He used his tractor to make over ten thousand 2-inch high terraces to stop erosion. Then, to make a seed bed, he spread cedar leaf litter on the terraces.

DAVID AND MARGARET BAMBERGER proudly stand on grass they restored from land that used to look exactly like their neighbor's across the fence. Fifteen thousand visitors a year come to Selah Ranch to learn ways to be both a successful rancher and a land conservationist. *Johnson City, Texas. October 15.*

He contracted with a nearby seed company to gather and clean the seed of grasses native to his county. To make the expensive seed go as far as possible, he developed the "tennis court" technique. By sowing an area the size of one tennis court in every 20 acres, he found that wind and water dispersed the seed and covered the whole area within a very few years. He also discovered that finely cut cedar branches thrown over the seedbed protected it from erosion and grazing.

David started with grass seed, hoping that forbs would follow on their own, but the original seed bank had eroded along with the soil. Forbs will have to be added from locally hand-collected seed to produce a full prairie restoration.

David's best advice is not to get discouraged. Grass burs seemed the only result for the first three years. But springs appeared the fifth year, and then the golden-cheeked warblers returned.

On the restored grassland, 18 acres can support a cow where it used to take 41 acres. Dry creeks are now flowing, springs are abundant, and the wells drilled to fill the stock tanks are no longer needed. The deer, once underfed, actually doubled in size, and hunting leases now bring in twelve times more income than before the restoration.

Chapter 4

Prairie restoration is not a substitute for conserving existing native prairie areas. These areas are the benchmarks from which any restoration starts. In our lifetimes, at least, even the best restored prairie will pale in comparison to the real thing that took centuries to evolve.

RESTORING CANADA'S NATIVE PRAIRIES

Using Preserved and Replicated Prairies as Models

CORDGRASS likes lowlands and standing water, and little bluestem likes uplands and good drainage. The other tallgrass species arrange themselves somewhere in between, being drawn to where they are best adapted. Shortgrass prairie species have a similar gradient, with cattails in the wettest spot. Only the most common species are shown.

IF YOU WANT YOUR PRAIRIE GARDEN to be an ecological and horticultural success, you need to copy a nearby prairie that has the same kind of soil and topography as your own garden site. There may be a prairie a block away, but if it is a wetland prairie, and you live on a dry hilltop, it is not going to help you. Wetland prairie species on your hilltop will become sickly and overrun with weeds. Find a dry hilltop prairie (within a radius of 50 miles, if possible) to serve as your source of inspiration. If you do not already know of a suitable prairie, call one of the local resources listed in the back of the book.

When first confronted with a prairie, you may find it bewildering. Years ago, when I became interested in this subject, I often mistook a field of non-native grasses for a prairie, and I certainly could not tell the difference between well-designed reconstructions and bad ones. It took about six weeks of looking at original prairies before I came to appreciate their marvelous harmony and complexity.

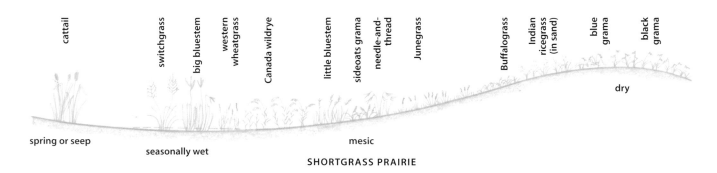

cattail · switchgrass · big bluestem · western wheatgrass · Canada wildrye · little bluestem · sideoats grama · needle-and-thread · Junegrass · Buffalograss · Indian ricegrass (in sand) · blue grama · black grama

dry

spring or seep

seasonally wet

mesic

SHORTGRASS PRAIRIE

This chapter is designed to help you recognize the real thing when you see it. It will help you distinguish the character of a wet prairie from that of a mesic one or a dry one. When deciding which plants to use, the key is to figure out where your soil is wet, mesic, or dry, and to gather together a mixture of plants adapted to those habitats.

This sounds tricky at first. In traditional gardening, we never had to match the plants to the site. We just bought what the nursery sold (invariably, non-native and ill-suited), stuck it in the ground, and then gave it lots of TLC.

But prairie requires a more discerning eye: while, at first glance, the terrain may look flat, in fact it has a gentle roll, and careful scrutiny reveals that the upside will have a slightly different plant palette from the downside. The same is true of the north and south sides of the roll.

AT THE BRADLEY STREET PRAIRIE, sedges, rushes, wild rose, and silverweed (*Argentina anserina*) grow out of sphagnum moss. *Winnipeg, Manitoba. June 25.*

■ LOWLAND PRAIRIES

Lowland prairies collect water. Depending on rainfall and evaporation rates, lowland prairies may be wet all year or just for a few days after a rain. Where they are wet all year, they are often bordering a lake, stream, or spring. One kind of wet prairie, called a calcareous fen, is kept moist by water constantly oozing over a slightly buried shelf of limestone or shale. Admittedly, this is not the sort of arrangement ordinarily found on a suburban lot, but we did see a beautifully crafted calcareous fen garden at Chicago Botanic Garden.

The Bradley Street Prairie in Winnipeg, Manitoba, managed by the Living Prairie Museum, is another kind of wet prairie—one that is highly acid. At first glance, it seemed to be a sedge meadow, backed by a wall of willow. As I walked out on this prairie, I was surprised to feel a springy, lumpy substance under my feet. Parting the stems of the sedges, I saw several inches of sphagnum moss completely covering the ground. Although it was a cold, cloudy day, the sphagnum moss that characterizes this kind of wet prairie was warm to the touch.

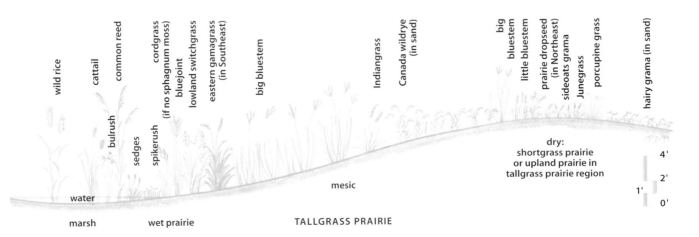

wild rice
cattail
common reed
bulrush
sedges
spikerush
cordgrass (if no sphagnum moss)
bluejoint
lowland switchgrass
eastern gamagrass (in Southeast)
big bluestem
Indiangrass
Canada wildrye (in sand)
big bluestem
little bluestem
prairie dropseed (in Northeast)
sideoats grama
Junegrass
porcupine grass
hairy grama (in sand)

dry: shortgrass prairie or upland prairie in tallgrass prairie region

4'
2'
1'
0'

mesic

water

marsh   wet prairie   TALLGRASS PRAIRIE

BEFORE MAN INTERFERED, many of the northern prairies were wet in the spring, attracting flocks of migrating waterbirds such as sandhill cranes, whooping cranes (now almost extinct), and geese. Farmers laid tiles under these fields to drain off the water. Here is an untiled field on the Blackfeet Reservation, Browning, Montana. *June 19.*

IN MORE ARID SHORTGRASS PRAIRIE REGIONS, the low places do not hold water. They just get extra runoff and are marked by the pale blue green hue of western wheatgrass. Before the great drought of the 1930s and before overgrazing, many of these draws were filled with big bluestem and Indiangrass. South of the Cheyenne River in eastern Wyoming. *June 17.*

In northern prairies, most wet spots are potholes or deep swales that hold water in the spring and are marshy in the summer. Field horsetail (*Equisetum arvense*) often acts as a "ground cover," which forms a fluffy blanket punctuated by the taller stems of sweet-grass, bluejoint, cordgrass, rushes, and an assortment of sedges.

In the South and the West, prairie wet spots seem to be wet only after a heavy rain. On the shortgrass plains from northwest Texas to Oklahoma, Colorado, and Kansas, rain collects in playa lakes, about one per square mile. The land is so flat, water cannot run off. It has nowhere to go, so it stands and supports reeds (*Scirpus*), arrowhead (*Sagittaria*), and other species until the water dries up. Ringing the edges of the playas are buffalograss or western wheatgrass with various forbs.

You can see that a wet spot in your prairie garden could vary greatly according to what part of the country you live in. To help you translate scenes this vast into an ordinary home garden, here are some examples of gardeners who have used lowland prairie in the landscape.

The Hesselton-Gillespie prairie garden in Maple Grove, Minnesota, borders Eagle Lake. Swamp milkweed and oxeye sunflower crowd the lakeshore along with bluejoint, cordgrass, and volunteer sedges. As the ground gets slightly drier toward the lawn, big bluestem, Indiangrass, switchgrass, and Canada wildrye are gaining hold. Forbs seeded here include northern blue flag, agastache (*Agastache foeniculum*), Joe-Pye weed, blue vervain, and golden Alexanders.

Instead of burning every year, Prairie Restorations cuts down the prairie in late fall or early spring when the wet spongy ground is frozen hard enough to hold the weight of the flail mower. The mower mulches and distributes seeds, helping the prairie to thicken up.

THE HESSELTON-GILLESPIE wet prairie garden borders Eagle Lake. The owners planted upland prairie species because they wanted a shortgrass prairie, but the prairie corrected itself by volunteering swamp milkweed and sedges. *Maple Grove, Minnesota. June 28.*

A BIT OF WET PRAIRIE can be tiny. Rochelle Whiteman had a few square feet of poor drainage next to the driveway. She observed which flowers grew in ditches and other wild wet spots in the Milwaukee area, and using that palette, planted a colorful composition of great blue lobelia, cardinal flower, sneezeweed, an ornamental sedge, big bluestem, and New England aster. *Milwaukee, Wisconsin. September 19.*

— A wet prairie can encircle a pond. At Sweet Grass Gardens in Hagersville, Ontario, a native plant nursery owned by Native Americans Ken and Linda Parker, sedges and other wet prairie species were placed around the demonstration water garden. This pond planting is not a replication of a natural wet spot but is rather a lovely garden using a hodgepodge of showy and ceremonially useful plants from northern wet prairies. In the water is sweetflag (*Acorus calamus*). Foxsedge, a plantain (*Plantago eripoda)*, and field horsetail are on the banks that are more moist than wet. Farther still from the pond, but where the soil stays damp, is a planting of sweetgrass, wild hibiscus (*Hibiscus laevis*), swamp milkweed, queen of the prairie, and glade mallow.

■ MESIC PRAIRIES

Mesic tallgrass prairies are not too wet and not too dry. Most of the photos in chapter 2, "A Gallery of Home Prairie Gardens," are examples of mesic tallgrass prairie gardens. To achieve mesic conditions in shortgrass areas where the prairie would normally be dry, you can channel rain runoff from roofs and paved surfaces into your planting areas.

In mesic prairies, big bluestem and Indiangrass are always present, although they may not be dominant. Well-drained mesic prairies are dominated by prairie dropseed in the North and by little bluestem in the South and West. Of course, a mesic prairie in Chicago, with its average annual rainfall measuring 32 to 33 inches, and a mesic prairie in Dallas, with similar rainfall, are pretty different; a higher evaporation rate and a longer growing season take a lot more moisture out of the soil in Dallas than in Chicago. A mesic prairie in Nebraska can have as little as 23 inches of rain for an annual average.

Soil type is also important. A mesic prairie usually has deep root-permeable soil consisting of a minimum of 6 inches of porous topsoil rich with humus and oxygen, a dense subsoil to hold moisture, and a loose parent soil in which roots can penetrate deep down to find the stable temperatures and moisture that are present even in drought years.

Because mesic prairies are on rolling ground, they harbor both wet and dry species. Lowland prairie species are found in swales, which hold water for a short time after a heavy rain, and upland prairie species are found on the higher spots. In this way, a mesic prairie is always ready to adjust to wetter or drier climate cycles. A mixture of wet and mesic species is called wet-mesic, and a mixture of dry and mesic species is called dry-mesic.

Schaefer Prairie, west of Minneapolis, Minnesota, is a silty mesic prairie with both wet and dry areas. It was sold to The Nature Conservancy in 1967 by Lula Schaefer Leonard. Her family had bought the land from a Wapatan Sioux in 1885, and while Lula harvested the hay, she never allowed the land to be plowed or grazed by domestic animals until her brothers forced her to lease the southern end to raise money to pay taxes on it. This prairie was saved because of Lula's steadfast dedication to it.

During the last ice age, Schaefer Prairie was covered by a glacier. Pollen studies show that 12,000 years ago it was a forest of spruce and tamarack. Ten thousand years ago it was a forest of pine and broadleaf trees. About 8,000 years ago it evolved into a rich-soiled prairie. Now, it hosts 245 native species of plants and 30 non-native species. It is mostly mesic prairie, but it has an area of wet prairie (marked by clumps of willow) and a gravel esker with an interesting patch of dry prairie. Bird species include song sparrow, American goldfinch, bobolink, and common yellowthroat.

A DRY-MESIC PORTION of Schaefer Prairie in autumn is lovely with several species of goldenrod and aster. Showy goldenrod predominates with smooth blue aster and Indiangrass. Both mesic and dry prairies have foliage that is bright green, yellow green, and silver. Here the gray velvety leaves of leadplant are echoed by the almost hidden silver leaves of Louisiana sage. *Schaefer Prairie. Brownton, Minnesota. September 15.*

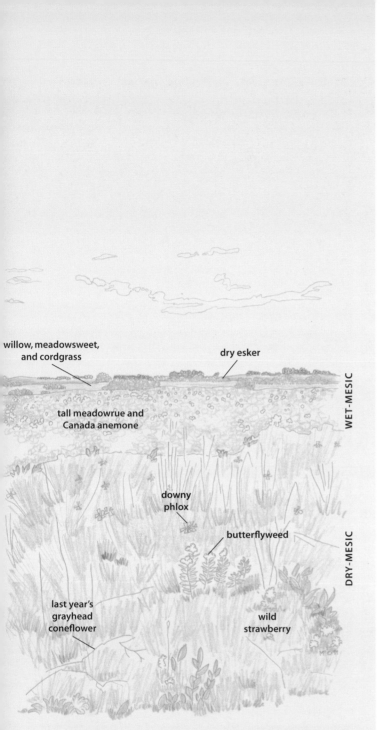

willow, meadowsweet, and cordgrass

dry esker

WET-MESIC

tall meadowrue and Canada anemone

downy phlox

butterflyweed

DRY-MESIC

last year's grayhead coneflower

wild strawberry

MESIC PRAIRIE arranges itself in broad stripes, with dry-mesic plants at the top of a roll and wet-mesic plants in the trough. In this northern tallgrass prairie, the foreground is dry-mesic prairie, which is pink with downy phlox and a ground layer of wild strawberry. The gentle dip beyond is wet-mesic prairie, and it is white with tall meadowrue and a ground layer of Canada anemone. The dots of willow in the background indicate a wet prairie dominated by cordgrass. The ridge beyond the willows is a gravelly esker, which is covered with dry shortgrass prairie species. Trees are visible behind the esker. In the foreground, tall tan stems of grayhead coneflower are left over from last year's vegetative growth. *Schaefer Prairie. Brownton, Minnesota. June 26.*

HEATH ASTER, skyblue aster, smooth blue aster, stiff goldenrod, gray goldenrod, big bluestem, Indiangrass, and the maroon autumn leaves of spring-blooming golden Alexanders make this human-made prairie garden especially beautiful in fall. This prairie and bur oak savanna are maintained by volunteers headed by curator Chase Cornelius. *Minnesota Landscape Arboretum. Chanhassen, Minnesota. September 15.*

— A human-made mesic prairie garden within an hour's drive of Schaefer Prairie can be seen at the Minnesota Landscape Arboretum. The site had been pasture previous to its restoration. Although bur oaks were still present, the native grasses and forbs had been grazed out, and the land had been replanted with exotic farm crops, such as quackgrass and crown vetch. The reconstruction was inspired by a Wisconsin prairie, and the seed was gathered from a mesic site just over the state line in Iowa. For budgetary reasons, the prairie grasses and forbs were sown only along paths and in a few designated spots to give color. The hillside was burned but never planted. The soil was not disturbed with glyphosate, tilling, or mulching. To everyone's amazement and delight, the prairie spread uphill *against* gravity and the prevailing wind, so that it now extends beyond the bur oaks at the top of the hill.

— Scuppernong Prairie in southern Wisconsin used to be wet-mesic, but it was drained a few decades ago, making it dry-mesic. The dominant grass is now prairie dropseed.

FORB LEAVES contrast beautifully with the fine texture of prairie dropseed's extremely narrow yellow green blades. Large-leaved prairie dock and shrublike cream wild indigo are the most eye-catching, but thirteen other distinctly different kinds of leaves are visible in this photo. *Scuppernong Prairie. Waukesha County, Wisconsin. July 5.*

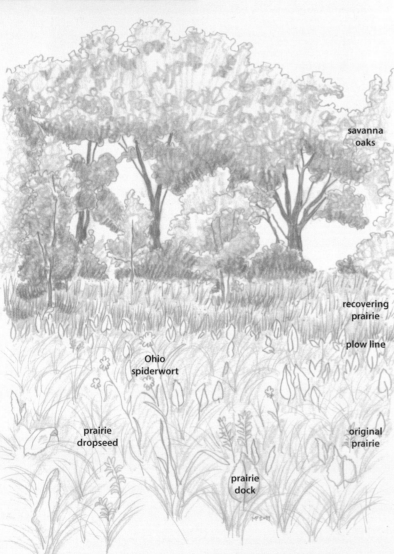

savanna oaks

recovering prairie

plow line

Ohio spiderwort

prairie dropseed

prairie dock

original prairie

IN THE FOREGROUND is original prairie composed of prairie dropseed, along with Ohio spiderwort, prairie dock, and prairie alum-root. In the background are large savanna oaks with northern bedstraw blooming beneath them. In between, notice how much coarser the texture is. This is prairie recovering on its own. Twenty to fifty years ago, this area was a plowed field. The "new" prairie is dominated not by prairie dropseed but by little bluestem and showy tick trefoil. *Scuppernong Prairie. Waukesha County, Wisconsin. July 5.*

Many northern dry-mesic prairies are dominated by long-lived prairie dropseed, a much shorter grass than big bluestem, or Indiangrass. Prairie dropseed has extremely narrow weeping leaves that give it a fine, elegant texture.

— A prairie dominated by prairie dropseed takes a long time to develop on its own. But when it is planted as a garden, it is almost immediately aesthetically rewarding. To see excellent re-creations, go to the Ray Schulenberg Prairie at the Morton Arboretum near Chicago or to the Greene Prairie at the university arboretum in Madison, Wisconsin. This kind of prairie garden is appropriate only for those who live in northern tallgrass prairie zones and in the northern Great Plains, and it is easiest for those who live in an area bounded by southern Manitoba, Nebraska, and Indiana.

THE SCHULENBERG PRAIRIE of the Morton Arboretum is the best replication we saw. Among the clumps of prairie dropseed are the contrasting leaves of two silphiums—prairie dock and compass plant—and the yuccalike leaves of rattlesnake master. The flowers of the moment are stiff goldenrod, gray goldenrod, and an aster. The dark red seed heads are of roundhead bush-clover with a few solitary round seed heads of pale coneflower. The coppery grasses in the background belong to a wet-mesic prairie dominated by big bluestem. *Ray Schulenberg Prairie, Morton Arboretum. Lisle, Illinois. September 23.*

IN 1989 Bill Davit designed and planted a 9-acre tallgrass prairie at a Missouri Botanical Garden site in St. Louis. On deep, rich, moist soil, this wet-mesic prairie is as tall as those described in pioneer's stories. See my hand just right of center? I was holding my arm straight up over my head, and I am 5½ feet tall. *July 17.*

— Eastern Missouri has high humidity, hot summers, and comparatively mild winters. In St. Louis bottomlands, we finally saw a tallgrass prairie that was over our heads. From pioneer reports, I had expected this to be the norm, but this was the only one we saw anywhere in our travels. Ecologists surmise that these really tall prairies were on the richest land and so were the first to be plowed. The one we visited was a replicated prairie designed and planted by Bill Davit of the Missouri Botanical Garden.

Andy wanted to take a photo of me standing in the prairie to show its height. At first I was apprehensive about walking in where I could see no more then 3 inches in front of my face. It was actually OK—better than OK. There was far more room in the prairie than I had expected, and the soil under my feet was clean and bare. The stems and leaves did not grab at me, not even those

THE MESIC SOUTHERN TALLGRASS PRAIRIE at Shaw Arboretum west of St. Louis is on shallower soil. Restored by Bill Davit, it is dominated by big and little bluestem, blazing star, rattlesnake master, and oxeye sunflower. About 5 feet tall, it gets burned yearly. *Shaw Arboretum, Gray Summit, Missouri. August 14.*

of the little bluestem, which was only half as tall as the big bluestem, eastern gamagrass, rosinweed, and wild bergamot. The temperature was cooler and more pleasant inside the prairie, and the scents that surrounded me were of live green things and the fresh mintiness of wild bergamot. It was also unexpectedly quiet, except for the buzzing of bees. Just eight steps into the prairie, and I was in a private, sheltered world.

— The Colony Prairie in Denton County, Texas, is about 30 miles north of Dallas. This rich piece of Blackland Prairie was a cotton farm for more than a century. In 1989, when IBM decided to restore it to mesic tallgrass prairie, the only bits of prairie visible were four clumps of big bluestem by some toppled headstones in the old graveyard.

Bill Neiman, owner of Native American Seed in Junction, Texas, plowed and disced in late winter. He let a few rains break up the heavy black clay clods, and then he harrowed to prepare a seedbed. He planted before Easter with a specially adapted seeder. One 10-acre area had to be seeded in midsummer because it was too wet to plow in the spring. Called a "slick spot," it seemed to be a naturally occurring salt fault that the farmers had given up on. The seedlings took a long time to appear, but now it has completely blended in with the rest of the prairie.

ALTHOUGH BILL NEIMAN COLLECTS, grows, and sells local handpicked prairie seed, he was on a tight budget for this project, so he had to resort to using brand-name seeds of little bluestem, big bluestem, Indiangrass, and switchgrass, the "big four" grasses of the Blackland Prairie. No forbs were planted, but they started appearing on their own after the prairie was burned in the fourth year; the same year plovers were seen for the first time in decades. *Denton County, Texas. October.*

■ UPLAND PRAIRIES

Upland prairies are always well drained and are the driest prairies in their area. On the Great Plains, the majority of the prairies could be termed upland or dry prairies because they never hold standing water—not even for an hour. Commonly called shortgrass prairie, upland prairies are usually knee-high, with species ranging from ankle- to waist-high, depending on rainfall. Characteristic species are little bluestem, sideoats grama, and needlegrasses, with an understory of buffalograss, blue grama, or black grama.

With domestic grazing or drought, buffalograss and blue grama become dominant. When grass cover is not continuous, rocks, pussytoes, or reindeer moss show between the clumps of grasses and forbs. In the Southwest, shortgrass prairie blends into desert grasslands and yucca savannas. Farther north, it blends into sagebrush steppes and ponderosa pine savannas. By the time shortgrass prairie washes up against the Canadian Rockies, it has mixed with Idaho and California species, and native fescues are the dominant grasses.

East of the 100th meridian, upland prairies are found on steep hillsides composed of porous, fast-draining soil, or on gentle hilltops where the soil is very shallow. Prairie dropseed, little bluestem, and hairy grama are considered to be upland prairie species because they do not tolerate poor drainage or heavy wet soil. The sandy prairies attached to black oak savannas are composed of dry upland species. The Konza Prairie in the Flint Hills of eastern Kansas, although considered a tallgrass prairie, has many dry upland species where bedrock is covered by only a few inches of soil.

West of the 100th meridian, average annual rainfall is too scant to support trees except in creek bottoms. The 100th meridian is an arbitrary line, cutting through Manitoba, the Dakotas, Nebraska, Kansas, Oklahoma, and Texas. Trees appear on Highway 1 in Manitoba near Brandon. During the drought of the 1930s, J. E. Weaver determined the line in Nebraska to be at 98°30'. In Texas, trees—even mesquites—become shrub size west of Abilene.

Between the 97th and 102d meridians, tallgrass and shortgrass species struggle for dominance, depending on rain cycles, so some scientists refer to this area as midgrass

IN SOUTHEASTERN NEBRASKA, we found this little bluestem prairie in its fall colors of tangerine and lime. The airy tarnished gold of Indiangrass is evident in a band of slightly moister soil. Forbs easy to spot in this photo are common ironweed, stiff goldenrod, and round-head lespedeza. The Oregon Trail runs right through this prairie. *Rock Creek Station Historical Park, Jefferson County, Nebraska. September 11.*

BUFFALOGRASS and a shrubby thicket of roughleaf dogwood, elm, and coralberry are rooted in the cool, moist limestone cracks found at the edge of a bluff at Konza Prairie. This area was burned two years ago but had not been burned at all during the previous twenty-five years. Dotted gayfeather, stiff goldenrod, and tall boneset are in bloom. Black Sampson and roundhead bushclover, wild indigo, and sideoats grama are already in seed, along with the white juicy fruits of roughleaf dogwood. Louisiana sage grows between the clumps of little bluestem. *Konza Prairie, Manhattan, Kansas. September 11.*

prairie. Of course, no scientist draws these maps with straight lines. The vegetative boundaries hop and skip and interweave according to soil, drainage, available information, and interpretation. The result is that no two maps look remotely the same. *If I lived in this area, I would experiment in my garden with both tallgrass and shortgrass species, and end up with whatever survived on rainfall alone.*

Rock Creek Station Historical Park in Jefferson County, Nebraska, around the 97th meridian, is an old stagecoach station at a ford on the Oregon Trail. Little bluestem is the dominant grass, and the height of this prairie at the end of its growing season was just under waist-high. The tracks of the old trail show that the soil was deep and porous in some areas and only a foot or so deep over solid rock in others. I found this prairie very similar in some respects to prairies near Dallas, Texas, 500 miles south but also close to the 97th meridian. It is easy to see why there is a lot of confusion in this area about whether to call these prairies tallgrass, midgrass, or mixedgrass.

— Konza Prairie, also close to the 97th meridian, is in the Flint Hills of eastern Kansas. Managed by the University of Kansas at Manhattan, it is one of the best studied tallgrass prairies in the nation, especially with regard to the effects of grazing bison and fire. The tallgrass prairie species are knee-high on the hilltops, where just a few inches of soil cover the bedrock. Even the airy purplish stems of big bluestem are barely chest-high. On some west-facing slopes, we saw almost pure stands of buffalograss and other shortgrass species. On deep soils, we saw northern tallgrass species.

— Hay meadows in western Kansas preserve prairie remnants. The one at Thistle Hill Bed and Breakfast, just east of the 100th meridian, has never been plowed, and the buffalo wallows are still visible. Buffalograss, sideoats grama, needlegrass, western wheatgrass, and blue grama

LITTLE BLUESTEM is still dormant in spring when bluebonnets, prairie verbena, and Indian paintbrush are in bloom. Landscape designer Kathy Taylor added indigenous forbs to this little bluestem remnant prairie bordering a wooded limestone creek. A tiny buffalograss lawn between the restored prairie and the house acts as both a path and open area. *Romero home, Gruene, Texas. April 8.*

THIS SHIN-HIGH SHORTGRASS PRAIRIE at Thistle Hill Bed and Breakfast in west-central Kansas has never been plowed, but it has been grazed year-round for more than a century. Is this really a mesic prairie that looks like a shortgrass prairie because of frequent

are punctuated by dotted gayfeather, broom snakeweed (*Gutierrezia sarothrae*), snow-on-the-mountain, Mexican hat, curlycup gumweed (*Grindelia squarrosa*), false boneset, and pasture sage. There are also rosettes of winecup, a spring forb. The original prairie probably contained big bluestem, little bluestem, and Indiangrass. These three grasses are chest-high on the ungrazed side of the fence, where they were planted as part of the government-subsidized Restoration Conservation Program (RCP).

— We wish we could show you a great photo of typical northern Great Plains shortgrass prairie. Unfortunately, wherever we went on national grasslands and private grounds, where we had been told shortgrass prairie still existed, all we saw was crested wheatgrass—a non-native sown onto northern shortgrass prairies after they have been grazed down to bare soil.

In eastern Montana we found evidence of grazed-down buffalograss, needlegrass, and western wheatgrass. Forbs uneaten by domestic cattle were plains yucca or beargrass (*Yucca glauca*), prickly pear (*Opuntia fragilis*), and dwarf sagebrush. On the ungrazed sides of fences we found western wild rose, scarlet globemallow, Mexican hat, silvery lupine, sego lily, scarlet gaura, skeletonweed (*Lygodesmia juncea*), and prairie onion, with buffaloberry and cottonwood in the ditches. When these forbs and grasses grew together and flowered, it must have been a breathtaking sight.

SHORTGRASS PRAIRIE on the Great Plains in eastern New Mexico starts mingling with oneseed juniper as it rises toward the Rocky Mountains. Honey mesquite, cholla (*Opuntia imbricata*), and buffalo gourd (*Cucurbita foetidissima*), plentiful on the Great Plains, peter out halfway up this pass. Water losses from evaporation and transpiration are about 70 inches a year, while rainfall is close to 10 inches a year. *David's Pass, New Mexico. April 20.*

JANET AND DAVIS PRICE transplanted buffalograss, plains yucca, prickly pear, and pink evening primrose from their parents' ranches near Canyon, Texas. Note how the Prices planted the yucca and cactus directly in the grass, just as they found them in the original prairie. *Lubbock, Texas. May 18.*

On the Blackfeet Reservation in north-central Montana, snuggled against the east side of the Rocky Mountains, we found a tiny jewel of a prairie. Prominent in late June were Junegrass and other grasses just starting to green up. Forbs we saw were pasque flower in plumy seed, prairie smoke, death camas, biscuitroot (*Lomatium ambiguum*), lupines, and pale yellow beardtongue (*Penstemon confertus*).

Although it has been grazed, shortgrass prairie in eastern New Mexico is better preserved than farther north and east because much of it has never been plowed. From a distance, it probably looks the way it looked three hundred years ago. Up close, it varies considerably from year to year. In a normal year, it gets shin-high. In a dry year, it never greens up or grows at all. After abundant late summer rains, it is waist-high with Indiangrass and big bluestem—at least one or the other every square yard. More prevalent are little bluestem, grama grasses, needlegrasses, and other drought-tolerant native grasses not covered in this book, along with several non-natives. In other words, shortgrass prairie contains both dry and mesic prairie species; the dominant plant palette depends on how much rain falls in a given year.

■ SAND PRAIRIES

Sand prairies have perfect drainage, so they support dry prairie species. But because they also have dependable moisture 5 to 7 feet deep, western sand prairies display mesic species normally found in areas of much higher rainfall. Some grasses and forbs grow only in deep loose sand. These are not included in the plant profiles but are vital to sand prairie restoration.

Some species important to the sandhills of the Great Plains from Nebraska to Texas are blowoutgrass (*Redfieldia flexuosa*), sandhill muhly (*Muhlenbergia pungens*), sandreed (*Calamovilfa gigantea*), and sand bluestem, along with plains yucca (*Yucca glauca*) and bush morning glory (*Ipomoea leptophylla*). These have extremely long taproots that can survive for over a century. Slightly less long-lived and drought-tolerant are blue grama and needle-and-thread. Pioneer species that are shorter-lived with shallow root systems are

Junegrass, sunsedge, and sand lovegrass (*Eragrostis trichodes*) in Nebraska and purple lovegrass (*Eragrostis spectabilis*) in Texas. The numerical importance of each species varies from north to south.

■ SAVANNAS

Prairies are often bordered by savannas. *Savanna* is a term borrowed from the now extinct Arawak Indians of the Greater Antilles and Bahamas, and originally meant a forest opening or prairie. It did not come to mean a mixture of scattered trees over a ground cover of grasses until E. J. Dyksterhuis published a paper on the subject in 1957. In the 1800s, savannas were often called barrens, because they were nearly barren of trees. In truth, savannas are ecologically rich. It is estimated that a post oak savanna in the Ozarks may have as many as 350 different kinds of wildflowers, sedges, and grasses.

The savannas we are most concerned with in this book are the midwestern oak savannas. Accounts written by early European settlers praised the beauty of these savannas. They used phrases like "stately orchard," "magnificent grove," and "a sight of unparalleled beauty." Oak savannas, also called oak openings, were the transition between eastern forests and midwestern prairies. Tallgrass prairies existed primarily along the Mississippi and Missouri River watersheds. To the east of these prairies, approximately along 95° longitude, was a zone that had enough rainfall to become an eastern deciduous forest, except that it burned every three or four years along with the adjacent prairie. This zone of burned forest was called savanna. The thick corky bark of the savanna oaks and their ability to resprout from the roots enabled them to evolve with prairie fires.

MINNEHAHA FALLS CITY PARK has a formal garden made up of prairie and savanna wildflowers. Beneath a bur oak are indigenous savanna plants, which include fall-blooming, sweet-smelling heartleaf aster and zigzag goldenrod. *Minneapolis, Minnesota. September 14.*

BUR OAK SAVANNAS are usually found on heavy alkaline soil. This restored savanna is continuously grassy except on the north sides of the trees, where *Rubus*, dogwood, prairie dock, golden Alexanders, sawtooth sunflower (*Helianthus grosseserratus*), prairie blazing star, and a shade-tolerant goldenrod change the texture. Big bluestem, Indiangrass, and white wild indigo dominate at this time of year. *Prairie at Minnesota Landscape Arboretum, Chanhassen, Minnesota. June 26.*

Oak savannas were generally composed of at least two species of oak, one of which was always dominant and particularly long-lived, giving its name to designate that type of savanna. Hickories were often present, also having thick fire-resistant bark.

According to John T. Curtis, white oaks (*Quercus alba*) were the savanna trees of eastern North America, often growing with shagbark hickory (*Carya ovata*). As late as the 1920s, broad old specimens, with the low horizontal branches characteristic of savanna trees, could still be observed in Princeton, New Jersey, and on Long Island, New York.

In the Midwest, bur oak savannas gradually replaced the less drought-tolerant white oaks, especially in rich alkaline clay loam. In central Texas, where savannas still exist, escarpment live oaks replace bur oaks on upland sites, and the bur oaks drop down along the creeks, where moisture is more dependable. Bur oaks become creekside trees exclusively as they go west from the 95th to the 100th parallels. These bur oak riparian woodlands, on the southern and western edges of bur oak's range, were historically narrow, sunny, and accessible to fire, so their understory was composed of savanna plants rather than forest species.

From Ontario southward, black oak savannas still claim acid sandy lands. In parts of Minnesota and Wisconsin, black oaks hybridize with northern pin oaks. In savannas as far south as Missouri, the drier sands are occupied by post oak savannas instead of black

oak savannas, and in east Texas, black oaks are just an
occasional specimen in the post oak savannas. Black oak
and post oak savannas are sometimes called the sandy oak
savannas, and the eastern ranges of these habitats often
have pines growing with them: white pine (*Pinus strobus*)
with black oak, and shortleaf pine (*Pinus echinata*) with
post oak.

Not all the eastern savannas bordering the central
American prairies are dominated by oaks. To either side
of the Mississippi River, on old sandy beaches in the Gulf
Coast states, are longleaf pine savannas. Where they continue on into the Carolinas, they have an understory of
turkey oak (*Quercus laevis*). On exposed limestone knolls,
there are cedar glades with dots and clumps of eastern red
cedar. The transition from boreal forest to prairie is not
oak but aspen parkland—*parkland* being the Canadian
term for savanna.

There are also savannas on the western edges of the
Great Plains. Aspen parkland interfaces with prairie
across the Canadian prairie provinces from Manitoba to
Alberta, and continues down the Rocky Mountains. At
the western edge of the Great Plains in the rain shadow
of the Rockies, elevation, not latitude, determines moisture. The aspens form the highest savanna-like meadows.

Below the aspens are heavily grazed and logged ponderosa savannas with a bunchgrass understory of species
such as little bluestem, Indiangrass, *Muhlenbergia*, and big
bluestem with a burnable woody understory of Gambel
oak and snowberry.

At lower elevations, below the ponderosas, are pinyon
grasslands with needle-and-thread, blue grama, and Indian
ricegrass, and below them, grading into the driest shortgrass
prairies, are juniper grasslands. In Texas, New Mexico,
and Arizona, mesquite grasslands occupy foothills above
the Chihuahuan and Sonoran deserts.

In the coniferous savannas of the Rocky Mountains, the adjacent prairies are sometimes called intermountain grasslands and sometimes called shrub steppe. Here the shrubby artemisias, or sagebrush, are mixed in with cool season grasses, such as Junegrass, western wheatgrass, and needle-and-thread, along with reindeer lichen, pussytoes, blue grama, and hairy grama.

Recent research is showing that although savanna does knit together forest and prairie, it deserves to be studied as a separate ecosystem. Dr. Stephen Glass at the University of Wisconsin-Madison Arboretum has discovered that savanna understory species will not move into woodland sites—even those a few feet away that were deliberately burned—because fire alone does not remove mature canopy, and savanna understory seeds need more light to germinate.

Dr. Mark Leach, also at the University of Wisconsin-Madison Arboretum, has found that savanna understory is richer in diversity than either prairie or forest, as it consists of prairie species, forest species, and species that seem to be peculiar to savannas. Dr. Leach has also found that a savanna on nutrient-poor dry soil, such as sand, or on a very thin soil is basically a grassland dotted with trees. The species in the shade do not differ radically from those in the sun, although the shady grasses are often wetland prairie species as opposed to dry prairie species. But a savanna on rich silty soil that is mesic to wet will have sharp divisions between sun and shade. The tall grasses in the sun are replaced by forbs and shrubs and a few sedges in the shade, making the shady areas more of a "forb-land" than a grassland.

■ THICKET SHRUBS

All our savannas seem to have understory composed of grasses, woodland sedges, legumes, milkweeds, asters, goldenrods, and blazing stars, as well as short flowering trees and shrubs that easily resprout from the roots following a fire. These thicket shrubs used to hang from cliffs or would fill hollows and ravines where fire or deer did not reach. Now they are often out of control and overshade prairie grasses.

While most prairie restorationists consider thicket shrubs to be enemies of prairie, a small amount of thicket is necessary for wildlife. Thickets are the favorite nesting height for catbirds, cardinals, song sparrows, and red-winged blackbirds. Rabbits, foxes, and weasels dig burrows under their roots. Deer and elk browse the leaves and twigs into gracefully rounded shapes. Thicket shrubs produce juicy plums, cherries, and blackberries that ripen in time for sum-

THE UNIVERSITY OF WISCONSIN at Madison has done extensive work with a dry-soil oak savanna attached to the Greene Prairie. The trees are bur oak, white oak, black oak, Hill's oak, and hybrids of these species. Many of the shrubs in this photo are waist-high oak grubs that are really root sprouts. They are probably a natural part of this kind of savanna, as they were recorded by pioneers. Smooth sumac in red fall color, Indiangrass, little bluestem, and gray goldenrod indicate that frost is soon to come. *Greene Prairie, University of Wisconsin at Madison. September 17.*

POST OAK SAVANNAS are found in fast-draining soils south of black oak savannas. Tree ring studies in the Ozarks indicate that many of Missouri's oak-hickory woodlands used to be grassy savannas maintained by bison, elk, and fire. After noticing that Missouri's carefully preserved savannas were deteriorating after decades of no burns, the Missouri Department of Conservation, the Missouri Department of Natural Resources, and The Nature Conservancy in Missouri banded together to start using fire to restore post oak savannas. The one we visited had a rich understory of moss, woodland sedge, Virginia wildrye, little bluestem, Indiangrass, and a host of herbs I was familiar with from post oak areas in East Texas, as well as black oak savannas farther north. Because the soil is so nutrient-poor, a large proportion of the herbs are nitrogen-producing legumes. *Bennett Springs State Park, Missouri. October 1.*

mer fledglings and fall migration, as well as rose hips, hazelnuts, and other "dry" fruits that winter well. If you want to see birds, plant a thicket.

■ HAVING TROUBLE FINDING A PRAIRIE TO COPY?

It is shocking how few of our native prairies and savannas remain. On Long Island, a few miles from Manhattan, we visited Hempstead Plains. This was the easternmost prairie we saw, and for more than four hundred years it has suffered from overgrazing by European domestic animals and the disregard of city dwellers. Andy's Aunt Inka has lived within fifteen minutes of Hempstead Plains for over forty years, and she did not even know it existed.

When Europeans landed, Hempstead Plains comprised some 60,000 acres. The last remaining 20 acres is managed by The Nature Conservancy and, of that, only 3 acres are in "pretty good" shape, according to Bob Zeremba of The Nature Conservancy in Albany. That these 20 acres exist at all is because they served as an air base and a golf course when the rest of the plains were being turned into Levittowns after World War II.

The midwestern oak savannas once occupied about 20 million hectares along the eastern boundary of the Great Plains. However, until 1985, when a group of volunteers led by Steve Packard, now with The Nature Conservancy, started restoring Vestal Grove in Cook County, Illinois, north of Chicago, oak savannas had been obliterated for so long that botanists no longer thought of them as a habitat in themselves. They were believed to be "merely" a transition zone where forest and prairie meet.

AROUND THE SIGN are non-native weeds. We had to walk out about 50 yards before we started seeing native prairie plants such as sphagnum moss, roundhead bushclover, Indiangrass, graystem goldenrod, and tall boneset. The big bluestem and asters are long gone, according to Bob Zeremba of The Nature Conservancy, but two endemics on the endangered list are still present. Surrounded by a shopping mall, a coliseum, a hotel, and an interstate, this prairie no longer sees night sky unless there is an electrical blackout. *Hempstead Plains, Long Island, New York. September 26.*

ONE GOOD PLACE to look for prairie remnants is in pioneer graveyards. The Smith Cemetery must originally have been bur oak savanna. The white marble stone belongs to Elizaphon Holycross, who died March 25, 1855, aged twenty-three years old. The big bluestem prairie was 6 feet tall in the sun, and only 3 to 4 feet tall under the bur oaks, where savanna species such as grape, carrionvine, and a dry-woodland sedge mixed with the prairie. The whole graveyard is 18 inches higher than the black clay loam farmland that surrounds it, showing how much soil has been eroded by 140 years of plowing. *Smith Cemetery, Madison County, Darby Township, Ohio. September 30.*

In Ohio, as in many other prairie states, some of the best prairie remnants are in old cemeteries. The land was put aside for burials—usually an acre at the top of a hill with an existing bur oak—and so it was never plowed. However, only a few cemeteries have escaped being mowed too often. Frequent mowing kills prairie plants.

Scott Weber of Bluestem Farm in Baraboo, Wisconsin, tells the following story:

> Back in the late 1970s, I saw a local news station congratulating itself for solving a problem: a resident was alarmed that an old cemetery had not been mowed and was unsightly. The "before" picture, to my amazement, as well as shock, showed a cemetery full of Indian grass, compass plant, and other species of virgin prairie. Here was a prairie relic, saved from the plow by a pioneer grave site. The "after" picture, predictably, showed the site mowed to the ground. How ironic that a news station in "The Prairie State" would report such a deed as a public relations victory, when the real news was that such a site still existed right in the heart of the city.

Today many restorationists gather their seeds along railroad tracks. When the railroads moved westward, they were viewed as a magnificent example of American know-how and dynamic growth. Yet, a few concerned voices were raised denouncing the railroads for destroying native vegetation and for scattering western seeds in midwestern cities. Today, you can find many shortgrass species not native to Illinois that have naturalized along train tracks in that state. While some of these rights-of-way are not true to the original prairies, they are prairies, and they have valuable repositories of native American seed.

THE MURALT PRAIRIE owes its existence to its being a dry prairie on a long narrow hill too steep to plow. Showy goldenrod, smooth sumac with its brilliant red leaves, Indiangrass, little bluestem, sideoats grama, and sprouts of wild black cherry are prominent in this picture. *Muralt Prairie, Green County, Wisconsin. September 18.*

As the old rails are dismantled, environmentalists and farmers fight over who gets to use the land. Where environmentalists have won, the railroad rights-of-way have become jogging trails or wildlife corridors. In other areas, such as near Kitchener, Ontario, where the farmers won, the railroad prairies were plowed to extend the farm fields.

Old country roads are also sometimes bordered with prairie remnants, especially in very poor counties where mowing takes place only once or twice a year. In Texas, a sterile mowed roadside may stop at the county line and erupt into dozens of native grasses and forbs, simply because the flowery county was saving money while the sterile county was trying to please people who thought the wildflowers looked "messy."

It could be that all our remnant prairies are not representative of typical mesic prairies. The mesic prairies with rich soil were the first to be plowed. Then the wet prairies were drained. Except for rare instances, only the dry prairies remain. We may never know exactly what the mesic prairies looked like, as written records are sketchy, and the soil for doing pollen tests has long since eroded away.

THIS BEAUTEOUS QUARTER-ACRE of roadside is on sandy soil in central Wisconsin. Road maintenance is steadily destroying the edges. We stood on mowed big bluestem to take the picture; the news that big bluestem cannot survive frequent mowings obviously never reached the maintenance crews and their bosses. The regularly mowed margin alongside the road was already filling with weeds. Still, this beleaguered bit was vibrant with showy goldenrod, skyblue aster, little bluestem, Indiangrass, and closed gentian. State Highway 21 *near Cutler, Wisconsin. September 16.*

Chapter 5

It required only a few wild acres for J. E. Weaver to discover why prairie flora is more drought resistant than the agronomic flora which supplanted it. Weaver found that the prairie species practice "team work" underground by distributing their root systems to cover all levels, whereas the species comprising the agronomic rotation overdraw one level and neglect another, thus building up cumulative deficits.

    ALDO LEOPOLD, Sand County Almanac, *1949*

Anatomy of a Prairie

BEFORE PLANTING A PRAIRIE, it is helpful to know which plants to use, how far apart they should be spaced, how fast they germinate and grow, and how long they are likely to live. Thanks largely to the work of J. E. Weaver, we know a lot about the depth and width of prairie roots, how they interact, how they differ from tallgrass to shortgrass sites, and how sod prevents erosion. We have data from long-vanished prairies about which plants were dominant in uplands and which in lowlands, and the proportions of grasses to forbs. And we also have valuable information about how prairie behaved during the great drought from 1933 to 1940.

◼ J. E. WEAVER

John Ernest Weaver earned his B.S. and M.S. from the University of Nebraska and his Ph.D. from the University of Minnesota. In the period between his M.S. and Ph.D., he spent some time in the now extinct Palouse Prairie in southeastern Washington. There he learned the painstaking technique of exposing and drawing a network of roots in situ. He was fascinated by the depth, intricacy, and efficiency of prairie roots. As soon as he joined the teaching staff at the University of Nebraska at Lincoln in 1915, he set out to examine 140 species from twenty-five prairie plots in Kansas, Colorado, South Dakota, and Nebraska. The results of his studies were published in 1919, in his tenth paper since 1914. During his lifetime he authored or coauthored 105 publications, including 12 monographs and 8 books.

    A dedicated workaholic, Weaver was passionate about prairies and his work. He

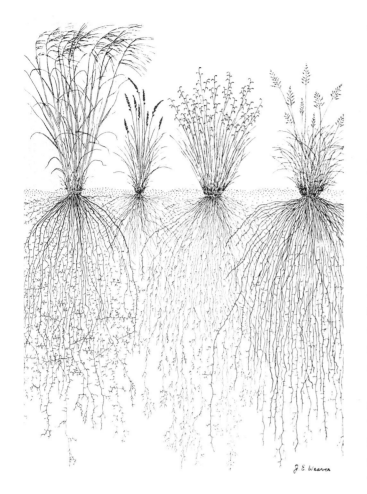

ONE OF J. E. WEAVER'S MANY ROOT DRAWINGS shows a 1-inch-thick slice of the tops and roots of four bunchgrasses common to upland prairie communities. Species from *left* to *right* are porcupine grass, Junegrass, little bluestem, and prairie dropseed. Weaver noted "that the tops are only about half as high as the roots are deep."

quickly developed a prestigious reputation that attracted both grants ($1,000 a year per student) and graduate students. In 1928, Weaver himself earned $3,000 a year, more than any other botany professor at the university, but he spent almost all of the money on his own research. Edsko J. Dyksterhuis was his most famous student, and Weaver characterized him as his "worst student" because Dyksterhuis had the temerity to argue with him. Weaver's son earned his master's with him, later going on to Chicago for his Ph.D. In all, Weaver had forty-seven graduate students who completed their degrees under him, five of them women, from 1923 to 1952.

Standing in the prairie, dressed in a three-piece suit and a green eyeshade, Weaver would direct the students to dig a trench, 2.5 feet wide, 5 to 10 feet long, and as much as 15 feet deep, to trace the roots of selected grasses and forbs. Then the students would climb down into the pit, stretch a grid with string and nails, and draw the roots. The students were paid 25 cents an hour.

Between 1953, when Weaver retired, and June 6, 1966, when he died at the age of eighty-two, he continued to study prairies, producing eleven papers and four books. Pete Jensen, his best friend in later years, recalled Weaver lying in his coffin: "It was open casket, and Weaver as usual was dressed impeccably in a three-piece suit with a starched white shirt. His glasses were laid on his chest. His hands were clasped. With joy, I noticed his fingernails; they were black with prairie dirt."

■ SOIL AND ROOT LAYER

Root Depth

The roots of grasses and forbs arrange themselves in layers so that every cubic inch of soil is exploited for moisture and nutrients. Tallgrass species grow deeper, because soil moisture is deeper. Shortgrass species are unlikely to find moisture beyond the fourth foot of soil, so they rarely grow deeper. Root depth varies each year according to rainfall. During a drought, in those places where soil moisture was nonexistent 2.5 feet down, Weaver found no roots below that depth.

Weaver found that the most long-lived tallgrass prairie plants have roots 5 to 23 feet deep. These include big bluestem, Indiangrass, prairie cordgrass, switchgrass, blazing star, wild indigo, rosinweed, wild rose, wild licorice, and leadplant. Little bluestem, heath aster, astragalus, and pale coneflower monopolize moisture and nutrients in the

J. E. WEAVER was a dynamic lecturer, pacing back and forth in front of the class, gesturing with his hands and waving his arms. He was a serious man—no jokes, no drinking, very proper, and extremely conservative politically. He read only technical literature and never engaged in small talk. Even his wife, a warm friendly woman, called him Dr. Weaver.

NINE MILE PRAIRIE is exactly 9 miles from Bessey Hall, where Weaver worked at the University of Nebraska in Lincoln. Weaver rented it for $10 a year, and although he worked at many other local prairies, it has been said that Nine Mile was the most studied prairie in the world at that time. In 1928 it consisted of 800 acres covered with 345 species. By 1975, 230 acres were left unplowed, but they had been overgrazed, many of the forbs had been treated with herbicide, and smooth brome was invading from adjacent fields. In 1979 the Audubon Society leased the prairie to save it, and in 1982, with the help of the state legislature and a benefactor, the land was bought by the University Foundation. Ernie Rousek, a soil scientist, inventor, and the Audubon member who fought hardest to save Nine Mile Prairie, burns the prairie on a three-year rotation the first week in May, as that is the time of year that fire is most likely to hurt smooth brome. *Lancaster County, Nebraska. September 12.*

band of soil 2 to 5 feet deep. A third group, which includes Junegrass, takes advantage of the top 2 feet of soil.

In the shortgrass and mixedgrass prairies of the Great Plains, the deep-rooted species go 5 to 7 feet deep. These include buffalograss, blue grama, western wheatgrass, sideoats grama, locoweed (*Oxytropis*), scurfy pea, yucca, and stoneseed. In areas of low rainfall, these deep-rooted prairie species also have extensive surface roots to take advantage of showers. Roots of forbs that specialize in surface absorption, such as broom snakeweed (*Gutierrezia sarothrae*) and pasture sage, might cover over 20 square feet of ground.

When a prairie is fully developed, root competition is so fierce that all the grasses and forbs are shortened and skimpy, and nothing is allowed to be aggressive. This makes a very pretty, friendly prairie to walk in.

Mycorrhizal Fungi

Since Weaver's time, scientists have continued to study prairie roots, and it is now evident that the thready end parts of roots are really mycorrhizal (my-ko-RYE-zal) fungi. The fungi acquire their carbon from the plant and, in return, act as an extension of the root system, improving the absorption of minerals, water, and nutrients and aiding the plant in resisting disease, improving soil structure, and recycling organic matter. There are many different species of mycorrhizae; common species grow on row crops while more sophisticated species are required by conservative prairie grasses and forbs. Warm season grasses are more dependent on mycorrhizal fungi than cool season grasses. Research is going on to determine whether mycorrhizae, sometimes called inoculants, need to be added to the soil to create a high-quality prairie.

Soil Nitrogen

For many years it was thought that legumes were nature's way of replenishing nitrogen in soil. More recent research has shown that it is the bacteria in legume root nodules that have the nitrogen-fixing properties. Blue-green algae growing on soil surfaces are also important in adding nitrogen to the soil.

FIELD HORSETAIL (*Equisetum arvense*) is native to the Northern Hemisphere and is useful in the treatment of prostate and kidney problems. We saw it often as a ground layer in ancient prairies and as a volunteer in moist home prairie gardens.

■ GROUND LAYER

Sod Layer

The layer of soil that sits above the roots in a prairie is called the ground layer. On some prairies it looks like bare soil, clean and pure, and can be seen between stalks of forbs and grasses. This soil is actually well-developed sod that lets rain soak in and allows almost no runoff. If during a frog-strangler, there is runoff, it is clear water; no soil erosion takes place. On overgrazed prairie, however, where the sod layer has been severely damaged, five tons of soil per acre can be eroded in a single storm.

Ground Covers

Covering the soil is often a low-growing ground cover or, in Weaver's words, a "mat-former." From wet sites to dry, we saw sphagnum moss, field horsetail, Canada anemone,

STRANGE CRUSTY LICHENS are a natural part of dry prairies. *Caprock Canyons State Park, Texas. May 27.*

wild strawberry, different species of pussytoes, reindeer lichen, and other species of mosses or lichens. Where conditions were really dry and the land was grazed down to bare earth, we saw desert "pavement," that is, a skin or crust of small rocks that resists wind and water erosion and moderates temperatures.

Understory Grasses

In the best remnant prairies, there are shorter understory grasses growing under the taller grasses. In tallgrass prairie, the probably non-native Canada bluegrass (*Poa compressa*) and the maybe-native-along-the-Canadian-border Kentucky bluegrass (*Poa pratensis*) are common, but we also found prairie panicgrass. Where little bluestem is the tallest grass, between its clumps is an understory of Scribner's panicgrass, buffalograss, blue grama, black grama, or purple lovegrass (*Eragrostis spectabilis*).

Understory Sedges

In all types of prairies, various species of small shade-tolerant sedges, *Carex*, are common. These are sometimes the same species found in abundance in savannas. Dry woodland sedges seem to be the ground layers of choice for savannas. Usually there are several species, but one is likely to be dominant.

■ GRASSES AND GRASSLIKE PLANTS

Grass Dominance

There would be no prairies without grasses. In tallgrass prairie, Weaver found that eleven species of grasses accounted for 80 percent of the vegetation. In some prairies, 90 percent or more of all the foliage is big bluestem. Yet, even when big bluestem dominates to that extent, it occupies less than 14 percent of the total ground area. The individual clumps are large, but between clumps is plenty of room for other species.

Grass Categories

Not only can grasses be divided into short grasses and tall grasses, but they can also be divided by season: cool season grasses are green as soon as temperatures rise above freezing, and they bloom in spring or early summer. Warm season grasses grow in the heat of summer and bloom in late summer or early fall. Grasses can be further divided into C_3 plants and C_4 plants, depending on whether the plant uses carbon dioxide directly from the air in photosynthesis (C_3 plants), or whether it takes up carbon dioxide at night and stores it for use during

WHERE BLACK OAK SAVANNA had not been burned for a hundred years, the ground layer consisted of nasty brown clumps of non-native fescue surrounded by bare ground. An accidental fire the year before produced lush, 8-inch clumps of a native sedge. The forbs growing through this sedge were healthy and had bloomed. The buds of those growing beside the fescue had been ravaged by insects. *High Park, Toronto, Ontario. July 11.*

AFTER A SPRING BURN, it is easy to see why big bluestem dominates a prairie. Look at how huge this grass clump is compared to the other grasses and forbs. *Oak Hammock Wildlife Management Area, Red River Valley, Manitoba. June 24.*

the day (C_4 plants). C_3 plants are woody plants, annuals, and cool season grasses. Needlegrasses, for example, are C_3 grasses that evolved on the edges of glaciers. C_4 plants include warm season grasses and forbs that evolved in the southern United States and Mexico. C_4 plants, such as the bluestems, have a higher rate of photosynthesis at high temperatures and use water more efficiently.

Grasslike Plants

The grasses belong, not surprisingly, to the grass family, but there are many grass*like* plants, mostly sedges and rushes, such as *Carex*, *Juncus*, and *Scirpus*. Most grow in wet prairies or in savannas.

■ FORBS

Forbs are all the nongrassy herbs in a prairie or savanna. Lilies, gentians, asters, sunflowers, and goldenrods are forbs. Sometimes nonherbaceous shrubby plants, such as roses and leadplant, are counted as forbs, because they are an integral part of prairie and they regularly burn to the ground and resprout.

Bloom Times

Forbs bloom continuously from early spring to frost, but there are four distinct climaxes of color: early spring, late spring, summer, and fall. In any one area, about twelve species are found flowering in early spring, forty bloom in late spring, seventy flower in summer, and another forty, mostly goldenrods and asters, appear in autumn, indicating that frost is not far away.

Height

The early spring flowers are very short. After all, the grasses are either short at that stage, or dormant. By midsummer, rosinweeds, sunflowers, stenosiphon, and bergamot need to be 5 or 6 feet tall, as tall as the grasses, to reach sunlight. Then, interestingly, in autumn the gentians, gayfeathers, and some of the goldenrods and asters are knee-height, down among the shrinking grasses, which are developing shades of red, rust, coral, and gold.

■ SHAPERS OF PRAIRIE

Fire

Fire affects prairies in several important ways. It eliminates trees. It cleans up vegetative debris so that forbs do not get smothered by thatch, and sunlight can reach the ground to germinate new seedlings. It returns nutrients to the soil in ash. And considering how mature plants magically appear after the first fire in decades, it could be that fire revitalizes roots or mycorrhizae.

Lightning strikes used to be the only cause of prairie fires, but when Native Americans observed how beneficial fires were to prairies and savannas, they started lighting them themselves.

Wind

Without trees to act as windbreaks, wind is inevitable. But scientists are beginning to see that prairie plants do not just endure wind, but use it to their advantage. Wind disperses pollen and seeds. Wind slows down grasshoppers; after all, they can eat only so much while holding to a stem for dear life. The next time you are in a prairie, notice how tricky the wind is, coming in spurts and gusts and constantly shifting direction.

Prairie plants have an advantage over trees when it comes to withstanding wind. The grasses get tossed around like waves, but they do not get permanently bent to one side the way a tree would. A prairie can withstand a tornado that would uproot an oak tree.

Grazing Mammals

North American prairies evolved 25 million years ago as the Rockies arose and created drier conditions. As the grasslands evolved, so too did horses, camels, and rhinos. They developed longer teeth because grazing (eating grass) wears teeth down faster than browsing (eating shrubs and tree twigs). Mammoths, sloths, pronghorn antelopes, and aurochs also feasted on the prairies.

All but the pronghorn became extinct about 11,500 years ago when Clovis man arrived during an interglacial. As Richard Manning writes in *Grasslands*, "The stratigraphy announces a stiff fact: The spear points appear suddenly, and above them there are no bones of native megafauna. No mammoths, no sloths, horses, camels, dire wolf, no *Bison antiquus*. The thin black line is the demarcation of extinction. The spears came and the animals went."

A BISON stands next to a buffalo wallow at Konza Prairie. The wallows are used to rub off shaggy winter coats. They also seem to serve as the arena for the foreplay that precedes a power battle. The bowl of bare earth catches moisture and gives fresh seeds a place to germinate.

PRONGHORN ANTELOPE are skittish and can run as fast as 70 miles an hour for as long as three minutes. Their speed and endurance are probably why they are the only native North American megafauna to have survived Clovis man.

Bison, elk, deer, moose, grizzly bear, black bear, and caribou, which had immigrated from Asia earlier, survived. Prairies continued to evolve under the management of Native Americans.

Bison, popularly known as buffalo, eat grasses that domestic cattle do not. At the Intertribal Bison Co-op in South Dakota, we watched a herd feasting on native western wheatgrass and needle-and-thread. I had always been told that needle-and-thread was not grazeable, so I was glad to hear that bison do eat it and was very curious to see their method. One cow seemed happy to oblige and demonstrated the process for me. She turned her head and looked at me from time to time to make sure I was paying attention. First she placed her mouth on the middle section of a clump of needlegrass and pulled it out by the roots. Then she carefully positioned it in her mouth so that all the barbs were pointing away from her. Finally, she sucked in the whole bunch in one clean gulp and chewed.

Insects

The prairie is not a feast just for bison and pronghorn and elk; it also feeds butterflies, moths, bees, ants, beetles, and a host of other insects.

While Andy was photographing in the Konza Prairie at sunset one September evening, I sat and observed what was going on. I first spotted a slantface grasshopper on a stem of grass. He was pale green with a maroon streak, and so was the grass stem he was perched on. He held very still, watching me watch him. Then I became aware of countless flying and crawling insects as they whirred and buzzed and clattered all around us.

THIS SCARLET-BODIED DRAGONFLY has black dots on the tips of its wings and a black pattern on the bottom of its red abdomen.

Penstemon leaves were so chewed on that it was hard to tell if they were once smooth on the edges or toothed. Rose hips got half eaten before they were fully ripe, and rose leaves were curled, spotty, and discolored. The tops were devoured out of many gayfeathers.

A double-winged dragonfly sailed by, as big as a hummingbird. Dragonflies eat mosquitoes and other insects and are omnipresent in prairies. A dickcissel or a lark sparrow (my eyes do not focus fast enough) swooped down and arose with a bug in its beak. The silkiness of a spider web gleamed in the late light, a moth caught in its sticky grasp.

Burrowing Creatures

Prairie soil must be turned, churned, aerated, and exposed so that shorter-lived forbs and grasses get a chance to replace themselves. The sharp hooves of bison accomplished this, as did buffalo wallows. But the task also falls to smaller, burrowing animals. Prairie dogs, gophers, and toads are the most common, but there are others—some of them quite strange. For example, in north Texas one finds prairie crayfish, which are believed to help aerate clay prairies.

Plains pocket gophers are reported to move two tons of earth in a year. At Schaefer Prairie, on the mesic to dry parts, there are an average of five plains pocket gopher mounds per acre. Chase Cornelius, our guide and a frequent visitor to Schaefer Prairie,

THE MOUNDS of plains pocket gophers are one of nature's methods for turning the soil and giving a place for seed to germinate. Also note how it gives smooth brome a chance to invade this ancient prairie. *Schaefer Prairie. Brownton, Minnesota. June 26.*

told us these gophers never seem to come above ground, and he has never actually seen one.

Another kind of prairie mound is the Mima mound. These low hillocks are 2 to 4 feet high and 30 to 100 feet wide, and they cover wet northern prairies at the rate of about one to an acre. On Schaefer Prairie, there are about 2,500 Mima mounds bordering Ice Lake, an old pothole left by the glacier. In winter, they are home to hibernating Manitoba toads. Because the soil is so loose and precipitation drains through so rapidly, the Mima mounds are typically covered with low-growing thicket shrubs rather than prairie sod.

Prairie dogs once inhabited 2 million acres; now at least 98 percent of them are gone because of loss of habitat or because they were deliberately poisoned for eating grass. Prairie dogs actually like seeds and fruits, but they will eat anything around their burrows that obstructs their view of predators.

If you want to make your prairie dogs move on before their town reaches the bare earth stage, Cheyenne River Sioux Pete Longbrake recommends setting up a temporary fence. Once they cannot see their enemies approaching, prairie dogs will move to a new site. A woman in Denver has developed a technique for transporting them to an entirely different property. She sucks them out of their holes with an industrial-sized vacuum cleaner and trucks them—physically unharmed (who knows how this affects their psyches)—to where they are more welcome.

PRAIRIE DOGS help prairie by eating woody plants that interfere with their ability to spot hawks and other predators.

PART TWO

Design, Installation

Visually, our yard is not traditional. Observations of natural settings have guided aesthetic choices, and our earth care practices. Once an apple orchard, trees in a row, short mowed grass, nature held in check with every apple, leaf, and twig removed, our land is now an organic adventure.

ROCHELLE WHITEMAN,
Milwaukee, Wisconsin

and Maintenance

PREVIOUSLY, WE HAVE DESCRIBED prairies and prairie gardens in a wide array of situations and locales, and we have discussed broad-stroke, basic ideas. From here on we will provide the specifics you need to create and maintain a prairie garden of your own.

To help you place plants to achieve the right texture and density, and to get the most from their seasonal colors, here are five planting plans. A sixth plan shows an actual landscape that gracefully combines prairie and woodland.

For those of you who have a hard time reading plans—about half the population—I have included a few eye-level views to give you an idea of what the gardens would look like.

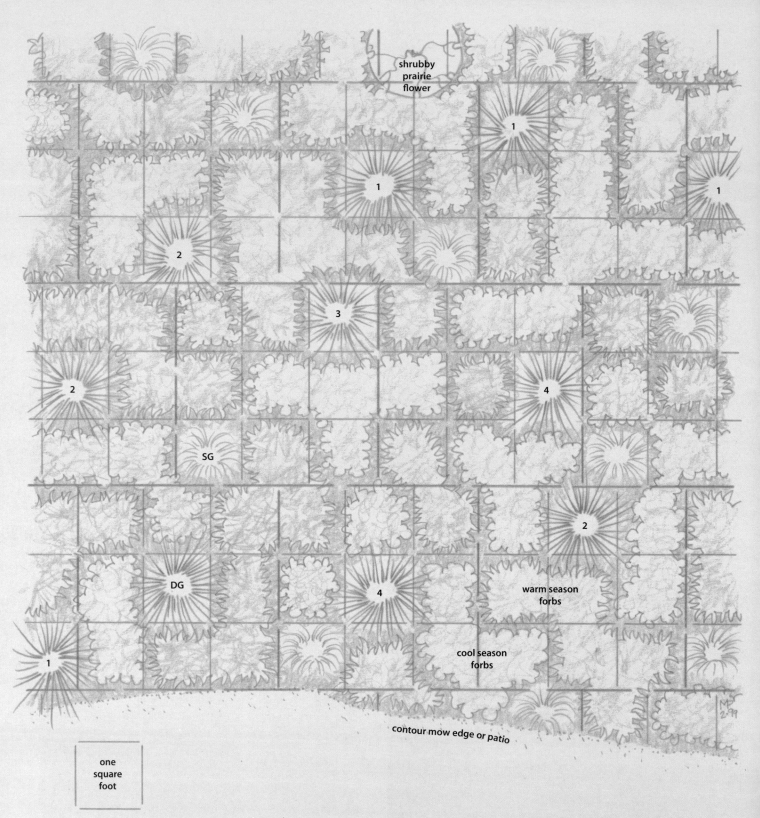

shrubby prairie flower

1

1

1

2

3

2

4

SG

2

DG

4

warm season forbs

cool season forbs

1

contour mow edge or patio

one square foot

PLANT ONE DOMINANT GRASS, sedge, or rush (DG) per square yard or square meter. Do *not* plant them in a discernable grid. There are usually one to four species of dominant grasses for each kind of prairie, here numbered 1 to 4. Notice that each species is planted in a random pattern so that when that species is most eye-catching, nothing will look lined up and artificial. For every DG, plant one subsidiary grass, sedge, or rush (SG). For every ten DGs, plant a shrubby prairie flower such as a leadplant, sagebrush, rose, or New Jersey tea (but not dense thicket shrubs such as snowberry, plum, or sumac). Now, choose four different species of cool season forbs and four species of warm season forbs for each DG and place them in drifts. Lastly, broadcast seeds of pioneer forbs to help cut down on weeds. Rows make it easier to read the plan, but the less lined up anything is, the better. As soon as the rhizomatous plants start to spread and everything seeds out, this grid should disappear altogether.

Chapter 6

The value of small "postage stamp" prairies and savannas should not be underestimated. Remnant prairies as small as one fourth acre have been shown to harbor an amazing diversity of insects, including rare species that do not occur in adjacent agricultural fields.

VIRGINIA KLINE, The Tallgrass Restoration Handbook

Designing Prairie Gardens

■ POCKET PRAIRIE

A planting plan for a pocket prairie is the most basic and important plan in the book for those of you who intend to plant container-grown plugs instead of sowing seed. Prairie has its own special texture, and this plan graphically shows you how to achieve it. Planting plugs is desirable in clay soil where seed is slow to germinate, or in small front gardens where you always want to look good for the sake of the neighbors.

Watering is a matter of geography. In Canada, when I asked gardeners how often and how long it was necessary to water their transplants, I was told that this was done only occasionally, right after planting. In Texas, where I have lived most of my life, it is a different story. Transplants, even nursery-grown ones with excellent root systems, have to be watered daily for two weeks, gradually being weaned to weekly waterings throughout the first summer (after all, it might not rain at all that summer), and then once a month through the second summer. In the Southwest, year-round waterings are recommended.

Top mulching with 1 to 2 inches of compost in June and again in November helps keep moisture in and weeds out. If you are going to sow seed in addition to the plugs, sow the seed into the mulch. Otherwise, wait until the seedlings are 3 or 4 inches high before you mulch.

KIM TYSON wanted her front-yard prairie garden to look good from the start, so she prepared approximately 120 square feet as she would for a flower bed, and planted plugs. The new garden shown here is only two weeks old. *Winnipeg, Manitoba. June 25.*

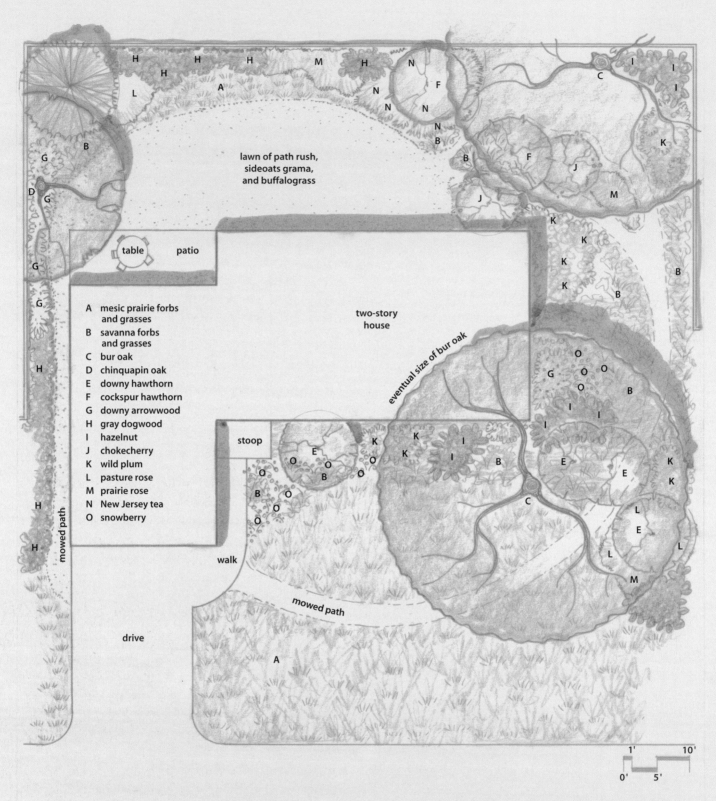

A mesic prairie forbs
   and grasses
B savanna forbs
   and grasses
C bur oak
D chinquapin oak
E downy hawthorn
F cockspur hawthorn
G downy arrowwood
H gray dogwood
I hazelnut
J chokecherry
K wild plum
L pasture rose
M prairie rose
N New Jersey tea
O snowberry

lawn of path rush,
sideoats grama,
and buffalograss

table   patio

two-story
house

eventual size of bur oak

stoop

walk

drive

mowed path

mowed path

1'   10'

0'   5'

THIS PLAN shows you how to place woody plants to create a bird thicket. To make a sample plan, I pretended that I lived on a mostly
level lot in a Chicago suburb with heavy soil suitable for bur oaks. From chapter 12, I picked out those plants listed in the categories
labeled Mesic Prairie or Bur Oak Savanna in the Northern Tallgrass Prairie quadrant. I eliminated those plants that were not native to
the Chicago area, those that needed slopes or extra moisture, and those that seemed too aggressive for a small yard. Then I arranged
the savanna trees and shrubs that are equally happy in either sun or shade in the areas that are currently sunny, and the shade-loving
savanna species in the predominantly shady spots. To choose the nonwoody savanna plants—grasses, sedges, and forbs—use the same
process, consulting chapters 9, 10, and 11. To install a bird thicket like this, prepare the soil where needed, and place the large shrubs and
small trees 5 to 7 feet apart, the small shrubs 2 to 3 feet apart, and the nursery-grown herbaceous plants 1 foot apart.

SASKATOON BERRY and willow grow together in a thicket on a steep-sloped prairie at a city park. *Calgary, Alberta. June 21.*

If you obtained your transplants from the wild during a plant rescue, you will increase their chances of survival if you cover them for a few days with a tent made from shade cloth or a screen of branches. Being transplanted is a stressful experience; by shading the leaves to reduce evaporation, you give the roots time to recover, and they do not have to get to work right away bringing up water and nutrients.

In general, it you follow the same methods you would use for planting a flower garden in your region, you will be successful in establishing a prairie garden.

■ BIRD THICKET AND SAVANNA

The texture of thickets is complex. You do not want them to look like a hedge, even though that is exactly what they are replacing. The thicket should look natural—no straight lines or boxy cuts. Furthermore, the best thickets are composed of several different species. Each thicket ought to provide spring flowers for nectar, fall fruits for migrating birds, thorns to protect nesting birds, and a dense network of roots and healthy soil to provide homes for shrews, rabbits, toads, and other creatures at the bottom of the food chain.

A garden like this creates a much needed sanctuary for prairie birds. The U.S. Fish and Wildlife Service reports that from 1966 to 1987 populations of bobolinks fell 90 percent; grasshopper sparrows, 56 percent; field sparrows, 56 percent; and savannah sparrows, 58.9 percent. Henslow's sparrows were too few to count. Other prairie birds struggling with loss of habitat are lark buntings and prairie chickens.

Most prairie birds like wide-open spaces. While spacious lawns deliver the open space, they do not provide unpoisoned insects, forb seeds, grass seeds, and thicket fruits. They do not provide tall grasses to hide the nest of a prairie chicken.

Just a few of the desirable species we want to help are bluebirds, shrikes, dickcissel, lark sparrow, savannah sparrow, grasshopper sparrow, lark bunting, meadowlarks, Brewer's blackbird, and American goldfinch. Some, such as Lapland longspur and snow bunting, nest in the Arctic and then winter over in our prairies, so it is important to let some ripe grasses, heavy with seed, stand all winter.

As a bird thicket matures, its roots can be aggressive. Mowing regularly can keep a thicket in bounds, but it will hurt prairie grasses even more. A better form of control is to hand-cut the woody stems where they are not wanted each summer. Do not paint herbicide on the freshly cut stems, as this poisons the whole thicket.

A FEMALE RED-WINGED BLACKBIRD, drably colored compared to her mate, guards their nest in a meadowsweet.

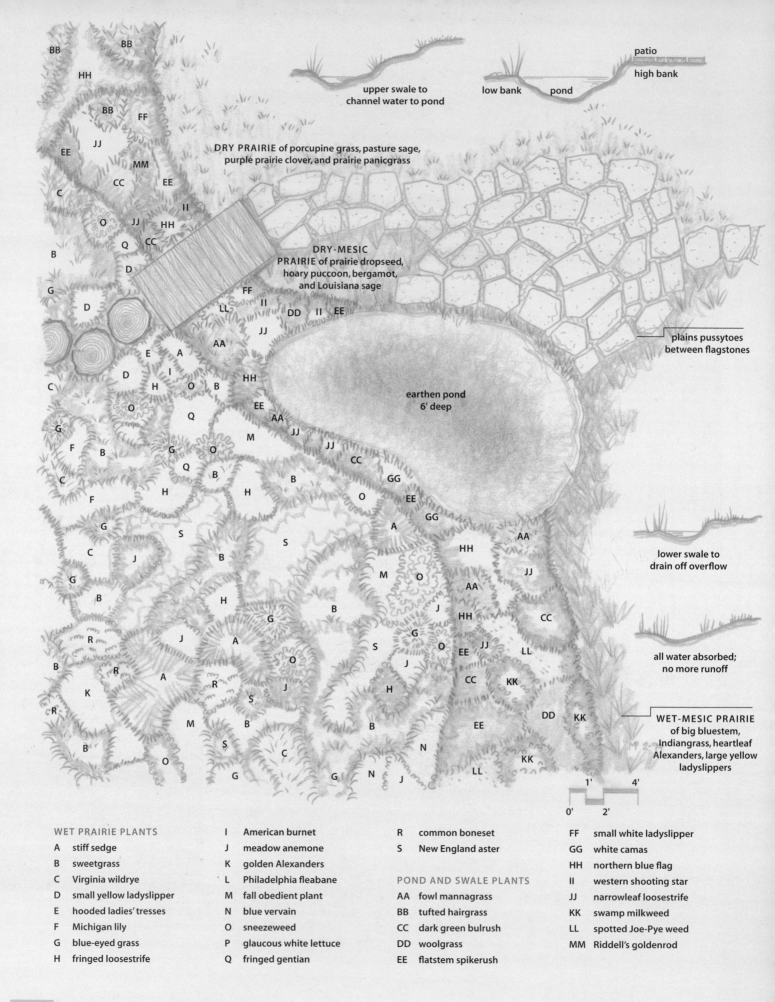

upper swale to channel water to pond

low bank pond patio high bank

DRY PRAIRIE of porcupine grass, pasture sage, purple prairie clover, and prairie panicgrass

DRY-MESIC PRAIRIE of prairie dropseed, hoary puccoon, bergamot, and Louisiana sage

earthen pond 6' deep

plains pussytoes between flagstones

lower swale to drain off overflow

all water absorbed; no more runoff

WET-MESIC PRAIRIE of big bluestem, Indiangrass, heartleaf Alexanders, large yellow ladyslippers

0' 1' 2' 4'

WET PRAIRIE PLANTS

A stiff sedge
B sweetgrass
C Virginia wildrye
D small yellow ladyslipper
E hooded ladies' tresses
F Michigan lily
G blue-eyed grass
H fringed loosestrife
I American burnet
J meadow anemone
K golden Alexanders
L Philadelphia fleabane
M fall obedient plant
N blue vervain
O sneezeweed
P glaucous white lettuce
Q fringed gentian
R common boneset
S New England aster

POND AND SWALE PLANTS

AA fowl mannagrass
BB tufted hairgrass
CC dark green bulrush
DD woolgrass
EE flatstem spikerush
FF small white ladyslipper
GG white camas
HH northern blue flag
II western shooting star
JJ narrowleaf loosestrife
KK swamp milkweed
LL spotted Joe-Pye weed
MM Riddell's goldenrod

PRAIRIE FORBS and grasses tumble down a steep bank to line the edges of a water garden ornamented with wet prairie species of iris, rush, sedge, and fern. Design and maintenance are by curator Scott Woodberry. *The Whitmire Wildflower Garden, Shaw Arboretum of the Missouri Botanical Garden, Gray Summit, Missouri. August 14.*

■ WET PRAIRIE GARDEN

For a backyard pond and wet prairie, here is a planting plan that arranges the most desirable wet prairie species for the northeastern prairie quadrant from most wet to least wet. Adapt this plan to your region by making your own list of wet prairie species. Examine wet places near you to figure out which species need water all year and which can survive seasonal drought.

Wet prairie species can be used on a small scale, for example, by planting a wet prairie over the home septic field, or by creating a swale for the gutters to empty into. Or they

THIS PLANTING PLAN (left) would be suitable for southern Manitoba around Winnipeg. The plants chosen are among the most polite and desirable of the wet prairie species. The pond and swale plants like being wet all year. The wet prairie plants can be wet some of the year and merely moist the rest of the year, with the most drought-tolerant species placed farthest from the pond. The idea is to plant the plugs of grasses, sedges, rushes, and forbs where they are most likely to succeed. Expect them to spread out into the interstices and even into the adjoining habitats, so that within a few years the smooth texture of prairie is achieved. The pond must be earthen to allow water to seep out and keep the surrounding prairie wet to moist. There is no need to plant in the water, as many species will seed in on their own. You can then pull out what is unwanted.

SWAMP LOUSEWORT (*Pedicularis lanceolata*), also known as marsh betony, seems to keep giant bulrush from taking over a wet garden. Native from Maine to southern Saskatchewan south to Nebraska, Missouri, and eastern North Carolina, this attractive flower is found in bogs, marshes, calcareous fens, wet prairies, and soggy roadside ditches. Here it is shown at the end of its long blooming season.

can beautify storm-water management for a whole subdivision.

A small pond enhances the diversity of wildlife considerably. Some desirable species you will probably not attract without water are dragonflies and damselflies, frogs and toads, and waterbirds.

Dragonflies and damselflies eat mosquitoes and other insects. Their eggs are laid in or close to water, and the naiads—which look vaguely shrimplike—eat tadpoles and other small aquatic creatures.

Frogs and toads, once common, are now developing birth defects worldwide. By providing healthy habitat gardens, we may be helping them to survive. Some prairie-associated amphibians are the plains spadefoot, the crawfish frog, and the northern leopard frog.

Whooping cranes, sandhill cranes, trumpeter swans, ducks, and geese tend to travel in large flocks and feed on large ponds, but you can expect the occasional stray to visit your small pond, along with solitary water birds, such as herons and egrets.

I put wild rice (*Zizania aquatica*) into this plan and the food garden plan because it makes such a beautiful transition from pond to wet prairie. An annual, it grows tall, over one's head, and produces rice in midsummer.

■ NECTAR GARDEN

This plan shows how to use prairie plants in a traditional flower garden to attract hummingbirds, sphinx moths, bees, beelike tachinid flies, and butterflies. These pollinators are a delight to gardeners and are important indicators of the health of our planet. Each requires an absence of pesticides and an abundance of nectar-rich flowers.

Butterflies feed during the day on flowers warmed by the sun. The tiny Karner's blue

THE NECTAR-RICH FLOWER GARDEN (right) in the center is packed with species especially attractive to butterflies. The surrounding prairie and thicket are composed of plants that nurture the caterpillars and provide safe places for the chrysalids. Within the flower garden are extra plantings of milkweed and members of the parsley family, which are also larval plants. The plants are arranged from *A*, the first of the nectar-rich cool season forbs to bloom, to *U*, the last of the warm season forbs. To make this plan work for you, turn to the plant section represented by each letter—for example, *L* indicates the milkweed family—and write in the name of the milkweed best adapted for you. If several milkweeds will work, fill each spot marked *L* on the plan with a different kind. The greater the variety, the more dependable will be the supply of nectar throughout the butterfly season. This design was inspired by the butterfly garden of Doris and Jim Kimball of Appleton, Wisconsin.

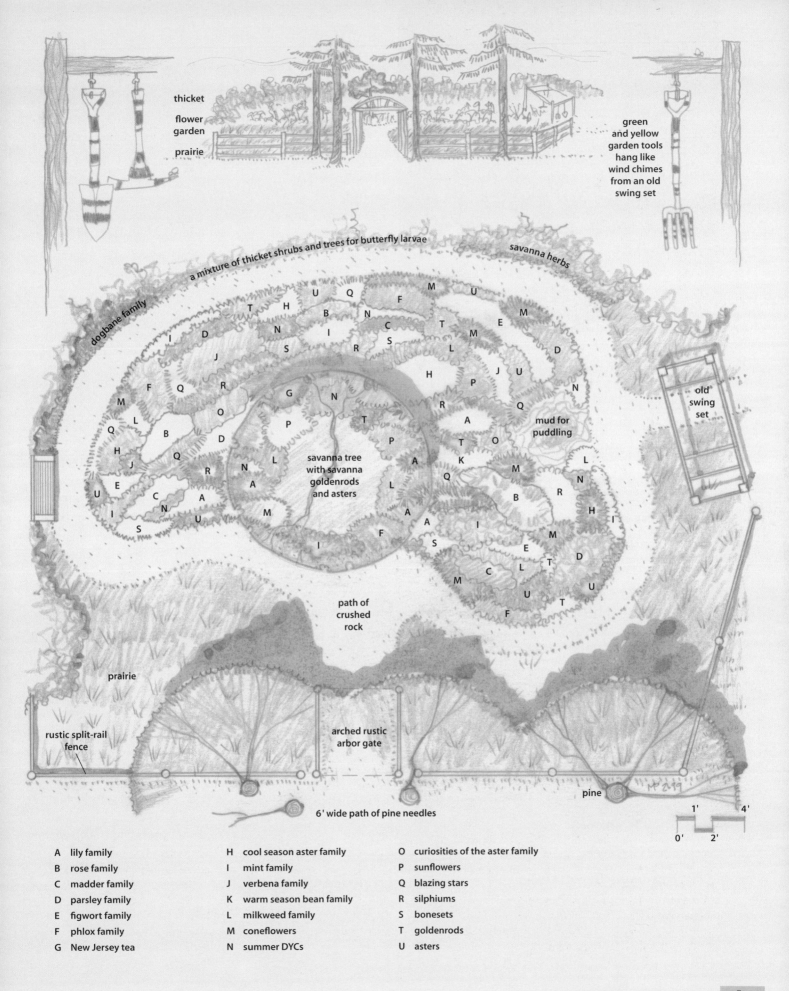

thicket

flower garden

prairie

green and yellow garden tools hang like wind chimes from an old swing set

a mixture of thicket shrubs and trees for butterfly larvae

savanna herbs

dogbane family

old swing set

mud for puddling

savanna tree with savanna goldenrods and asters

path of crushed rock

prairie

rustic split-rail fence

arched rustic arbor gate

pine

6' wide path of pine needles

1'   4'

0'   2'

A lily family	H cool season aster family	O curiosities of the aster family
B rose family	I mint family	P sunflowers
C madder family	J verbena family	Q blazing stars
D parsley family	K warm season bean family	R silphiums
E figwort family	L milkweed family	S bonesets
F phlox family	M coneflowers	T goldenrods
G New Jersey tea	N summer DYCs	U asters

A MONARCH BUTTERFLY feeds on an oval milkweed, possibly the very same plant it fed on in the larval stage.

butterfly is the most famous of the many endangered prairie butterflies, but butterfly counts show that other blues, monarchs, fritillaries, sulphurs, and swallowtails are declining in numbers.

Larval plants are necessary for the caterpillar stage. The blues feed on the bean family. Swallowtails require the parsley family, willow, plum, artemisia, and others. Host plants for other butterflies are members of the rose family, the milkweed family, mallows, asters, pussytoes, violets, and sedges. The larvae of skippers are found on big bluestem, little bluestem, and switchgrass.

The sphinx moths, also called hawk moths, feed mostly at night, except for the small daytime humming-bird moth. Larval plants for nectar-feeding moths include viburnum, snowberry, evening primrose, northern bedstraw, the willow family, and the nightshade family.

When people think of bees, they think of the domesticated European honeybee or the bumblebee or the infamous non-native killer bees. These three all live in colonies and store honey. But there are more than 3,500 species of bees native to North America, many of them solitary bees, and some, like the green metallic bees, are very pretty.

The beelike tachinid fly feeds on coneflowers, and its larvae feed on caterpillars. This very large fly has a round red or amber body that is beautifully translucent and decorated by rows of black bristles.

Ruby-throated hummingbirds are common in tallgrass habitats, while the black-chinned variety is seen throughout the range of shortgrass prairies. Hummingbirds are known to love red deep-throated flowers, such as penstemons, but they also feed on annual sunflowers and oozing tree sap.

■ FOOD AND MEDICINE GARDEN

Many native foods, medicines, and ceremonial plants are diminishing in the wild. Ken and Linda Parker of Sweet Grass Gardens in Hagersville, Ontario, founded the first Native American–owned nursery to grow the plants First Nation people still like to use.

Besides fruits and nuts, other popular foods are Jerusalem artichoke, the asparagus-like spring shoots of swamp milkweed, Indian breadroot, the seeds of blue flax, which are used as seasoning, and New Jersey tea, which really does make an excellent tea.

Medicinal plants, ignored for the past few decades, are now making a comeback. For modern details on how to prepare and administer these plants, I recommend *Medicinal Wild Plants of the Prairie* by Kelly Kindscher, or any of the medicinal plant books by Michael Moore. *Uses of Plants by the Indians of the Missouri River Region* by Melvin R. Gilmore, originally published in 1914, is a classic because he was able to interview many elderly medicine men and women.

THE BUDS, flowers, fruits, and padded leaves of eastern prickly pear (*Opuntia humifusa*) and other cacti are still used as food.

SWEETGRASS, shown freshly picked in a switch and also in a dried braid, is burned to invite helpful spirits. The bundle of sage (*Artemisia*) wrapped in gut is burned to drive out evil spirits. Both plants have aromatic leaves that smell wonderful, whether fresh, dried, or smoldering.

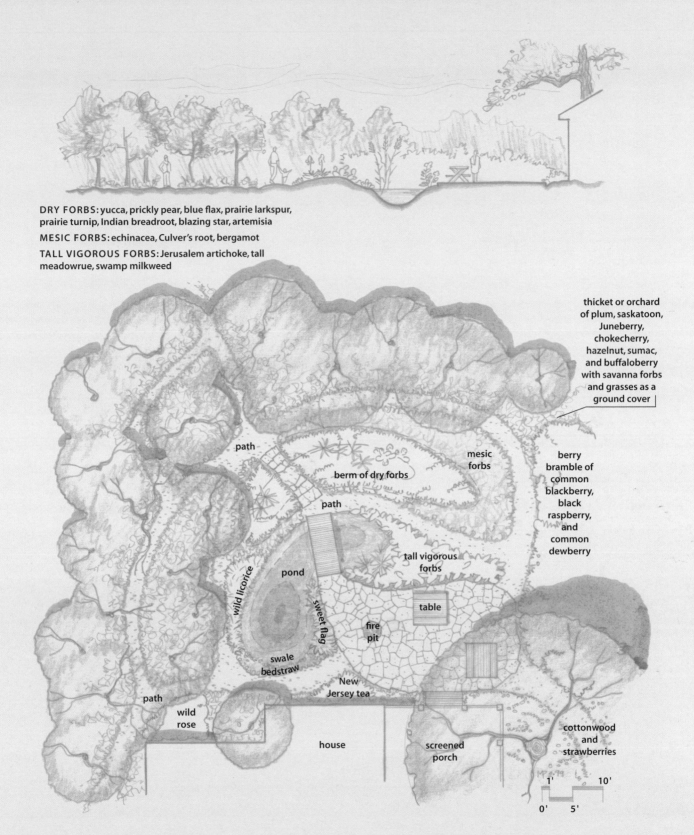

DRY FORBS: yucca, prickly pear, blue flax, prairie larkspur, prairie turnip, Indian breadroot, blazing star, artemisia
MESIC FORBS: echinacea, Culver's root, bergamot
TALL VIGOROUS FORBS: Jerusalem artichoke, tall meadowrue, swamp milkweed

thicket or orchard of plum, saskatoon, Juneberry, chokecherry, hazelnut, sumac, and buffaloberry with savanna forbs and grasses as a ground cover

path

mesic forbs

berm of dry forbs

path

berry bramble of common blackberry, black raspberry, and common dewberry

wild licorice

pond

tall vigorous forbs

sweet flag

table

fire pit

swale bedstraw

New Jersey tea

path

wild rose

cottonwood and strawberries

house

screened porch

1'   10'

0'   5'

A GARDEN for food, medicine, dyes, and ceremonial rites can be beautiful as well as functional. In this plan, set in an ordinary South Dakota backyard, a flat lawn is transformed into a berm and pond with plenty of paths for easy gathering. The berm is where you will grow the plants that require excellent drainage, while the swale is home to those plants that like extra moisture. This planting plan is not strictly indigenous, as traditionally these plants were gathered by Native Americans roaming throughout an area that covered several hundred square miles. Delicious native fruits—many of which are now entering commercial production—include saskatoon, buffaloberry, and choke-cherry. Sweetgrass, important in aboriginal ceremonies and fragrant in rooms and drawers, is becoming scarce in the wild, so growing your own helps both you and nature. Native herbs that are grown in good poison-free soil make valuable home medicines.

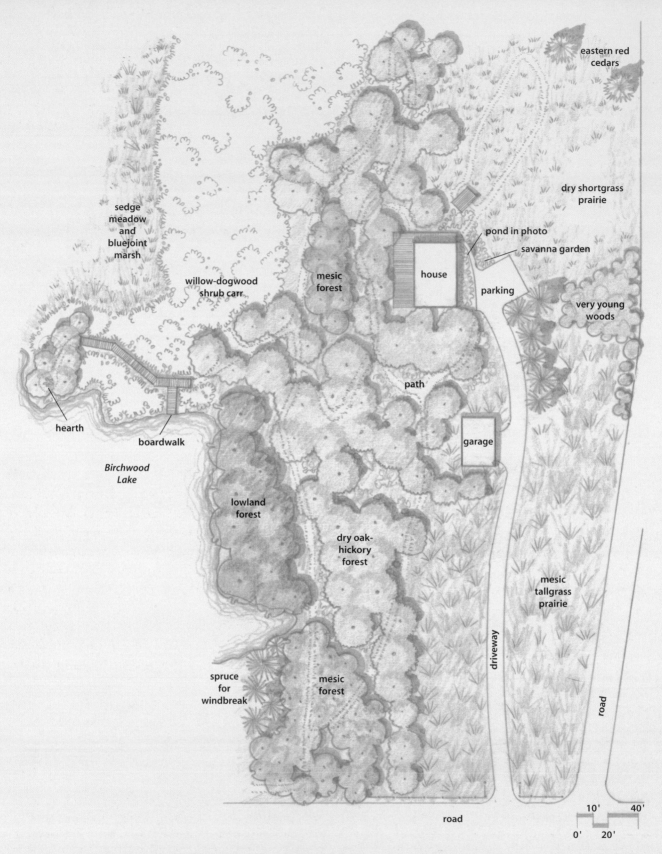

eastern red cedars

dry shortgrass prairie

pond in photo

savanna garden

parking

very young woods

house

mesic forest

sedge meadow and bluejoint marsh

willow-dogwood shrub carr

path

garage

hearth

boardwalk

Birchwood Lake

lowland forest

dry oak-hickory forest

mesic tallgrass prairie

spruce for windbreak

mesic forest

driveway

road

10'   40'

0'   20'

road

FIFTEEN YEARS AGO this 10-acre lot consisted of a cornfield and native woodlands that had been grazed and trampled down to mostly bare soil or a cover of buckthorn, Asian honeysuckle, farm weeds, and aggressive native species such as prickly ash and box elder (*Acer negundo*). As Bill Volkert identified native woodland species, he would scatter their seed, or bring in seed from woodlands nearby. Sometimes just removing weedy competition was enough to let the native understory restore itself. Connie Ramthun replicated dry and mesic prairies by gathering local seed, sowing, weeding, planting contract-grown seedlings, weeding some more, mowing, weeding yet again, and finally burning. Bill has now documented 540 species of native plants and animals on their property.

Dye plants make use of buds, bark, roots, leafy stems, or flowers. Cottonwood buds, smooth sumac roots, and milkweed stems make yellow dyes; bedstraw stems or juniper berries, a tan dye; blackberries, a light purple or blue; prairie larkspur flowers, a pale green; wild plum bark, a soft pink; and prickly pear fruits, a strong red or magenta.

Yucca root makes an excellent shampoo, and sunflower seed oil gives a shine to dry hair. Fresh and pleasant sachets can be made of wild bergamot (those with weak stems have a superior scent), the dry seed capsules of prickly ash, or the leaves of sweet flag.

There is also good horse food and medicine here. Cottonwood stems and *Liatris* flowers allegedly make horses swift and healthy. A poultice of wild licorice leaves can relieve a horse's sore back.

■ DESIGNING WITH PRAIRIE AND WOODS

Connie Ramthun and Bill Volkert bought 10 acres of old farm adjacent to a 32-acre lake and the northern Kettle Moraine ecosystem. Bill has been taking an inventory of prairie remnants in his area since 1980 and in the Kettle Moraine State Forest since 1983. Connie specializes in prairie restoration for this sensitive area with seed she has collected herself. Together, they set out to restore their land to its natural habitats. Where there were already woods, they removed exotic and native weeds, and, in most instances, the native woodland forbs started reappearing. Where there had been cornfields, Connie tested her skills at restoring prairie. In one abandoned field, juniper was already trying to turn old field into forest, and they are allowing natural succession to take place there.

CONNIE RAMTHUN specializes in prairie restoration in the northern Kettle Moraine area of Wisconsin, but having plenty of shade in her own yard, she is also interested in woodland and savanna species. Here in the semishade between her house and a prairie, she has put in a pond for wildlife and savanna species to attract birds. Ohio spiderwort is in bloom. Other important species are Pennsylvania sedge, yellow avens (*Geum aleppicum*), bottlebrush grass, smilacina or false Solomon's seal (*Maianthemum racemosum* ssp. *racemosum*), thimbleweed, and arrow aster (*Symphyotrichum urophyllum*). *July 3.*

Chapter 7

It still surprises me when people who should know better assume that landscaping with native plants should be cheap. The cost of a lawn is accepted, like death and taxes, but actually paying for a wild landscape seems wrong because those plants should "be there anyway." Well, the days are gone when we could dig up a few plants from Grampa's woods and start our own little nostalgic garden. Why should the endangered wildlings, plants that can't be raised on an assembly line and won't grow in every soil, come back for free?

    WENDY WALCOTT, Milwaukee, Wisconsin

Installing Prairie Gardens

INITIALLY, and not surprisingly, installing a prairie is more complicated than seeding a lawn. Most people start off slowly and do not try to convert all their property at once. If you do take on a several-acre project like the Wondras did, then it is a good idea to adopt their sensible attitude of doing what they can while it is still enjoyable and quitting when it gets to feel like work. A prairie system is a slowly changing organic process. It takes lots of time, so you can too.

■ HISTORY OF PRAIRIE GARDENING

Weaver's documentation of the interaction between grasses and forbs provides some of our earliest information on how the whole system works. Weaver, however, studied prairies; he never tried to plant one.

The first person to plant a prairie or savanna for landscape aesthetics was Jens Jensen. In 1881, as the frontier was officially closed and as Europeans were going gaga over American plants, several prominent landscape designers started using native plants. In Chicago, this practice was called the "prairie school" of landscape gardening. But they were using native plants only in conventional ways in combination with non-native plants.

Planting native flora in naturalistic configurations was a revolutionary idea developed by Jensen, a Dane who came to Chicago in 1886. He wanted landscapes to have a regional flavor, and he wanted Chicagoans to appreciate the many beauties of a land that was rapidly succumbing to urbanization.

He first worked in the West Parks system, but in 1902 he started a private practice using native flowers and hedgerow shrubs such as hawthorn. His home landscapes evoked the open expanse of prairie and the shrub-woodland edge but were seldom purely native. As Jensen researcher Colston Burrell said, "I can find no evidence to indicate that Jensen ever created a true prairie on any site, even though he used prairie species throughout his career." The closest he came to re-creating a prairie, as far as we know, was at Columbus Park, where Burrell said he found references to prairie grasses in Jensen's notes, and later, when Jensen was seventy-six, at Lincoln Memorial Garden.

Jensen was certainly aware of the importance of matching plants to habitat, as evidenced by this 1938 letter about Lincoln Memorial Garden sent to a Mrs. T. J. Knudson. He wrote, "As for the lead plant, yes, it is native to Illinois, but it is a plant that grows in rocky and sandy soil. . . . If you had a steep bank I would have introduced it, but I would not introduce it into the gentle rolling landscape because it does not belong. . . . The idea is not to make an arboretum out of the Garden, nor a museum, but to *plant the things that fit and are in harmony with each other and in harmony with the contours of the Garden and the country surrounding*" (our emphasis).

The first person to advocate the actual replication or restoration of prairie was Aldo Leopold. Inspired by Weaver, and appalled by our eroded farms and the thoughtless destruction of natural landscapes, he decided in 1935 to see if degraded land could be restored. The Leopold farm was in Baraboo, Wisconsin, in Sauk County in the Wisconsin sand hills. The book for which Leopold is famous, *Sand County Almanac*, describes the sandy low-nutrient soil that resulted when northern European farming techniques stripped off the organic topsoil.

The Leopold legacy is based on both practical experiments and inspirational philosophy. On old farmland around the family "shack" (previously a chicken coop), Leopold planted little bluestem and prairie forbs between groves of shagbark hickory, bitternut, and black oak to restore the land's natural mixture of prairie and savanna. But Leopold was no purist. A forester by training, he planted red pine and other non-native trees as well.

He also invented controlled burns. Native Americans had a long history of burning prairies to keep them healthy, but they set wildfires, and it did not matter where the fires went or how long they burned. Leopold understood that on farms and in the suburbs, it mattered very much that the fire not escape the boundaries of one's property. Today, modifications of his techniques are used by all prairie restorationists.

But Leopold's greatest gift to us is the eloquent way he voiced his conservation ethic. "We abuse land because we regard it as a commodity belonging to us. When we see land as a community to which we belong, we may begin to use it with love and respect. There is no other way for land to survive the impact of man." He also pointed out that "If the biota, in the course of aeons, has built something we like but do not understand, then who but a fool would discard seemingly useless parts? To keep every cog and wheel is the first precaution of intelligent tinkering."

The Curtis Prairie at the University of Wisconsin at Madison was inspired by Leopold. In fact, he was a consultant for that restoration project for a number of years. Under the direction of prairie ecologist Theodore Sperry, the Curtis Prairie—our oldest reconstructed prairie—was planted by the Civil Conservation Corps (CCC) from 1935 to 1941. Civic and university leaders raised the money to house, feed, and pay each CCC member $3.00 a month. To assist in the restoration, Jane and John Curtis, botanists for whom the prairie was named, traveled the state with a number of their botany students, searching for prairie remnants and rare plants.

ALDO LEOPOLD landscaped the family vacation shack with little bluestem prairie and woodlands. In 1949 he wrote about his observations in *Sand County Almanac*, now the bible for most midwestern conservationists. His family founded the Aldo Leopold Foundation, which funds research, education, and active restoration on the old farm site as well as on the lands of other participating landowners in the area. *Sauk County, Wisconsin. July 1.*

Today, the Curtis Prairie is healthy and intact, although the placement of individual plants appears somewhat crude compared to how nature does it. To see if placement could more closely mimic nature, Professor Henry C. Greene single-handedly, from 1945 to 1950, reconstructed a prairie on a campus farm field. The Greene Prairie at the University of Wisconsin at Madison and the Schulenberg Prairie at the Morton Arboretum near Chicago are the two most beautifully reconstructed public prairies to date. Both are predominately prairie dropseed prairies.

■ PREPARING A SEEDBED

As any gardener knows, seed must be on or in the soil for germination to take place. Farmers plow before they plant crops. Home owners till before planting either a lawn or a vegetable garden from seed. So, it was natural for the early prairie gardeners, both home owners and restorationists, to till or plow before planting prairie seed. Recently, however, prairie gardeners have discovered no-till methods that work better because they do not destroy native vegetation or encourage alien aggressive weeds.

When to Till

Tilling is effective on old farm fields. Patricia Armstrong of Prairie Sun Consultants in Naperville, Illinois, sowed her home landscape on an abandoned farm field. She tilled deeply to bring up the rhizomes of smooth brome and expose them to the killing effects of a frigid winter. This method worked well for her as that winter was especially severe.

When Not to Till

Pastures, savannas, and steep slopes are best not tilled, as tilling can destroy existing prairie species, hurt tree roots, and create erosion. Woodland forbs and grasses that are already there may be few in number, and some may exist only as dormant seed, but they are important. They are indigenous to the site and form the basis for the restoration.

To expose the soil enough for the seed to reach it, the previous year's dried standing vegetation is removed either by burning or mowing very close to the ground (scalping).

After the soil is exposed, seed is broadcast by hand. This is called interseeding, and it is the process favored by restorationists when the land has been too abused by grazing, absence of fire, and the encroachment of non-native weeds to heal on its own.

Weeds are best eradicated *before* planting or sowing, because they outcompete slow-growing prairie seedlings and shade them to death. There are several methods of weed eradication favored by restorationists. Burning or scalping in spring when the cool season Eurasian grasses are about 6 inches high damages these most invasive prairie weeds. It will not eradicate them, but it slows them down. If this is done prior to interseeding, the native species start outcompeting the non-natives by the sixth summer, according to *The Tallgrass Restoration Handbook* (Packard and Mutel, eds.).

When to Use Herbicides

If the weeds still seem to be winning, restorationists turn to herbicides. Randy Powers of Prairie FUTURE Seed in Wisconsin gives one example of using herbicides to create prairie:

> It was a new subdivision, on an old oak savanna and a filled wetland, heartbreaking as usual. The owners wanted a "wildflower meadow" under the big old oak tree on a hill covered with thick reed canary grass. In the fall, on our advice, they sprayed with a herbicide that kills only grass. After the grass turned brown, they raked out the heavy thatch, and sprayed the regrowth, killing the grass tillers. In the spring, rare prairie trillium, bellwort, and wild geranium—long suppressed by the grass—were up and blooming! Scraping, tilling, or smothering, or any other method of killing the grass roots would have destroyed the wild forbs as well.

A few years ago, my response to the question of using herbicides was immediate and passionate: "Do not poison our environment with *any* toxics! No way! Never!" But since then I have toured through prairies, and I have seen firsthand how a seemingly unstoppable army of invasive weeds can take over. And so I advise using the *least* toxic, *shortest-lived* herbicides, as *sparingly* as possible, as *carefully* as possible, and only on those weedy invasives that are long-lived, aggressive, and unfazed by hand-weeding.

Be aware that pre-emergent herbicides are dangerous to prairie seeds. The purpose of a pre-emergent is to prevent weed seeds from germinating. These herbicides will also prevent prairie seeds from germinating. If you have been using a chemical lawn service, check to see whether pre-emergents have been applied before you sow a prairie garden. These sprays can also drift over from a neighbor's yard if applied on a windy day.

No Tilling and No Herbicides

Here are two methods for planting a prairie garden that involve no tilling and no herbicides.

Smothering is a popular technique for small areas of bluegrass or St. Augustine lawn. First cut the grass very low. Then lay down sheets of newspaper. The thickness varies from

"THE PRAIRIES" is a newly built golf course in Cahokia, Illinois. The garden around the clubhouse is appropriately landscaped with prairie plants: 60 percent grasses and 40 percent forbs. The design, installation, and maintenance are by Dianne O'Connell of St. Louis, Missouri. Dianne selected seed to be contract grown six to nine months before the estimated installation date. To prepare the soil left by the builder, she did not till. She used two applications of glyphosate and drilled with Tanaka augers for 2-inch, 4-inch, or 2-gallon plants. The drill pulverized the soil so there were no lumps. Then she top-dressed with 3 inches of shredded bark mulch to hold in moisture and keep out weeds. *July 16.*

PATRICIA ARMSTRONG covered the lawn at the Lincoln Elementary School with newspaper and clean, coarse sand in May 1994. The lawn underneath was neither herbicided nor tilled. In less than three months, the roots of the nursery-grown prairie plants were already growing through the newspaper, through the dead lawn, and into the rich soil below. *Elmhurst, Illinois. July 31.*

two sheets to twelve. Use at least ten sheets over aggressive weeds. In windy areas, roofing nails may be needed to hold down the paper as you work. On windless days, wetting down the paper is sufficient. Spread 4 to 6 inches of sand or a mixture of sand and compost on top of the paper. Plant plugs and seeds directly into this mixture. The roots grow through the newspaper with no problem, and the loose planting medium acts as a mulch and makes pulling weeds a breeze. This technique does not work on bermudagrass.

We have talked about sowing on old pastures and abandoned farm fields, but what if the farmland is still active or has only just been harvested? With this kind of existing farm field, the transition to prairie is easy, because weeds do not get the chance to become established. Cindy Hildebrand and Roger Maddux of Ames, Iowa, are converting the soybean fields around their home to prairie. Their first choice is to plant in November over the stubble that remains after harvesting the soybeans. They hand-scatter seed that they collect themselves, with permission, from local remnant prairies. Then they roll the field with a garden tractor. The result is an almost weed-free, completely indigenous prairie. There is one danger here: if Atrazine™ or a trifluralin chemical has been used within three years, these poisons will inhibit the germination and growth of prairie seed.

Enriching the Soil

Pioneer prairie vegetation can thrive in worn-out or abused soil conditions that would make conventional nursery stock very unhappy. And when these pioneer species die, they decompose and enrich the soil for the conservative species that follow. Periodic prairie fires also help enrich the soil because ash makes the minerals in the organic matter more water soluble. That is why restorationists normally do not do anything to enrich the soil.

However, if your prairie garden replaces a conventionally "well-cared-for" lawn, the necessary soil microorganisms may have been killed by synthetic fertilizers, pesticides, and herbicides. If you do not get that special smell just after rain hits dry soil, that is an indication that the soil is probably dead. In tallgrass areas, if you dig a hole and do not find any earthworms, that is another clue. Digging that hole may also be difficult because the ground has become terribly compacted from years of overwatering and mowing.

Before you try to establish a prairie garden, such soil is going to need some serious first aid. In tallgrass areas, begin by working in several inches of compost. Do not use more synthetic fertilizer; that is what contributed to the problem in the first place. I have had good luck adding commercial compost starter—granules of microorganisms that help organic material decompose. Research is also being done on ways to add exactly the right mycorrhizal fungi for particular habitats.

In dry shortgrass areas or on sandy soils, the indigenous prairie species will not be happy in rich organic soil, so do not add compost, or add only very small amounts.

If you are planting plugs in an abused prairie remnant or under a tree in a savanna setting, disturbing the soil by working in organic matter would be just as bad as tilling. If the soil seems depleted, you can top-mulch with an inch or more of compost after planting plugs. Do not add a mulch if you plant seed, as you will smother the seed. For a planting under a tree in a savanna garden, quit raking the leaves and let them decompose, and the soil will heal itself.

If your home is in a new subdivision, you may need to add organic matter because the topsoil has been scraped away and a clay subsoil remains. It is much better to pile on 6 inches of compost than to bring in topsoil. Even topsoil that is "guaranteed" to be weed-free usually harbors nasty invasives.

Doing Next to Nothing

There is one final approach to establishing a prairie garden, and it requires a minimum of effort on your part. Basically, you allow the land to heal itself. This method would drive a purist crazy, because non-natives might always be part of the plant palette, but the benefits of establishing a wildlife habitat and enjoying low maintenance are met within a year or so.

Understand, we are not talking about letting a weed patch develop. You have to do some work. But instead of mowing your lawn every week, you mow or have a controlled burn once a year. For a savanna garden, you quit raking leaves, and during the dormant season, you clear out any unsightly dried forb stalks. *In other words, you skip all the installation and prep work, and go straight to prairie and savanna maintenance.*

Mandy Ploch was not trying for an indigenous prairie—a pure example of what had been here before her ancestors immigrated from Europe. She just wanted the benefits of

MANDY PLOCH simply stopped mowing her bluegrass lawn and is now adding prairie species. Note the fence and mowed parkway that let the casual observer know that this is a planned landscape. *Milwaukee, Wisconsin. August 6.*

Design, Installation, and Maintenance

prairie. When she and her husband bought a house with a 3-acre lawn, Mandy decided to continue mowing the parkway and a small amount around the house to create a curving path and a small rounded sitting area; the rest she let go. Queen Anne's lace (a short-lived non-native), a daylily (non-native), Canada goldenrod (a native weed), and New England aster volunteered immediately in the knee-high grasses. They looked pretty and Mandy left them. She adds nursery-grown prairie grasses and forbs as she feels she can afford them. Mandy could also have been adding native seed, and this would have cost even less money. All in all, this is a cheap and easy way to get started, and still have the benefits of no mowing, no watering, no run-off, and no poisons, and have a landscape hospitable to wildlife.

John Morgan in Argyle, Manitoba, did not mow a weedy part of his lawn one year because of a drought. By the end of the summer, big bluestem showed up. Encouraged, he did not mow the next year either, and counted twelve prairie species by the end of that summer. By the third year, he burned, and was able to identify forty more native prairie species. By the tenth year, he had ladyslippers, an indicator of mature prairie.

■ WHAT TO PLANT

Just as in a true prairie, your prairie garden should be composed of a good balance of forbs and grasses. A high-quality mesic or dry prairie possesses well over two hundred species. Generally, there will be twenty species of grasses, constituting 10 percent of the prairie species. There will also be some fifty species of aster family composites (25 percent), ten to thirty species from the bean family (5 to 15 percent), with the higher percentage if the soil is sandy and nutrient-poor, three to ten species each from the rose, milkweed, mint, and lily families, and then another hundred miscellaneous species. Admittedly, developing this intricate a palette would take years of combing your area for appropriate seed, but your home garden can be much simpler. Remember, having a prairie garden is supposed to be a pleasure.

To make getting started easy, the plant profiles in part III are laid out so that if you choose at least one plant suitable for your region and habitat from every group, you should have the proper mix. This will be forty to fifty species in roughly the proportions recommended—a good start on a prairie. Furthermore, the groups are laid out so that you will have something flowering at every season.

Although it is more expensive to plant fifty species instead of twelve right away, everyone agrees that the long-term costs are lower. For one thing, you will have fewer weeds in a planting that possesses a wide diversity of species. According to Wendy Walcott, "Out of every five species you plant, one or two will do well no matter what the timing, weather, or soil conditions. With the wild seeds, some species seem to need others in order to germinate at all. Putting them all in at once is better than trying to add the more unusual or slow-developing ones later."

How to Match the Plant to the Habitat

If your soil is either clay loam or sandy loam and can retain moisture in the top few inches for a week or so, you have mesic soil. Mesic soil can hold lots of organic matter, which is why it was so quickly turned into rich farmland. If it grades from mesic to dry mesic because of a slope, stony soil, or a fast-draining pocket of sand or gravel, make up separate lists for each site. If one area holds water a day or two after a rain, and you have rain at least once or twice a month, it can become a lowland prairie. If you have a big tree, choose savanna species to grow in the shade. If your yard is boringly flat, you can create a swale and a berm to give yourself different habitats.

Choosing When to Be Purist

This topic is hotly debated in native plant circles. Whether you are doing a restoration or a replication, the rule is to use only local genotypes, that is, seed from indigenous plants that are growing geographically close to you. When gathering seed from a plant such as switchgrass that grows both in wet sloughs and on upland prairies, choose seed from a plant from the same type of habitat you are restoring. The idea is to pull together the same genetic material that might have been on your site before it lost native species and got infested by weeds. To add inappropriate genotypes to an existing healthy prairie, or even to land adjoining a pristine prairie, would be criminal according to current restoration theory, because it would contaminate the local indigenous gene pool.

Some prairie gardeners are not so purist. They figure that as long as the plant is native to North America and it can grow in the wild on its own, that is all that matters.

A reasonable approach for home gardeners is simply to use whatever prairie plants can be found, as long as they can survive in the garden without pampering. But for restorationists, every effort should be made to be purist and to preserve the genetic diversity of the local species.

What Is Native for You?

In the plant profiles, the individual species maps let you know if the plant is native to your state. The tables at the end of each plant profile chapter match the plant to habitats in your area. Between the two, you should be able to figure out what is *likely* to be native to your site. For a serious restoration, you might want to consult with a local botanist to identify those plants that are not found in this book.

Seeds or Transplants?

Sowing seed is much less expensive than installing plugs or transplants, and much less work, too. If you are doing a big project, seed is the way to go. There are some excellent nurseries that specialize in local seed. If you are not near such a nursery and you want to do a purist reconstruction, you will need to hand-gather seed locally.

Seeds of annuals, biennials, short-lived perennials, and all weeds tend to germinate quickly and easily. The seeds of high-quality perennials often require healthy soil with the right mycorrhizae.

The general consensus is that sowing in sand produces easy germination, and sowing in clay is sometimes a bust, or at least is not so immediately rewarding. For clay soil jobs of over an acre, special machinery that drills tiny holes in the ground and deposits the seed can greatly increase germination. For small gardens in clay, putting in transplants or plugs is the best way to go.

Taking transplants from the wild is a major no-no unless you are part of a native plant organization that is conducting a plant rescue. The wildlands are having a hard enough time without having holes dug in them and important (possibly endangered) plants removed.

If you want plugs purely of local genetic material, you can gather your own seed and then start seedlings on your windowsill or under a grow light. Or you can contract with a local nursery to grow your seed into plugs for you.

Although buying plants from a nursery can increase the cost of your garden, for

IN JUNE, Patricia Cooper decided to convert part of the front lawn into a prairie garden, but her husband, Richard Edlich, was not so sure. One quick way to demonstrate how great prairie looks is to use plant plugs instead of seed. Three months later, Richard was an enthusiastic convert to native plants, and we were taking this photo. Design and installation were by Andy Sudbrock of Minneapolis. *St. Anthony, Minnesota. September 14.*

instant results in a small area, this is a good option. Some people do a combination of seed and transplants, depending on what is available.

Collecting Your Own Seed

Just as flowers appear from spring to frost, so does ripe seed. You will begin collecting the seeds of cool season grasses and forbs in early summer, and continue collecting various species all summer, finishing up with the seeds of some of the warm season grasses and forbs. These late-developing seeds ripen just before first frost and can sustain several frosts unharmed.

It takes a few years to learn how to identify each plant in both flower and seed. To make sure the seed you are gathering is the seed you want, first notice the flower in bloom. Then check on it during the days and weeks that it takes for the seed to ripen. Often, you will see a long flower stalk with flowers at the top still blooming and ripe seed at the bottom, ready to be sown.

Be sure you have permission to gather seed on private property. Joining a Nature Conservancy volunteer group, the Wild Ones, the Native Prairies Association of Texas, or a similar group will put you in touch with local experts and also give you entrée to some of the best prairies in your area. Warning: be sure to learn the weeds first so you do not gather those seeds by mistake.

As a rule of thumb, when you gather seed in the wild, you never take more than 10 percent of what is available. (No, this does not mean that ten people can *each* gather 10 percent.) If one species is bountiful one year, gather the full 10 percent that year, if you need it, because you may not see that much of it again for three years, or even twenty years.

Most seed collected in the "soft dough" stage and planted immediately germinates quickly and easily. This soft dough stage is the earliest period of ripeness, when the seed capsule is turning from green to tan, and the plant has stopped sending nutrients to the seed, but the seed is still pale and gummy. Just a few days later, the seed coat will harden into a capsule that can protect the tender germ of life from heat, drought, and cold—for decades if need be. Once the seed coat has hardened, experiencing prolonged cold, alternate freezing and thawing, passing through the gut of a bird or mammal, having an acid bath, or other conditions are sometimes necessary to crack the seed coat and allow rain to seep in and trigger the signal to begin germination.

Most restorationists collect one kind of seed at a time, gather it in paper bags, and check to see if insects are already eating away at the seed. If they are, cut a half inch off your pet's flea collar and drop the piece into the bag. Then you can separate the seed from the debris at your leisure. Fresh, cleaned seed can be sown immediately or stored in a cool, dry place until you are ready to use it. The vegetable drawer in the refrigerator is the preferred storage place for many horticulturists. Label and date each species clearly, and do not trust your memory. I also like to add the exact location where I collected the seed.

When I am not planting large areas, I collect all the seed from one habitat in one bag, as it is much easier to pass through the collecting area just once holding one large sack instead of ten or twenty small ones. Since my prairie garden will be an amalgam of species, intermingled just as they are in nature, it does not matter if they get all mixed up in my sack, as long as I do not mix seeds from different habitats.

When collecting seed, there is often a lot of chaff and fluff present that is not seed. Seeds themselves are usually dark, heavy, and dense, although some are pale or as minuscule as finely ground pepper.

Many of the warm season prairie species have seeds with fluffy, silky parachutes attached. Seeds of little bluestem, goldenrods, asters, *Liatris* species, and milkweeds are some of the most conspicuous. Some of the cool season grasses have long threads called awns attached to the seeds. These attachments were developed to aid in seed dispersal: the parachutes are wind-borne, and the awns cling to animal fur. But in your seed sack, the silky threads can get tangled into a ball. Pull the balls apart and mix the seeds in a bucket with clean sand or compost to keep them separate and ready to sow. The seeds will not enter the soil at the proper angle unless they are separated.

How Many of Each Species Do I Choose?

Although forbs account for only 4 percent of the cover in a typical prairie, their showy flowers, dramatic leaves, and attractiveness to butterflies make them the favorite part of prairie for most people. So, prairie gardeners often plant 80 percent forb seeds and 20 percent grass seeds. That is by number. By weight, these proportions come out to 50:50, as forb seed on average is smaller and lighter than grass seed.

Because seeds differ widely in size, weight, and viability, nurseries that sell seed have (or should have) charts that show you how much you need of a particular species to cover a given area. You want to plant thickly enough so that prairie plants give weeds no room to grow, but you do not want to plant so thickly that all your prairie plants become too stunted to bloom. Scott Weber of Bluestem Farm, Baraboo, Wisconsin, recommends fifteen to thirty seeds per square foot.

If you are hand-gathering seed, you will plant what you can find.

■ HOW TO PLANT

Sowing Seed

For a huge project, use farm machinery specially adapted to prairie seed. Most states have at least one nursery that specializes in 100-acre plantings and has the right equipment. These machines can plant in a bare-soil field, or they can drill into existing sod. They are specially adapted to handle both the fluffy seeds and the tiny seeds typical of many prairie species, both of which are quite different from crop seeds.

On a small job, mix the seed half and half in a bucket with potting soil or children's play sand—something sterile and a contrasting color to the soil—and then broadcast it by hand. Scatter about one cup for every 100 square feet. Put just a pinch of the very fine or the very rare seeds in each bucket so they get distributed evenly. Then rake the seedbed, roll it, drag a board or a harrow over it, or have dozens of children walk on it (or one child walk on it dozens of times). These are all ways to insure that the seed gets pressed into the soil. A firm seedbed that barely shows footprints will hold in moisture and protect the seed from birds and insects.

For interseeding, mix the seed the same way and scatter it in the bare spots. If the soil is hard, rough it up with a rake and then press in the seed with your foot. If you time it right, a good thunderstorm can sometimes pound the seed in just right—on level ground, that is. On a slope, it can wash all the seed down somewhere else. I always plant most of my seed at the top of a slope and let gravity take care of the bottom.

Wendy Walcott, land manager for native plants at Schlitz Audubon Nature Center, is a strong believer in sowing with a cover or nurse crop when the seed is going onto tilled ground. The purpose of a cover crop is to fill bare soil with harmless annuals so there is no room for harmful weeds to germinate. This works best if harmful weeds are not already present in the soil. Wendy likes to use buckwheat, moth mullein, annual flax, wild rye, and oats. She mixes both the cover crop seeds and the prairie seeds with compost, and then spreads the seed-compost like mulch.

Bob Ahrenhoerster also likes a cover crop, but prefers an all-native one: common evening primrose (*Oenothera biennis*), black-eyed Susan, and nodding wildrye are good for south-central Wisconsin. Purple threeawn and Mexican hat work well in the South and Southwest, especially in fast-draining sandy or gravelly soil.

Seed does not need to be watered at all in most of the country, but in Texas and the southwest quadrant, one to three waterings in a dry spring, once the soil has warmed up, speeds up germination. Otherwise, you might have to wait several years to get enough rain at the right time.

In places where droughts make successful germination difficult, seed balls are popular. Store-bought seed balls are full of non-native wildflowers. The best prairie seed balls are handmade, and you can do it yourself. The recipe is simple: take one part prairie seed, add this to three parts dry compost with live mycorrhizal fungi and soil inoculates, and then combine that with five parts finely sifted dry clay. Add one to two parts water, a tiny bit at a time until the consistency is right to form half-inch-diameter balls. Roll the balls between your palms until they feel round and smooth, and set them aside to dry for at least twenty-four hours. Then they can be broadcast on the planting area. In this form, the seed is protected from birds and rodents and will not try to germinate until there is sufficient rain to melt the clay ball. Ten to twenty seed balls are recommended per square yard.

Planting Plugs and Transplants

Prairie plugs or plants grown in pots or grow bags are planted the way you plant any nursery-grown ornamental. The root ball is placed so that the top of the potting soil is level with the top of the ground. Firm the fluffed-up soil around the plant, and then water to melt the soil around the roots and eliminate air pockets.

Bare-root perennials usually have larger root systems. Keep the roots moist at all times. I mix root stimulator in a bucket of water and plunge in the roots, letting them soak while I dig the holes. I make a firm cone of soil at the bottom of each hole and arrange the roots over it like a skirt. Be sure that the "crown" of the plant, where roots and stems meet, is at ground level. If the crown is buried, it can rot, and the plant dies. Firm the soil around the roots and water.

CINDY HILDEBRAND surrounds a transplant with a temporary cage to protect it from being eaten by deer and rabbits. *Ames, Iowa. September 13.*

Adding Plugs and Transplants

After your prairie is started, it is easy to increase diversity by adding species. When adding a plug or transplant, most gardeners give it a wire cage for protection or flag it so they can remember to water it. In the South, a bit of shade cloth is a good idea.

You want the new plant to be able to seed out on its own, so if at all possible, add at least three individuals of each new species so you will get fertile seed.

When to Plant

The optimum time to plant seed or plugs varies greatly according to geography. In Canada, springtime is best. As a rule, the time of year when you are statistically most likely to get a good rain is best of all. In northeastern tall-grass prairies, this is most likely to be May or June. In northern shortgrass prairies, April or May is better, after the snow has melted and the ground has thawed. One Colorado restorationist recommends sowing directly into a late spring snow, so that the seeds soak into the ground as the snow melts.

In Minnesota, Wisconsin, Iowa, and Colorado, several restorationists recommend seeding in November before the ground freezes. Don Vorpahl of Hilbert, Wisconsin, says he has found fall seeding to work well only in sand or gravel. He prefers seeding June to July for heavier soils. Plugs may be planted in spring or summer when there is no danger of frost.

In Missouri, Oklahoma, and Texas, seedings from September to November do well, although some fall-blooming forbs germinate best if they are sown in February or March. Southern summers are too hot and dry for germination, but winter soil is moist and easy to work. Transplants do best in fall, as they have all winter to grow roots, but very early spring plantings are also successful.

Chapter 8

Maintaining
Prairie Gardens

ONCE A PRAIRIE IS PLANTED, maintenance is the key to long-term success. An established prairie garden does not need watering, weekly mowing, herbicides, insecticides, or fungicides. It is definitely environmentally friendly. But it does depend on you for its life. In a home garden, once a year you have to burn or mow to mimic the work of bison, elk, deer, rabbits, grasshoppers, and wildfire—tools that traditionally removed woody plants, allowed sunlight to reach spring flowers, recycled organic debris into the soil, and kept insect populations in balance.

In a perfect world, burning and mowing would be all the maintenance required. But because so many alien seeds have been planted by home gardeners, farmers, ranchers, and highway departments, there is another side to maintenance—fighting weeds that have the power to demolish your prairie garden. We discussed how to get rid of as many weeds as possible before planting.

This chapter deals with fighting weeds as your prairie gets established and as a regular part of ongoing maintenance. Weeding is vital the first two years because that is when the weeds must be subdued to give prairie grasses and forbs a chance to get established. Admittedly, weeding is not fun, but each year it gets easier.

■ WEEDS

Before Europeans arrived, there were no weeds in prairies. Weedy-looking, rambunctious annuals, like giant ragweed, prevented erosion and were quickly taken out by perennials. Thuggish early-succession perennials, such as Canada goldenrod, were eventually out-

THE MINNESOTA VALLEY NATIONAL WILDLIFE REFUGE landscaped around two sides of its building and its parking area with prairie. Although native plants and natural ecosystems do not require weekly maintenance, they do require some upkeep. At the time we visited, the prairie was clearly in need of a cleanup. Moreover, the shrubbery against the building, which was originally all snowberry, was being overtaken by weedy trees. The Minnesota Native Plant Society meets here each month, and one of the members, Andy Sudbrock, says they have volunteered to pay for this privilege with two work days a year to maintain the plantings. Even with less than minimal maintenance and a gloomy sky, the fall color of Anoka sandplain little bluestem looks beautifully pink in contrast to the coppery spires of big bluestem. *Bloomington, Minnesota. September 14.*

competed by conservative prairie plants. Thicket trees and shrubs that border prairie and invade it, such as smooth sumac, were traditionally held at bay by regular fires, browsing, and the roots of big bluestem.

Now our prairies are overrun by plants from other continents, and we call these plants "weeds." Most people think of weeds as ugly. In fact, some of the most vicious weeds are quite attractive. What makes them weeds is that when they come on the scene, they drive out all the other plants. Non-natives such as Queen Anne's lace, bluegrass, asparagus, bladder campion, hawkweed, chicory, dandelions, and flannel mullein are either short-lived or they are willing to share the whole prairie system in a way that is not harmful—except, of course, from the purist's standpoint of their not being authentically North American.

The problem weeds in our prairies are drought-tolerant prairie plants from other continents. They not only survive and thrive, they run amok because here they have none of the natural controls that kept them in balance where they came from.

Choosing Which Weeds to Fight

It is best to fight only those weeds that can cause tremendous trouble later. Most first-time prairie gardeners are diligent weed fighters, but they do not know the prairie plants from the weeds, and they do not know which weeds will go away on their own and which will act like Attila the Hun.

It is helpful to know what the prairie plants look like as they first germinate. You can do as the Wondras did and plant each seed in its own tiny labeled plot so the desirable prairie plants can be identified at all stages of growth. For those who live in the northern tallgrass area, I recommend buying *Restoring Canada's Native Prairies* by Morgan, Collicutt, and Thompson for its photographs of 119 northern prairie seedlings.

But it is even more helpful to learn the weeds. It is much easier to memorize the life cycles of three to twelve invasive weeds than those of a couple of hundred desirable prairie species.

Worst Weeds

As we interviewed prairie gardeners, we did a survey of their worst weeds. Thirteen of these seem never to be completely eradicated in northern prairies. Beating them back each year is the best one can hope for. But they are the ones it is most imperative to fight if you do not want to lose your whole prairie or savanna garden.

Attacking each weed at least twice a year works best. Hot fires at key times of the year, or in combination with herbicides, can be very effective. Cutting and bagging seed-bearing stalks also help if you are persistent enough. Old-fashioned weeding is effective right after the plants have germinated and before their root systems have begun to spread.

The weedy grasses and clovers are still being sold and planted by ranchers and farmers. But other weeds such as thistles, knapweeds, and leafy spurge can ruin farmland, so there are government programs to help fight them. Contact your local extension service for the latest information, or consult the chapter by Mary Kay Solecki on "Controlling Invasive Plants" in *The Tallgrass Restoration Handbook* (Packard and Mutel, eds.).

Noxious cool season rhizomatous grasses:

1. Smooth or Hungarian brome (*Bromus inermis*), native to Europe, Siberia, and China, is prairie enemy number one in the northern prairies. Its rhizomes exude a poison that kills neighboring plants.
2. Quackgrass (*Agropyron repens*), from Eurasia, is said to be equally noxious and is even more drought-tolerant.
3. Reed canary grass (*Phalaris arundinacea*) is native to wet northeastern prairies, but for some reason we brought in a Eurasian ecotype that forms a sod that excludes all other plants. It breaks dormancy early in the spring and then shades out other grasses and forbs.

Noxious perennial forbs:

4. Crown vetch (*Coronilla varia*), a legume native to Europe, southwest Asia, and northern Africa, is still planted for erosion control along highways. It is even sold in the Park Seed catalog. A long taproot makes it drought-tolerant, and its multibranched creeping roots can soon fill several hundred square feet.
5. Leafy spurge (*Euphorbia esula*), native to Europe, invades dry prairies, mesic prairies, and savannas in the north and along the Rockies. At the Curtis Prairie, one lone leafy spurge was ignored, and now it infects an entire acre of once healthy prairie.
6. Birdfoot trefoil (*Lotus corniculatus*), from Europe and Asia, is planted for forage and highway "beautification." It is most destructive of prairies in the northeastern quadrant.
7. Russian knapweed (*Centaurea repens*) is a thistlelike perennial whose rhizomes emit a poison that kills off other plants. It was accidentally introduced into North America in 1898 and is monitored in the northwestern Great Plains as a noxious weed.
8. Canada thistle (*Cirsium arvense*), native of southeastern Eurasia, is eventually outcompeted by big bluestem in northern tallgrass prairies but ruins shortgrass prairies.

Noxious biennials and short-lived perennials:

9. If you hand-weed wild parsnip (*Pastinaca sativa*), a native of Europe, you will likely get huge nasty blisters. This biennial invades moist waste places, mesic prairies, and savannas in the north.
10. Yellow sweet clover (*Melilotus officinalis*) and the later-blooming white

sweet clover (*Melilotus alba*) are natives of Eurasia. They disappear on their own in tallgrass prairies, but in shortgrass prairies, they shade out the neighboring prairie plants.

11. Spotted knapweed (*Centaurea maculata*) can be eradicated by persistent weeding.

12. Garlic mustard (*Allaria petiolata*), native to Europe, invades more ground each year in savannas and woodlands in the northeastern quadrant.

13. Common buckthorn (*Rhamnus cathartica*), a tall spiny shrub from Eurasia, chokes out northeastern savannas, and glossy buckthorn (*Rhamnus frangula*) invades wet prairies.

Other weeds people complained of in the Northeast are alfalfa, tall fescue, *Miscanthus* species, *Phragmites australis*, redtop, teasel, Dame's rocket, black medic, purple loosestrife, roundleaf bittersweet, porceline berry, alien bittersweet, creeping Charlie, red clover, perennial rye, field bindweed, burdock, curly dock, *Hypericum perforatum*, flowering rush, multiflora rose, bishopsweed, lily of the valley, garden heliotrope, Asian honeysuckles, Japanese barberry, Siberian elm, and Norway maple.

Many of these northeastern weeds are invasive all over the continent. But other prairie areas have additional weeds that can cause problems. Southern pests are hairy vetch, Japanese hops, Asian *Ligustrum* species, bermudagrass, johnsongrass, buffelgrass, and guineagrass. Out West beware of Russian olive, crested wheatgrass, and horehound.

How to Control Weeds the First Two Years

Let nonvicious annual weeds act as a cover crop and worry only about long-term weeds. If weeds are minimal, hand-weed only. If weeds are numerous, mow. Excessive hand-weeding in a newly planted prairie disturbs the soil and can dislodge too many tiny prairie seedlings.

The first year, mow whenever weeds grow over 10 inches tall. They will shade out prairie seedlings if you do not cut them back to 6 inches, the height of the prairie plants. Use a flail mower or a weed whip.

Prairie plants do not grow over 6 inches the first year, because they are too busy growing roots. *Liatris punctata*, for example, might be only 5 inches tall at the end of its first growing season and possess only two leaves. But Weaver found it to have a taproot 33 to 38 inches long.

In early spring of the second year, mow to the ground to allow ungerminated prairie seeds to sprout. Do not burn, as fire exposes the soil too much and causes increased weed growth.

Biennial weeds like spotted knapweed and sweet clover grow tall the second year. They can be mowed to 6 inches in late spring or early summer just as they are starting to bloom and before they set seed. This is somewhat damaging to your prairie plants, so most restorationists mow only if the biennials are too numerous to hand-weed.

■ INSECTS

The best way to handle insects is to do nothing at all. Resorting to chemical warfare kills off butterflies and birds. Less than 1 percent of garden insects are pests, and many of those metamorphose into desirable butterflies and nectar-feeding moths.

Over twenty years of no-pesticide management in our own gardens have taught

Andy and me that if you just let nature take its course, it all balances out, and nothing is harmed two years in a row. In fact, epidemics in our neighbors' gardens have passed us by.

■ WATERING

In the tallgrass areas, do not water your garden after it is established. If you continue to water, the plants that survive will be those that require extra water, and you are stuck watering forever. Or you have to let them die and start all over, because the plants that "belong" on your site—the ones that can live on rainfall—rotted because they got too wet or disappeared because they were outcompeted by more water-tolerant species.

In the shortgrass areas, and especially in a drought year, a watering every month or so may be necessary to keep your garden from going dormant. If you do not water, and your garden does go dormant, it is OK; nothing is likely to die.

■ FIRE

Fire is the traditional cleanup for prairies all over the globe. Prairies outcompete forests where rainfall is scant, so prairies get dry and become combustible. When lightning strikes a dry prairie, a fire is the result. Native Americans observed how beneficial the fires were and how the all-new tender green growth attracted bison the next year, so, cleverly, they set fires on their favorite prairies. According to Cabeza de Vaca, the sixteenth-century Spanish explorer, they burned some prairies and left others, so as to gather all their prey together on a convenient unburned prairie for the winter. Historical records indicate that Native Americans set fires most often around April or October, while lightning fires occurred in late summer.

The North American "wilderness" that the European explorers found was really a fire-managed landscape. In the 1970s, some scientists claimed that all the tales of Indians firing the prairies were apocryphal, but as S. J. Pyne wrote in 1982 in *Fire in America*, "The evidence for aboriginal burning in nearly every landscape of North America is so conclusive, and the consequences of fire suppression so visible, that it seems fantastic that a debate about aboriginal fire should ever have taken place."

The prettiest prairies we saw, with the highest abundance of orchids, lilies, and other high-quality climax spring plants, were always on Indian reservations, where fall fires are frequent. We were told that these prairies have been burned every year for as far back as anyone can remember. At Walpole Island, Ontario, they alternate annual fires between September and spring.

When to Burn

A burn can have both negative and positive effects on wildlife and plant composition depending on when you do it. For example, a burn in April can hurt nesting killdeer. One in May can harm nesting pheasants and most forbs. One in late summer is better for butterflies because they are not in the egg or caterpillar stage. A February or March fire increases spring soil temperature (black absorbs light), so the prairie greens up earlier than normal, but removes seeds and cover for overwintering birds and mammals, and kills insects, including butterflies, that are in the egg or pupal stage.

Fire also affects mycorrhizae and other soil invertebrates, and scientists suspect that frequent fires lower organic matter and nitrogen. These changes in the soil in turn affect plant composition, but hard data are not yet available.

FIRE is currently the preferred maintenance for tallgrass prairies. Stonewall Prairie was burned in May. Note how clean the black ash looks and how everything has already greened up. Also, notice how many plants exist per square foot, and how only a few of them get large at any one time of year. This is authentic prairie texture. *Stonewall, Manitoba. June 24.*

Several scientific studies on the effects of burn times on prairies are under way. Results so far indicate the following: Spring fires help warm season grasses. (If big blue-stem is taking over your prairie, do not burn in the spring.) Summer burns seem to harm woody species. Fall burns favor almost all forbs and cool season grasses. Winter fires seem to benefit both warm and cool season grasses. An ongoing Missouri study indicates that species diversity may be highest with fall burns (pre-frost), next highest with winter burns (dormant), and lowest with spring burns (post-emergence).

Design, Installation, and Maintenance

How Often to Burn

To minimize damage to wildlife and to increase plant diversity, people with large tallgrass prairies tend to burn only a third each year, and they vary the time of year they burn. In northern tallgrass areas, any time a fire occurs during the growing season, resprouts occur within days, and flowers start appearing in two weeks.

Fire studies at Konza Prairie in Kansas have found that species diversity is greatest when fires occur every four to five years. They have found that annual fires favor warm season grasses, and infrequent fires allow woody vegetation to increase. In the southern Great Plains, where woody plants are rare and fuel loads are low, fire should be very infrequent, as grasses cannot grow new leaves until they receive rain, and rain may not appear for months.

In a home landscape, if you decide to burn every three to five years, you will want to mow in the interim years. That way you will have no dead brown leaves and stems from the previous year detracting from the fresh green leaves and flowers of the current year.

How to Conduct a Safe Controlled Burn

You are now convinced that a burn will definitely benefit your prairie landscape. But common sense tells you that this is not something you can undertake without some instruction. You are right. It is a good idea to invite experienced helpers to be on-site for at least the first two burns.

Sometimes, native plant nurseries can be hired to do a burn. Prairie Restorations of Princeton, Minnesota, for example, does about sixty burns a year. On a large property and for a fee, The Nature Conservancy will sometimes show you how to do a burn.

Fire departments can be helpful and will have had experience in handling grass fires, although they may not understand the reasons for a prairie burn. Some local parks departments are developing these skills as well.

Here are some important tips:

— To start a fire, mass up a small bundle of dry grass, light it, and drag it along the ground using an iron garden rake or, better still, a specially designed fire rake, with a 12-inch metal extension between the rake head and the wooden handle.
— Have a fire-swatter handy. This is a 12-by-18-inch piece of reinforced rubber attached to a 5-foot handle, which is used to smother small grass fires. You can use it to extinguish the back fire. Do not slap with too much force or you will spread the fire.
— Have ample water handy, a garden hose under pressure, buckets of water, or a backpack pump that can shoot a stream of water 20 feet. Sometimes you can borrow equipment from the fire department.
— Do not wear synthetic clothing, which can burn and melt, and avoid clothing with frayed edges that can ignite. Wear gloves and long-sleeved shirts to protect your skin from radiant heat, and a hat to protect you from flying embers.
— Pick a day when the wind is light (3 to 15 mph) and the relative humidity is between 25 and 60 percent. Winds tend to be milder in the morning. Winds can also change directions; be prepared to handle this.
— Never burn by yourself; have at least one reliable partner who can help

you watch for flare-ups, and can keep your water supply topped off. More help is better.

— Do not get overconfident. With proper conditions of moisture and wind, you can control a burn. But fire is always dangerous, and if your mind wanders, your burn can get out of control.

■ GRAZING

It takes at least 8 acres of tallgrass prairie to support one bison in Kansas, and it could take as many as 100 acres of shortgrass prairie in New Mexico. These estimates take into account how much grass it takes to feed a bison for a year. A Native American told us that he could not imagine bison being happy if there were not at least three to five of them and they did not have a minimum of 100 acres to roam around in. Also, bison are wild animals with intelligence and survival instincts; they can be dangerous if not treated with respect. *Clearly, grazing bison cannot be a maintenance option for suburban homeowners.*

However, maintaining prairie with bison *is* an option for large tracts of land. This is partly why many reservations, ranches, and Nature Conservancy lands are now stocking bison and restoring prairie at the same time.

The Osage Prairie, in northeastern Oklahoma near Pawhuska, is managed by The Nature Conservancy. Bison were introduced in October 1993. All internal fences were removed so that the unmanaged interaction of bison, free range, and natural fires could be studied.

Fred Dubray, a Native American, founded the Intertribal Bison Co-op, a project to restore bison to tribal prairies for both the good of the prairies and to improve the diets of Native Americans. He started on the Cheyenne River Sioux Reservation by buying back land that had been ruined by northern European farming methods and stocking it with a herd of bison. He does not burn or mow; he lets the bison graze on all of it.

The question naturally arises as to whether bison are environmentally friendlier than domestic shorthorn cattle. The answer is a definite "maybe."

Dr. Gene Towne, research associate at Kansas State University, is very likely the only academic currently studying the effects of cattle and bison on the land, and thus far his work at Konza Prairie has resulted in several findings.

Bison pastures have more forb diversity because bison prefer grass. The forbs benefit because fewer of them get eaten and there is less competition from grass.

Bison tend to overgraze patches as large as a football field and ignore the surrounding prairie, while cattle graze uniformly throughout the prairie. Both the bison grazing areas and buffalo wallows expose bare earth, which is then invaded by annual pioneer forbs or alien weeds. Lacking sufficient fuel load to carry a fire, these areas can also be invaded by woody species.

Commercially, bison, although they take a year longer to be market-ready, have several advantages over domestic cattle. Bison are being sold to a growing health-conscious

THE GRAZING OF BISON may be the key to managing large prairies. *Intertribal Bison Cooperative, Cheyenne River Sioux Reservation, South Dakota. June 18.*

market as a leaner alternative to beef. Bud Griffith, who manages Ted Turner's 130,000-acre ranch in Montana, says that managing three thousand cattle would require a dozen cowboys, but three people can manage the same number of bison. Bison are able to live without supplemental feedings of farm crops, and they know how to survive blizzards. If our present ranch lands were grazed in a natural manner, they could probably support as many bison as cattle, and we could do away with farm subsidies, erosion, overgrazing, and aquifer depletion.

Domestic cattle can also be used to restore prairie, as evidenced by the Duncan Ranch in Shellytown, Texas, near Amarillo. In 1991, Patsy Ward began restoring both upland and lowland prairies on the family ranch. Her tool is the Allan Savory method of Holistic Resource Management, which advocates rotational grazing. She lets the cattle graze the grass down to about 6 inches and then moves them to another pasture. The litter of leaves and 3- to-4-inch stems left behind acts like a mulch and helps restore the soil.

She does no haying, no mowing, and no burning. Little bluestem, the principal upland grass, does not thicken up when burned. Other upland grasses are four kinds of grama grasses, silver bluestem, and purple threeawn. The lowland pastures are rich with big bluestem, silver bluestem, and Indiangrass on the floodplain, and along the banks and in White Deer Creek itself are switchgrass, alkali sacaton, and cordgrass.

I saw this ranch in October 1998, and it was impressive. Even the upland prairies were over 2 feet tall, grassy and rich with forbs, while most of the neighboring ranch lands were thick with yucca, and the only grasses I saw were inch-high tussocks.

■ MOWING

Mowing to keep prairies healthy and to cut back shrubs and trees is a substitute for burning or grazing. A flail or mulching mower leaves the prairie looking tidy and makes the dead stems and leaves easier to break down. If you use a scythe or a weed whip, you need to pick up the hay. To put it back down as mulch, you then need to put it through a shredder or a composter—obviously lots more work, unless your prairie garden is tiny.

Mowing should be done only once a year, except in the first year when you are combating weeds. Mowing more frequently favors non-native farm grasses and kills our native warm season grasses.

MOWING with a flail mower or baling hay once a year is more effective than fire for maintaining little bluestem prairies. Late-summer or fall mowings produce beautiful spring flowers like this. *Midlothian, Texas. May 12.*

PART THREE

Plant Profiles

Whether you start your restoration by introducing ten species of plants or one hundred, it is important to remember that each one has become adapted to a set of conditions over a long period of evolutionary time. A restorationist cannot change the adaptations; rather, the plants must be put into appropriate locations where their adaptations will let them succeed. Matching community to site is critical.

VIRGINIA M. KLINE,
The Tallgrass Restoration Handbook

THE PLANT PROFILES are set up to help you choose a suitable variety of plants for your prairie. They are divided into four chapters: grasses, sedges, and rushes; cool season forbs; warm season forbs; and savanna trees and thicket shrubs.

Within each chapter, there are groups of plants. If you choose a plant from as many groups as you can, you will have continuous flowers from spring to fall.

To make a list of the plants that will most likely succeed in your garden, first, determine what quadrant you live in by referring to the map of the prairies of North America in chapter 1. The western half of the prairie region is called the Great Plains. There, rainfall is scarce and shortgrasses predominate. The northwest quadrant is often called the Northern Plains, and the southwest quadrant may be referred to as the Southern Plains. The eastern half of the prairie region gets more rainfall, and it used to be dominated by tallgrasses and oak savannas. The northeast quadrant and the southeast quadrant are the north and south divisions of the tallgrass prairie region.

After you have found your quadrant, determine which habitat in your quadrant best reflects the moisture conditions of the garden you are designing. An explanation of the habitats is found on the following table.

Then, turn to the habitat tables at the end of each chapter. If you are planning a mesic prairie garden, list all the plants for a mesic habitat in your region.

To learn more about these plants, go back to the beginning of each chapter and read each plant profile. The plants are listed in the tables in the same order you will find them in each chapter.

The idea is to develop a list of all plants that are native to your area and habitat. Next to each plant profile, there is a map showing its native range. Be aware that within each state, a plant is native only to its specific habitat.

Green on the range map indicates fairly common distribution. *Yellow* indicates that the plant is rare—maybe only a few sites or individual plants are known to exist in the entire state. *Brown* means that there is historic documentation that the plant used to grow in that state, but that current fieldwork indicates that it is now extinct there. Some of the plants have naturalized beyond what was their native range a century ago. In the text, I attempted to indicate pre-European distribution where information was available.

Once you have your plant list, you are ready to design your prairie garden.

	NORTHWEST *Northern Plains Shortgrass Region*		NORTHEAST *Northern Tallgrass Prairie Region*		SOUTHWEST *Southern Plains Shortgrass Region*		SOUTHEAST *Southern Tallgrass Prairie Region*	
	Habitat	Dominants	Habitat	Dominants	Habitat	Dominants	Habitat	Dominants
LOWLAND PRAIRIE	Wet to moist all year, poorly drained	Sedges, fowl mannagrass, sweetgrass	Wet to moist all year, poorly drained	Prairie cordgrass, bluejoint, spikerush, sedges, rushes	Flooded once a year	Alkali sacaton, western wheatgrass, big bluestem	Wet to moist at root level all year	Lowland switchgrass, brushy bluestem
MESIC PRAIRIE	Moist at root level most years	Western wheatgrass, little bluestem, big bluestem, needle-and-thread (waist-high)	Moist at root level all year every year	Big bluestem, Indiangrass, switchgrass (man-high to "high as a man on a horse")	Moist at root level most of year	Little bluestem, needlegrasses, buffalograss, sideoats grama (waist-high)	Moist at root level most years	Big bluestem, switchgrass, Indiangrass, little bluestem (man-high)
UPLAND PRAIRIE	Well-drained, often dry at root level	Blue grama, needle-and-thread, Junegrass, little bluestem (knee-high)	Well-drained, moist at root level	Prairie dropseed, prairie panicgrass, little bluestem, porcupine grass (knee-high)	Dormant when no rain	Grama grasses, buffalograss, cactus, yucca (ankle-high to knee-high in flower)	Well-drained, never standing water	Little bluestem, sideoats grama (knee-high to waist-high)
SAND PRAIRIE	Moist at root level most years	Bluestem, sandreed, grama grasses, needlegrasses, Indian ricegrass (waist-high)			Moist at root level most years	Bluestems, grama grasses, sandsage (waist-high)		
BUR OAK SAVANNA			Clay, loam, or sand, mesic	Bur oak, white oak in east, woodland sedges, woodland brome, bottlebrush grass, big bluestem			Clay, loam, or limestone, mesic	Bur oak, chinquapin oak, big bluestem. In central Texas, escarpment live oak with little bluestem
BLACK OAK SAVANNA			Sand, well-drained even if moist	Black oak, northern pin oak in north, bracken fern, woodland sedge, little bluestem				
POST OAK SAVANNA							Sand, well-drained	Post oak, blackjack oak, hickories, little bluestem, legumes
ASPEN PARKLAND	Borders Canadian mesic prairie or mountain grasslands	Aspen, balsam poplar, rough fescue, needle-and-thread, little bluestem						
PONDEROSA SAVANNA					Mountain grasslands above pinyons	Ponderosa pine, shrubby oak, grama grasses, bluestems, needlegrasses		

Certain species of prairie grasses are so vigorous and abundant that their influence upon the habitat and effect upon other species determine to a large degree the condition under which all of the remaining species associated with them must develop. Such a species is called a dominant.

J. E. WEAVER, *North American Prairie*

Grasses, Sedges, and Rushes

THIS CHAPTER IS ARRANGED to help you choose four to nine grassy species for each of your prairie or savanna habitat gardens. The grasses (Poaceae) and grasslike plants such as sedges (Cyperaceae) and rushes (Juncaceae) are the prominent features of a prairie. Surprisingly, each local patch of prairie is dominated by only four to five grassy species. Then there are smaller numbers of a few other grasses or grasslike plants.

There are four species of grasses that are present in most of our prairies. Here is Ray Schulenberg's quick and easy way to tell them apart when they are not in flower or seed:

> If it's flat and smooth, it's little bluestem.
> If it's flat and fuzzy, it's big bluestem.
> If it's round and smooth, it's switchgrass.
> If it's round and fuzzy, it's Indiangrass.

"It" is the sheath around the stem or, botanically speaking, the culm of the grass right down at its base, where it may be as much white as green. Reach down into a big tuft of grass and grab one stem where it connects to the root and give a tug. In your hand will be a culm. The flatness of bluestems is very obvious. In cross section, a bluestem culm is a flattened oval, as opposed to the round cross section of switchgrass or Indiangrass. This rhyme works best where orchard grass, which also has a flat, smooth culm base, is not present.

Big bluestem and little bluestem are prairie dominants, suitable for nearly every prairie garden. Other bluestems that are especially lovely are bushy bluestem and sand bluestem. Early-succession bluestems that are likely to come in on their own without your having to plant them are broomsedge (*Andropogon virginicus*), silver bluestem (*Bothriochloa laguroides* ssp. *torreyana*), and cane bluestem (*Bothriochloa barbinodis*). There are several other native bluestems, but these are the most important ones.

Two non-native bluestems, KR (King Ranch) bluestem (*Bothriochloa ischaemum* var. *songarica*) from Eurasia, and Australian bluestem (*Bothriochloa bladhii*) from Australia, have naturalized and become pests in southern prairie plantings.

All North American bluestems used to be *Andropogons*, and in the 1986 edition of *Flora of the Great Plains*, they are still listed that way. However, most botanists have divided the family into several genera.

BIG BLUESTEM is also called old turkey foot because the long, slender spikes of purplish flowers reminded pioneers of turkey toes.

BIG BLUESTEM (*Andropogon gerardii* [an-dro-POE-gon jer-RAR-dee-eye]) is found in every tallgrass prairie from Canada to central Mexico, because it is tough, drought-tolerant, flood-tolerant, and long-lived. It is a warm season perennial bunchgrass that sometimes has short rhizomes and is aggressive in the long term. Use it sparingly in a tiny prairie, maybe only one for accent. In a large prairie, go light on the seed, or plant it only as a backdrop. Because it is unmowable, it can be killed if it is continually cut back during its growth period. You can slow it down by cutting it back a little every once in a while the way bison did. The chief beauty of big bluestem is its color: blue green to green in summer and reddish purple or russet in fall. The leaves usually arch over, especially at the base.

SAND BLUESTEM (*Andropogon hallii* [an-dro-POE-gon HAWL-ee-eye]), a warm season sod-forming tallgrass, is closely related to big bluestem and often interbreeds with it. The chief difference is that the roots of sand bluestem are aggressive enough to stabilize sand dunes.

understory grass to big bluestem in tallgrass prairie, and an overstory grass in shortgrass prairie where buffalograss and blue grama form the understory. Some botanists call it a midgrass. Paradoxically, while it

Sand bluestem

LITTLE BLUESTEM (*Schizachyrium scoparium* var. *scoparium* [skeh-zack-ee-REE-um sko-PARE-ee-um variety sko-PARE-ee-um]) is one of the most widespread and important of all the prairie grasses. It is typically 2 to 3 feet tall, which makes it an

Big bluestem

Little bluestem

dominates sites that are drier than where one would find big bluestem, during the droughts of the 1930s it was found to be less drought-tolerant than big bluestem because it is not as deep-rooted.

Little bluestem is a warm season perennial bunchgrass with ample space around its individual bunches to harbor a rich array of other grasses and forbs. It usually does not green up until summer, and it can-not survive frequent mowing. In the Southwest, it does not respond well to being burned annually.

Its seeds are on single spikes that are arranged loosely along a flowering stalk. As there are several stalks along each culm (stem), the total effect is both airy and showy. In dry savannas, little bluestem is found under bur oaks, black oaks, post oaks, and live oaks.

BUSHY BLUESTEM (*Andropogon glomeratus* [an-dro-POE-gon glom-er-AH-tus]) is a dramatically handsome grass year-round. It is a bunchgrass with blue green summer color and rich coppery winter color. Its flower and seed head are a dense showy plume of multiple spikes. Bushy bluestem grows in swales and ditches that are seasonally flooded, along pond banks, and in prairies where the water table is very close to the surface. It is native from Massachusetts down to the eastern half of Texas, and in moist spots either side of the Mexican border west to California.

Bushy bluestem

LITTLE BLUESTEM is especially attractive as it provides six months of fluffy silvery seed, plus blue green summer color and coppery winter color.

The grama grasses are a New World genus. There are about 40 species altogether, half of which are native to North America. These are primarily found west of the tallgrass prairies and east of the Rockies from southern Canada to northern Mexico. Sideoats grama, blue grama, and black grama are dominants in the shortgrass prairies of the Great Plains.

Even in a dried state, grama grasses are very attractive. Fall color is pale yellowish tan, and winter foliage is silver and often curly. These grasses are highly nutritious whether green or "cured" and can withstand frequent grazing, which is probably why the cattle-raising Spaniards named them *grama*, a Spanish word for grass.

The four grama grasses featured here are warm season perennials that can increase like pioneers during drought years and are stable and long-lived when the weather is normal. Because of their short stature and because they do not break dormancy until early summer, the grama grasses do not crowd out a wide array of short and colorful spring flowers.

SIDEOATS GRAMA is one of the easiest grasses to identify because its seeds, a favorite with juncos, tend to hang all on one side of the long, arching stems.

SIDEOATS GRAMA (*Bouteloua curtipendula* [boo-tuh-LOO-ah kur-tee-PEN-dew-lah]) is the tallest of our grama grasses, able to reach 3 feet, although it is usually half that

Sideoats grama

height. It is also the most tolerant of high rainfall and clay soil and is often found in loam along with little bluestem or buffalograss. Although sideoats grama is the most moisture-tolerant of the grama grasses, those of you who live in the northern tallgrass prairies must remember to think of it as a dry prairie grass. Sideoats grama has two growth habits, and on that basis it has been divided into two varieties.

Bouteloua curtipendula var. *curtipendula* has small tufts connected by rhizomes. This is the most widespread variety, native from southeastern Canada to Argentina. It makes a smooth mowed path or lawn and mixes well with buffalograss and other grama grasses.

Bouteloua curtipendula var. *caespitosa* (seas-peh-TOE-sah) is a bunchgrass and a prolific seed producer, making it an especially

handsome addition in a garden. It seems to be native primarily in the Southwest.

BLUE GRAMA (*Bouteloua gracilis* [boo-tuh-LOO-ah grah-SILL-iss]) is mat-forming, with short rhizomes, but in dry prairies the plants are separated into tufts. The leaves roll up when dormant, giving the tufts a

Blue grama

rather jolly look, like coarse curly hair that enjoys not being combed. When in flower, blue grama can be 2 feet high, but it is normally less than a foot tall, and the foliage is 3 to 4 inches high. Blue grama is more drought-tolerant than buffalograss, especially in sand, but it also grows on loam. In prairies, the two are usually growing together as understory beneath little bluestem, sideoats grama, and needle-and-thread. In Wisconsin and Illinois, it is native only on the western edges of those states.

HAIRY GRAMA (*Bouteloua hirsuta* [boo-tuh-LOO-ah here-SOO-tah]) is easy to identify because it is short and looks like blue grama with the addition of a long "hair" extending

a half inch beyond the flower spike. This grass is found primarily in sandy soil, although it can also be found on fast-draining rocky soil. Along the Gulf Coast, it grows in longleaf pine savannas, and in Wisconsin it is associated with black oak savannas. In the Great Plains, it is a dominant in sandy prairies and is more frequent in the south than in the north.

BLACK GRAMA (*Bouteloua eriopoda* [boo-tuh-LOO-ah err-ee-OPP-o-dah]), the most drought-tolerant, is also called woollyfoot grama because the lower stems may be covered with whitish fuzz. It is a short, tufted bunchgrass with no rhizomes, although sometimes the outer stems lie down and root at

Black grama

the nodes. Usually about a foot tall, black grama can get almost as tall as sideoats grama. Although it prefers full sun, it can survive in the shade of shrubs. It is more drought-tolerant than the other three gramas and is not native east of central Kansas.

Hairy grama

BLUE GRAMA has straight flower heads that later arch backward to force out the ripened seed, leaving distinctive curlicues that last until spring.

All of our needlegrasses used to be called *Stipa*. Worldwide, they are native to warm dry places. In North America, they are found from Massachusetts to California but mostly in western grasslands. At present, none of our species is called *Stipa*.

Those now called *Hesperostipa* (the western *Stipa*) are distinguished by their long, sharp, needlelike awns. Awns are hairs at the tip of the seed covering. Those with less exaggerated but still conspicuous awns, such as Texas wintergrass and the California needlegrasses, are called *Nassella*. Species with short awns were relegated to the ricegrasses, formally called *Oryzopsis*, but are now known by a host of other names. Indian ricegrass is the most widespread and important of this group. Blackseed oatgrass (*Piptochaetium avenaceum*), sometimes called blackseed needlegrass or blackseed speargrass, is widespread in sandy post oak savannas.

All the needlegrasses and their relatives are cool season grasses.

NEEDLE-AND-THREAD (*Hesperostipa comata* [hes-per-o-STY-pah koe-MAH-tah]) is a cool season bunchgrass that is usually slightly more than knee-high, although it can reach 4 feet. It has no rhizomes, so it depends on seed to renew

NEEDLE-AND-THREAD has a seed encased in a sharp-pointed "needle" with a long flexible awn attached that resembles a "thread."

Needle-and-thread

itself. Although short-lived like a pioneer, it is a dominant in mesic shortgrass prairies, especially sandy or rocky ones, along with little bluestem, grama grasses, or western wheatgrass. It also grows in juniper savanna. Its color is a pale bluish green. Ranchers hate it because domestic livestock cannot cope with the long awns, but bison relish it, especially in the spring when the warm season grasses are still

dormant. In a mass, needle-and-thread sways in the slightest wind with a motion like water, and the awns have a silvery cast. How the seed gets into the soil is remarkable. Wind blows the "needle" onto the soil. The threadlike 5-to-8-inch awn is twisted behind the needle, and as it unwinds, the seed is literally drilled into the soil to the proper depth.

PORCUPINE GRASS (*Hesperostipa spartea* [hes-per-o-STY-pah spar-TEE-ah]) is a slightly taller version of needle-and-thread. Because it requires more moisture, it is better adapted to more eastern grasslands. Both needle-and-thread and porcupine grass are found in the Canadian prairie provinces, Minnesota, the Dakotas, and Montana. But in Nebraska, Kansas, and Oklahoma, porcupine grass is found in the tall-grass areas on dry upland prairies with little bluestem and prairie dropseed, while needle-and-thread is found west of that line.

Porcupine grass

TEXAS WINTERGRASS (*Nassella leucotricha* [nuh-ZELL-ah loo-ko-TRICK-ah]) is an important perennial pioneer grass for the Blackland Prairie in Oklahoma and Texas, and a minor component of mature prairies. The sturdy awns, about 4 inches long, make excellent darts, so children often call this grass speargrass. It got the name wintergrass because it is a cool season grass

Texas wintergrass

that greens up in early January and remains short and green all winter. In the spring, it gains height and blossoms along with spring wildflowers. By early June, it has formed seed and turned dormant tan.

INDIAN RICEGRASS (*Achnatherum hymenoides* [ack-nuh-THEER-um hye-men-OY-deez]), also known as *Oryzopsis hymenoides*, is a conspicuous grass in dry, sandy grasslands in western North America along with needle-and-thread. It

Indian ricegrass

lacks the long awns indicative of a needlegrass and instead has fat seeds that dangle on wiry threads. A cool season perennial bunchgrass, it is usually knee-high and extremely attractive, as its dormant color is warm ivory. It is somewhat short-lived and depends on seed to maintain its presence in large numbers. It was an important grain for the Zuni, Hopi, and Navajo, and the foliage is tasty and nutritious to grazers.

INDIAN RICEGRASS owes its airy quality to a series of branching Ts, from the ends of which the seeds hang.

There are about 150 species of dropseeds throughout the warmer regions of the world. Most of our North American dropseeds are somewhat short-lived, but useful in sandy situations or as a pioneer cover crop. In contrast, prairie dropseed is one of our very finest long-lived prairie grasses. Alkali sacaton, another long-lived dropseed, is useful as a large, colorful focal point in alkali washes and desert grasslands.

PRAIRIE DROPSEED (*Sporobolus heterolepis* [spoe-ROB-o-luss het-ter-o-LEPP-iss]) is a dominant conservative warm season bunchgrass in mesic to dry prairies and savannas in both northern tallgrass prairie zones and the northern Great Plains. South of a line from Connecticut to Nebraska, it becomes infrequent to rare and in Colorado is found only in sandy soil or in tallgrass prairies at the base of the Front Range.

The clumps of leaves are less than knee-high, "weeping" as they get long, because the blades are thin, smooth, and less than ⅛ inch wide. The overall effect makes prairie dropseed one of our prettiest prairie grasses, even when it is not in flower or seed.

To some people the flowers of PRAIRIE DROPSEED smell like fresh popcorn.

PRAIRIE DROPSEED is a treasure in prairie gardens because of its fine texture, short stature, and golden green color.

Prairie dropseed

SAND DROPSEED (*Sporobolus cryptandrus* [spoe-ROB-o-luss krip-TAN-drus]) is a warm season pioneer perennial 1 to 4 feet tall that persists only in very sandy areas. The flowering panicles are usually wrapped tight and look, at first glance, like a stiff heavy-tipped stem. The spikes of hidden seeds hold on for a long time, making them important winter food for birds and small mammals.

Rough rushgrass

Sand dropseed

ROUGH RUSHGRASS (*Sporobolus clandestinus* [spoe-ROB-o-luss klan-DESS-tee-nus]) is a fairly high-quality dropseed. Like prairie dropseed, it has very narrow leaves that are rough to the touch, and a narrow flower spike. It grows in well-drained places in sand or on limestone and sometimes in oak savannas from east Texas to Wisconsin and eastward. It used to be lumped in with rough dropseed, *Sporobolus compositus*, and both were called *Sporobolus asper*. Rough dropseed is a somewhat weedy pioneer species that is likely to come in on its own.

ALKALI SACATON (*Sporobolus airoides* [spoe-ROB-o-luss err-ee-OY-deez]) is a warm season perennial bunchgrass primarily useful for grasslands in the southwestern states and Mexico. It prefers sandy or gravelly soil and is tolerant of salt, so it is often the dominant grass in saline flats. It can handle a wide range of moisture, from flooded to dry, including the ground over a septic tank. Typical heights range from 2 to 4 feet. Stiff leaves make up the lower third, and flowering panicles the upper two-thirds. The foliage is yellow green, or sometimes pale blue green, above which the fully opened panicles of seed look dark and dramatic.

Alkali sacaton

These three grasses are so widespread and numerous in our prairies that they are called co-dominants for some prairies. Yet, they each represent not a group of prairie plants, but the only species of their kind important in our North American prairies. Buffalograss is the only *Buchloe* known in the world. Junegrass, *Koeleria macrantha,* is the only *Koeleria* native to North America south of the Yukon. Although in some books you might find it called *Koeleria cristata* or *K. pyramidata* (or *K. gracilis, K. nitida, K. latifrons,* or *K. yukonensis*), it is all the same Junegrass. Indiangrass has cousins in the southeastern United States, but Indiangrass is the only *Sorghastrum* found in tallgrass prairies and on the Great Plains.

BUFFALOGRASS is typically male or female. Here is a male plant with flowers that are white with hints of pink, orange, and purple. Female plants have round burlike seeds that stay hidden close to the earth.

Buffalograss

BUFFALOGRASS (*Buchloe dactyloides* [buck-LOE-ee dack-tee-LOY-deez]) is a conservative warm season dominant of shortgrass prairies along with blue grama, which is even more drought-tolerant. When regularly mowed or grazed, these two grasses form continuous stands. Where unmowed or lightly grazed, they are understory to little bluestem, needle-and-thread, sideoats grama, Junegrass, or western wheatgrass, depending on soil and moisture.

For the most part, buffalograss is found west of the 97th meridian and east of the Rocky Mountains and desert grasslands. It grows as far north as southern Canada and south through the plains states to Puebla, Mexico.

Cultivars, developed for lawns, work fine in a prairie garden, but be aware that they are usually female. If you want dancing male flowers, gather your own local stock.

INDIANGRASS (*Sorghastrum nutans* [sar-GASS-trum NEW-tans]) is a conservative warm season perennial of tallgrass prairies whose habitat requirements are almost exactly the

INDIANGRASS is one of our more stunning grasses because of its blue stems and leaves and its golden flowers.

same as those of big bluestem. They are considered co-dominants, although there is always at least twice as much big bluestem as there is Indiangrass.

Indiangrass is native from Canada to Mexico. In rich, moist tallgrass prairie, Indiangrass is usually 6 to 9 feet tall. Where it appears in little bluestem prairie,

Indiangrass

it is usually 4 to 5 feet tall. Its rhizomes are so nonaggressive that it looks like a bunchgrass. Finches and sparrows feast on the seeds all winter.

JUNEGRASS (*Koeleria macrantha* [kee-LARE-ee-ah mah-KRAN-tha]) is a pioneer cool season perennial bunchgrass that is a dominant in northern shortgrass prairies where it is found with little bluestem, buffalograss, and needle-and-thread. In the northern tallgrass areas it grows on upland prairies and in woodlands on thin soils with little bluestem, prairie dropseed, and porcupine grass. It becomes sparse in the south.

Because it blooms soon after win

Junegrass

ter, when other grasses are short, it is only 1 to 2 feet high. The narrow flowering plumes are a yellowish or greenish white and quite showy. It is harmed by as few as two mowings a year.

JUNEGRASS blooms in June in Canada, but in Texas its silvery plumes appear in mid-April.

Wheat, rye, barley, and their wild relatives are divided into several related genera. All the domesticated ones are from Europe or Asia and have been hybridized and genetically tweaked for thousands of years. Our wild ones do not seem to have been as popular with Native Americans as corn, wild rice, Indian ricegrass, and dropseed. However, there is evidence that Canadian wildrye was used extensively by the Gosiute tribe in Utah.

The North American branch of this family used to be mainly *Elymus*, but then it was divided into *Elymus*, *Sitanion*, *Hystrix*, and *Agropyron*. Then *Agropyron* was divided into *Pascopyrum*, *Elytrigia*, and so forth. Now nearly everything has been lumped under *Elymus* again, although the mostly western *Elymus* have been named *Leymus*, and *Agropyron smithii* is the one and only *Pascopyrum*. Got it?

CANADA WILDRYE (*Elymus canadensis* [ELL-ee-mus kan-uh-DENSE-us]) is a pioneer cool season short-lived perennial bunchgrass in mesic tallgrass prairies along with bluestem and Indiangrass. Usually 2 to 3 feet tall, it can reach 6 feet. More plentiful in the north or at high altitudes, it prefers a porous soil with plenty of moisture, and it will tolerate a half day of

shade. Weaver found it to be slightly more drought-tolerant than western wheatgrass, and slightly less than Junegrass.

The silvery leaves and large pale nodding heads are very attractive, so Canada wildrye is a good grass to plant on bare ground, as it provides an aesthetically pleasing way to keep out weeds and prepare the soil for long-term grasses. Blooms and seed are prominent in midsummer. Even more beautiful, **silky wildrye** (*Elymus villosus*) grows in oak savannas from Toronto to Oklahoma.

CANADA WILDRYE, also called nodding wildrye, has silvery blue foliage.

Virginia wildrye

VIRGINIA WILDRYE (*Elymus virginicus* [ELL-ee-mus ver-JIN-uh-kus]) is very similar to Canada wildrye except that it is green rather than silvery blue, and the seed heads are upright rather than nodding and appear earlier in the season. Furthermore, it is shorter, even less drought-tolerant, and more shade-tolerant. It is often found in oak savannas.

BOTTLEBRUSH GRASS (*Elymus hystrix* [ELL-ee-mus HISS-trix]), also known as *Hystrix patula*, is a component of northeastern oak savannas, especially white oak

savannas. It increases if burned. This tall graceful grass is popular with gardeners because of the way its large open head catches sunlight, even in the shade.

Canada wildrye

Bottlebrush grass

BASIN WILDRYE (*Leymus cinereus* [LAY-mus suh-NARE-ee-us]), also known as *Elymus cinereus*, grows in moist lowlands in the western Great Plains. It is also called giant wildrye because it gets 3 to 6 feet tall. Its showy white flowers appear soon after Junegrass, and its foliage is a bright yellow green, despite its name *cinereus*, which means ashy.

Basin wildrye

WESTERN WHEATGRASS (*Pascopyrum smithii* [pass-ko-PIE-rum SMITH-ee-eye]) is a rhizomatous cool season perennial that often turns western swales, ditches, and other seasonally moist places to a beautiful silvery green. Aggressive at first, it soon gets squeezed back by other grasses and forbs. However, western wheatgrass can become aggressive again if it loses competition because its companion grasses have been destroyed by grazing, and if, at the same time, there is adequate spring rain.

Take care not to confuse western wheatgrass with the non-native and far more aggressive quackgrass (*Elymus repens*, also known as *Agropyron repens*). Here is how they differ: the leaves of western wheatgrass are blue green and less than ¼ inch wide, and they roll up long ways when dried with obvious ridges on the upper side of the leaf. The leaves of quackgrass are rarely blue and have thin white lines on the undersides, and they dry flat.

Western wheatgrass

BOTTLEBRUSH GRASS is a dramatic garden accent in partial shade.

The panicgrasses all used to be *Panicums*, but half are now *Dichantheliums*, and botanists are busy splintering off more genera to make this genus less large and confusing. That is, some botanists are. Others are putting the whole tribe back under *Panicum*, as they consider some of the differences to be arbitrary. *Dichantheliums* are supposed to be different in that they have a rosette of basal leaves in winter that sends up a few simple flowering stems in spring that often produce no viable seed, and then in fall they send up numerous short, branched stems that produce a bushy effect with a lot of fertile seed. The *Dichantheliums* featured here are short, polite bunchgrasses.

The true *Panicum*, switchgrass, is large and rambunctious.

PRAIRIE PANICGRASS (*Dichanthelium leibergii* [dick-an-THELL-ee-um lee-BURG-ee-eye]) is a perennial bunchgrass found in old preserved dry upland prairies and on the drier edge of mesic tallgrass prairies and savannas. It is native westward only to the eastern edges of the Dakotas and Kansas. Its spring show occurs at the same time that butterfly milkweed and porcupine grass are in bloom. Its height can be waist-high, but I have always seen it shin-high. Conspicuous round viable seeds are produced from June through fall above short, wide, bright green leaves. Prairie panicgrass looks similar to Scribner's panicgrass except that its stems, leaves, and seeds are all covered with fine hairs.

Prairie panicgrass

PRAIRIE PANICGRASS, despite its name, is not particularly high-strung.

SCRIBNER'S PANICGRASS
(*Dichanthelium oligosanthes* var. *scribnerianum* [dick-an-THELL-ee-um o-lig-o-SAN-theez variety skrib-nare-ee-A-num]) is a short perennial pioneer bunchgrass that grows in sandy prairies. It is native from Canada south into Coahuila, Mexico. Its height varies from 4 to 28 inches. Besides being shorter and less hairy than prairie panicgrass, Scribner's panicgrass usually has leaves up the stem to just under the

flowering spikelets. Even more drought-tolerant is **Wilcox rosette-grass** (*Dichanthelium wilcoxianum*), a very short, very hairy panicgrass that is native from Illinois to the Rocky Mountains.

SWITCHGRASS (*Panicum virgatum* [PAN-ee-kum ver-GAY-tum]) is one of our most common tallgrass prairie grasses. It is a warm season perennial with stout stems 3 to 9 feet tall and long scaly rhizomes that can make it aggressive in the long-term. It is found in mesic to wet prairies and alongside ponds and streams in a niche between big bluestem and cattails.

Some Texas botanists are now dividing switchgrass into two vari-

SWITCHGRASS is a big burly grass with large airy panicles that remain attractive all winter.

eties. One is the lowland switchgrass from which the exceedingly aggressive cultivar "Alamo" was selected. The other is called upland switchgrass because it inhabits drier sites. It is far more manageable in a small prairie as it is only waist-high and far less aggressive. Research is showing that these differences may be genetic rather than environmental.

Other genetic variables in switchgrass are showy pale green leaves, as opposed to ordinary green ones, and flowers that are pink instead of whitish. Nearly all switchgrasses turn a deep golden yellow in the fall, but some turn soft orange, and in some years fall color just does not happen, and switchgrass goes abruptly into its gentle winter tan.

The four genera represented here are localized outside the main prairie region and enter it only at one end. However, because of their local importance, you will definitely want to include the one native for you.

SWEETGRASS (*Hierochloe hirta* ssp. *arctica* [hire-uh-KLOE-ee HUR-tah subspecies ARK-tea-kah]) is the most southern member of the *Hierochloe*, nearly all of which live in grasslands circling the North Pole. The *Hierochloe* are called Holy Grass by the Anishinabe and Ojibway-Odawa. Legend says that these were the first plants to cover Mother Earth, and they may well

Sweetgrass

have been the dominant grasses in western North America when Native Americans migrated over the Bering Strait land bridge. Until recently, our prairie sweetgrass was lumped in with the circumpolar sweetgrass *Hierochloe odorata*.

Sweetgrass is extremely fragrant when dried. Bundles or braids of the leaves are either burned or hung in houses to purify the air. They are also woven into baskets, used as sachet, or boiled to make a medicinal tea.

A long-lived perennial knee-high rhizomatous conservative, sweetgrass is the first grass to bloom in a northern spring. Its golden flowers turn into tan seeds by the end of June, but its satiny, slightly sticky leaves remain bright green until winter.

EASTERN GAMAGRASS (*Tripsacum dactyloides* [TRIP-sah-kum dack-tee-LOY-deez]) has the most northern range of its family, the majority of which live around the Gulf of Mexico and southward. A conservative warm season grass of moist southern and eastern tallgrass prairies, eastern gamagrass is a relative of corn. It was eaten by the Ozark bluff-dwellers. Considered to

EASTERN GAMAGRASS forms a long spike of cornlike kernels that can be roasted and eaten as popcorn.

SWEETGRASS, which has sweet-smelling leaves, is native only to wet northern prairies.

Eastern gamagrass

be native from southern Iowa and southeastern Nebraska through Missouri, Kansas, Oklahoma, and Texas, it is thought to have been spread by Native Americans from Massachusetts and southern Michigan all the way down to Bolivia and Paraguay. This is a large stout grass that can get up to 10 feet tall, although 5 feet is more common.

PURPLE THREEAWN (*Aristida purpurea* var. *purpurea* [uh-RISS-tuh-dah pur-PUR-ee-ah]) is grown mostly for its beautiful flowers that shine red when backlit. Purple threeawn is a cool season short-lived perennial bunchgrass usually less than knee-high. From Colorado and Kansas south to Mexico, it is considered a co-dominant with little bluestem in dry midgrass prairies. It is invaluable for reconstructing dry sandy southern and western prairies where there is lots of bare earth showing.

Red threeawn

RED THREEAWN (*Aristida purpurea* var. *longiseta* [uh-RISS-tuh-dah pur-PUR-ee-ah variety lawn-juh-SEE-tah]) looks almost exactly like purple threeawn except that it is shorter and the awns are usually upright rather than nodding. It is significant in shortgrass prairies to the west of purple threeawn.

PRAIRIE SANDREED (*Calamovilfa longifolia* [kal-uh-moe-VILL-fah lawn-jee-FOLE-ee-ah]) is the

northernmost member of a genus of only five species, all endemic to North America. Chest-high, it is a strongly rhizomatous, warm season grass that is a co-dominant of sand-hill prairies. It also grows on dunes and in sandy black oak savannas. Leaf color ranges from dark green to shiny pale blue green. The flowery plumes are up to a foot long, becoming narrow as the seed ripens. The prairie sandreed around the Great Lakes *Calamovilfa longifolia* var. *magna* has looser plumes.

Purple threeawn

Prairie sandreed

RED THREEAWN, a cool season bunch-grass in western shortgrass prairies, may have showy red blooms three times a year, in spring, summer, and fall.

These grass genera represent some of the best of our savanna species, other than those, like Virginia wildrye, that are already covered elsewhere in this chapter. Those grasses with *woodland* in their common name grow in the most shade. The others prefer a daily mixture of bright sunlight and shade. Most require the extra moisture of floodplain, streamside, or bog to thrive in full sun.

A few can survive in dry, sunny prairies. One of my favorites is prairie satingrass (*Muhlenbergia cuspidata*). Native from Virginia to the Rocky Mountains, it is found in upland prairies or on thin limestone soil. The graceful prairie brome (*Bromus kalmii*), native primarily to states around the Great Lakes, grows in both wet and dry prairies, with cordgrass or with prairie dropseed.

TALL MELICGRASS (*Melica nitens* [MELL-eh-kah NYE-tens]), knee- to waist-high, is a cool season rhizomatous grass that grows with wild hyacinth in dry to mesic limestone woodlands under escarpment live oaks, bur oaks, or junipers. Given sufficient moisture, it grows in mesic prairies with rosinweed. **Porter's melicgrass** (*Melica porteri*) grows in southern ponderosa and aspen savannas, and **oniongrass** (*Melica bulbosa*) grows in northern ones. All are uncommon and exceptionally lovely.

Tall melicgrass

LEAFY SATINGRASS (*Muhlenbergia mexicana* [mew-lynn-BURG-ee-ah mex-uh-KANE-ah]), also called wirestem muhly, has very narrow dark green leaves. It grows in seeps and moist sandy woodlands in both tallgrass and shortgrass regions. This grass is warm season, rhizomatous, and fairly ubiquitous. Less so are similar-looking **rock muhly** (*Muhlenbergia sobolifera*), **woodland muhly** (*Muhlenbergia sylvatica*), and **slender muhly** (*Muhlenbergia tenuiflora*), all native to bur oak savannas. Lindheimer's muhly (*Muhlenbergia lind-*

TALL MELICGRASS has large clusters of white-green flowers that show beautifully in the shade of a savanna tree.

Leafy satingrass

heimeri) is a tall bunchgrass native to live oak savannas and floodplains in central Texas.

WOODLAND BROME (*Bromus pubescens* [BRO-mus pew-BESS-ens]), also called Canada brome, is a waist-high, cool season, perennial bunchgrass. Very common in the northern oak savannas, it has fuzzy gray green leaves and stems, and the stem hairs point downward. In the South, the leaves are sometimes glossy bright green, and this version is often separated out as *Bromus nottowayanus*. Equally delicate panicles of seed are found on **Porter's brome** (*Bromus porteri*), native to northern

Woodland brome

ponderosa savannas, and on **nodding brome** (*Bromus anomalus*), native to southern ones.

COMMON WOODREED (*Cinna arundinacea* [SIN-nah ah-run-dee-NAY-see-ah]) is a chest-high, warm season, perennial grass with a showy dense plume of flowers and seeds. The leaves, soft blue-green with a strong white stripe down the center, droop at the tip. Opposite to where the bottom leaves join the stem is a tiny pair of leafy "rabbit ears." Common woodreed is native to both bur oak and black oak savannas but only the moist ones. **Slender woodreed** (*Cinna latifolia*) is common throughout aspen parklands.

Common woodreed

LONGAWN WOODGRASS (*Brachyelytrum erectum* [brack-ee-ee-LEE-trum eh-RECK-tum]), a warm season clumping grass, has narrow erect heads of long seeds with even longer straight-up awns. Shin-high, it has many short narrow leaves alternating up the stem, sometimes with a spot of white at the base of each leaf. Native to savannas in the tallgrass region, it is more common in the North.

WOODLAND BROME stands out in early summer because of its heavy, dangling, flattened clusters of seed.

Longawn woodgrass

These grasses grow in marshes, bogs, and fens. They require moisture year-round and can even be partially submerged, at least part of the year. We saw these grasses used in home gardens over septic tanks, in seasonally wet swales and roadside ditches, and on the edges of streams and ponds. In large prairies, these grasses grow in ephemeral duck-beckoning lakes where water stands for weeks in the spring.

PRAIRIE CORDGRASS (*Spartina pectinata* [spar-TEEN-ah peck-tuh-NAY-tah]), also called marshgrass or sloughgrass, often forms a ribbon of monoculture in soggy ground below switchgrass but above reeds in standing water. As this rhizomatous warm season perennial advances into the southern parts of its range, it is gradually outcompeted by cattails. A slough of cordgrass is not fun to walk in because the ground is squishy and the blades slice up your skin. But it is very pretty when the gray green leaves curve over and toss in a breeze like waves on an ocean. The hollow stems get 8 feet long, and the roots go down 9 feet or more. As the flowers turn to purply pink seed, they twist tightly around the flower stalks.

Prairie cordgrass

ALKALI CORDGRASS (*Spartina gracilis* [spar-TEEN-ah grah-SILL-iss]) is half as tall and half as aggressive as prairie cordgrass. Native to alkaline marshes, meadows, and dry sandy soil, it is found primarily in northwestern North America. In late summer, its highly ornamental, snowy white flowers alternate up the main flowering stem on short twisting stalks. Alkali cordgrass

PRAIRIE CORDGRASS has distinctive horizontal spikes of pinkish flowers and leaves with sawtooth edges.

Alkali cordgrass

thrives over septic tanks where salt is added to soften the household water.

BLUEJOINT (*Calamagrostis canadensis* [kal-ah-muh-GROSS-tiss kan-ah-DEN-sis]), native to

Bluejoint

BLUEJOINT has blue green leaves at right angles and bronzy mauve flowers.

marshes, fens, bogs, and lakeshores, often makes a solid stand that excludes all other plants. This cool season rhizomatous perennial is highly variable in appearance, especially in the size of its flowers, but the variations grade into each other too much to make clear varieties. Its height ranges from 2 to 5 feet.

FOWL MANNAGRASS (*Glyceria striata* [gly-SEER-ee-ah stry-A-tah]) is a mildly rhizomatous cool season perennial native to marshes, calcareous fens, bogs, and moist woods in the North. In the South, it is found only where there is permanent, not seasonal, water. It is a delicate-looking grass with light green leaves and panicles of flower and seed that range from yellow green to rosy purple. Usually about 2 feet high, it can reach twice that.

Fowl mannagrass

Tufted hairgrass

FOWL MANNAGRASS has a lacy texture when in flower and seed.

TUFTED HAIRGRASS (*Deschampsia caespitosa* [des-KAMP-see-ah seas-pea-TOE-sah]) is a well-mannered bunchgrass. The straight hollow stems and the rolled leaves give a stiff, wiry appearance. One-to-3-feet-tall airy panicles of seed appear in early summer. Native to fertile wetlands, limestone seeps, or sandy lakeshores, this lovely water grass is becoming quite rare in parts of its range.

True sedges, *Carex*, compose the main genus in the sedge family (Cyperaceae). There are a multitude of sedges in almost every shady or wet habitat, and quite a few sedges in dry prairies also. They are generally short with straight-up narrow leaves, although common wood sedge (*Carex blanda*) has weeping tufts of wide leaves. Colors range from dark green to yellow green but never pale bluish green.

Sedges look a lot like grasses except that each flower is enclosed by one instead of two scales. It sometimes takes a magnifying glass to see this. There are easier although less sure ways to tell them apart. Grasses usually have hollow stems, and sedges usually have solid triangular stems. ("Sedges have edges," or "a sedge is a wedge.") Grass stems have joints, and sedge stems do not.

PRAIRIE SEDGE (*Carex bicknellii* [KARE-ex bick-NELL-ee-eye]) is also called copper-shouldered oval sedge because of the touches of copper on its oval-shaped fruits. It is frequently found in high-quality upland prairies with little bluestem and porcupine grass, in mesic tall-grass prairies with big bluestem and Indiangrass, and in open woodlands or savannas. It forms a slender

Prairie sedge

PRAIRIE SEDGE looks like a slender bunchgrass with tiny conelike flowers.

clump 1 to 4 feet tall of sharply triangular stems. In similar habitats with a more westerly distribution is **short beak sedge** (*Carex brevior*).

STIFF SEDGE (*Carex tetanica* [KARE-ex teh-TAN-ee-kah]) grows in wet sedge prairies with bluejoint or big bluestem, or in swales in mesic tallgrass prairies with a high water table. Its clump of rough, triangular stems is knee-high. The leaves have a white or yellow stripe that runs up one side. A more drought-tolerant

Stiff sedge

and rhizomatous version of this plant is **Mead's stiff sedge** (*Carex meadii*), which grows with little bluestem and big bluestem in the tallgrass region west to Saskatchewan.

BROWN FOX SEDGE (*Carex vulpinoidea* [KARE-ex vul-pin-OY-dee-ah]) is a weedy sedge that is usually only shin-high, although it can get waist-high. It has crisply triangular stems and leaves with a greenish white stripe. Because it is easily grown from seed and tolerates a wide range of conditions, from hillsides to swamps and lakeshores, it is very useful for starting a prairie.

Brown fox sedge

PENNSYLVANIA SEDGE (*Carex pensylvanica* [KARE-ex pen-sil-VAN-eh-kah]) is also called common oak sedge because it is ubiquitous in black oak savannas. Its triangular stems are usually only

Pennsylvania sedge

about ankle height and are sometimes reddish in color. In texture, it might look like a short lawn grass, or it might grow in clumps. It is also found in open woodlands and moist thickets.

SUNSEDGE (*Carex inops* ssp. *heliophila* [KARE-ex EYE-nops subspecies heel-ee-OFF-eh-la]), strongly sod-forming, is the western

Sunsedge

version of Pennsylvania sedge and is sometimes called *Carex pensylvanica* ssp. *heliophila*. Both of these sedges are ill suited to the heat and drought of woodlands in the southern Midwest. There you are more likely to find **reflexed sedge** (*Carex retroflexa*) or its close relative **Texas sedge** (*Carex texensis*), both of which grow under post oaks. In Texas, the most common woodland sedge is **cedar sedge** (*Carex planostachys*), a short, clumping sedge tolerant of limestone.

STIFF SEDGE, here bending over in an unstiff way, makes a uniformly fine yellow green texture at Scuppernong Prairie in Wisconsin.

Spikerushes (*Eleocharis*) and bulrushes (*Scirpus* and *Schoenoplectus*) are in the sedge family (Cyperaceae). These grasslike sedges can be found in bogs, marshes, fens, sloughs, and wet prairies.

The true rushes belong to the family Juncaceae. Their inconspicuous flowers are tiny tan cups of three petals and three sepals (under-petals) arranged in a circle. The fruit is a three-parted capsule filled with tiny seeds. Most *Juncus* are tall and at a glance look similar to *Scirpus*.

SPIKERUSHES (*Eleocharis* [ee-lee-OCK-uh-riss]) are native to moist or wet ground all over the earth. Most are perennial and rhizomatous, although some are annual. A few are over 4 feet tall, but most are under a foot. About half have a strong preference for sand, so if you need one for clay, be sure to collect from a clay site. The seed scatters as soon as it ripens in summer or early fall, so check the heads often until you find some ready to shatter. The brilliant yellow green color and fine

Spikerushes

upright texture make spikerushes a beautiful addition to a wet prairie, sedge meadow, ditch, septic tank, or pond edge.

Some spikerushes thrive in mesic prairies. **Flatstem spikerush** (*Eleocharis compressa*) grows in wet places but also in swales that are moist only some of the year, and in mesic prairies with Indiangrass and big bluestem.

DARK GREEN BULRUSH (*Scirpus atrovirens* [SKUR-pus ah-tro-VIRE-ens]) is a marsh plant common in the Northeast. By the time it reaches north Texas, it is rare. Dark green bulrush has very short rhizomes and is not aggressive,

SPIKERUSH stems are short, straight, numerous, and yellow green, topped with brown seed heads.

Dark green bulrush

DARK GREEN BULRUSH has clusters of seeds that ripen to the color of rich dark chocolate.

which makes it a comfortable addition to a small garden.

GREAT BULRUSH (*Schoenoplectus tabernaemontani* [skee-no-PLECK-tus tay-ber-nee-mon-TAN-ee]), also known as *Scirpus validus*, is native all over temperate North America. It does have aggressive rhizomes and can take over a wet prairie. Alan Wade of Prairie Moon Nursery accidentally discovered a way to counteract it. A pretty forb that likes the same wet conditions, swamp lousewort (*Pedicularis lanceolata*), seems to be semiparasitic on great bulrush, reducing it to a manageable amount that allows numer-

Great bulrush

ous other forbs and grasses to grow in harmony with it. The stems of great bulrush are as dark or darker than dark green bulrush. To tell them apart, split open the stem. The inside pith of great bulrush is pale, very soft, and divided into chambers.

WOOLGRASS (*Scirpus cyperinus* [SKUR-pus sye-PEER-ee-nus]) usually grows in clumps. The upright clusters of weeping coppery brown seeds are quite showy. It is native to sedge meadows, marshes, and bogs, primarily on the eastern edges of the tallgrass prairie region.

Woolgrass

PATH RUSH (*Juncus tenuis* [JUNK-us TEN-you-iss]) has a fine texture similar to spikerush, but it grows in drier sites and tolerates foot traffic.

Path rush

This rhizomatous perennial is found on compacted shaded paths and picnic areas in the northern tallgrass prairie region. Although widespread, it is not useful everywhere. In Texas, for instance, it grows only in east Texas woodlands and goes dormant in the summer.

DRYLAND SEDGES and rushes have a lovely fine texture, plus they can be mowed and walked on.

GRASSES, SEDGES, AND RUSHES

Species	NORTHWEST — Northern Plains Shortgrass Region					NORTHEAST — Northern Tallgrass Prairie Region					SOUTHWEST — Southern Plains Shortgrass Region					SOUTHEAST — Southern Tallgrass Prairie Region				
	Lowland prairie	Mesic prairie	Upland prairie	Sand prairie	Aspen parkland	Lowland prairie	Mesic prairie	Upland prairie	Bur oak savanna	Black oak savanna	Lowland prairie	Mesic prairie	Upland prairie	Sand prairie	Ponderosa savanna	Lowland prairie	Mesic prairie	Upland prairie	Bur oak savanna	Post oak savanna
BLUESTEM GRASSES																				
Big bluestem	■	■				■	■	■	■	■	■					■	■		■	
Sand bluestem				■										■				■		
Little bluestem		■	■	■			■		■		■		■			■	■	■		
Bushy bluestem											■					■				
GRAMA GRASSES																				
Sideoats grama		■			■			■	■			■						■		■
Blue grama			■									■								
Hairy grama				■			■		■					■					■	
Black grama														■						
NEEDLEGRASSES																				
Needle-and-thread		■	■	■								■	■							
Porcupine grass								■		■									■	
Texas wintergrass													■							
Indian ricegrass														■						
DROPSEEDS																				
Prairie dropseed					■	■	■	■							■					
Sand dropseed				■					■					■					■	
Rough rushgrass									■											
Alkali sacaton											■	■		■						
SINGLE FAMILY CO-DOMINANTS																				
Buffalograss		■	■								■	■	■							
Indiangrass							■	■	■	■				■		■	■		■	■
Junegrass		■	■	■	■			■		■			■	■				■		■
WILD WHEAT AND RYE																				
Canada wildrye				■			■		■					■		■	■			■
Silky wildrye									■										■	
Virginia wildrye				■		■			■										■	■
Bottlebrush grass									■	■										
Basin wildrye	■										■									
Western wheatgrass	■	■									■	■								
PANICGRASSES																				
Prairie panicgrass						■	■	■												
Scribner's panicgrass		■		■	■				■				■	■					■	■
Wilcox rosettegrass			■	■				■		■										
Switchgrass	■					■	■		■		■					■	■			
REGIONAL SPECIALTIES																				
Sweetgrass	■					■														
Eastern gamagrass						■												■		
Purple threeawn												■						■		■

Species	NORTHWEST Northern Plains Shortgrass Region					NORTHEAST Northern Tallgrass Prairie Region					SOUTHWEST Southern Plains Shortgrass Region					SOUTHEAST Southern Tallgrass Prairie Region				
	Lowland prairie	Mesic prairie	Upland prairie	Sand prairie	Aspen parkland	Lowland prairie	Mesic prairie	Upland prairie	Bur oak savanna	Black oak savanna	Lowland prairie	Mesic prairie	Upland prairie	Sand prairie	Ponderosa savanna	Lowland prairie	Mesic prairie	Upland prairie	Bur oak savanna	Post oak savanna
Red threeawn		■											■	■				■		
Prairie sandreed			■					■		■			■							
SAVANNA GRASSES																				
Tall melicgrass							■		■									■	■	
Porter's melicgrass					■															
Oniongrass					■															
Leafy satingrass						■			■	■					■					■
Rock muhly									■										■	
Woodland muhly									■										■	
Slender muhly									■											
Woodland brome					■				■	■									■	■
Porter's brome					■										■					
Nodding brome															■					
Common woodreed									■	■										
Slender woodreed					■															
Longawn woodgrass									■	■									■	
LOWLAND GRASSES																				
Prairie cordgrass	■					■					■					■				
Alkali cordgrass	■		■								■									
Bluejoint	■					■														
Fowl mannagrass	■					■														
Tufted hairgrass	■					■														
SEDGES																				
Prairie sedge						■	■	■	■							■	■			
Short beak sedge		■		■		■		■			■	■			■	■		■		
Stiff sedge						■														
Mead's stiff sedge		■						■										■		
Brown fox sedge	■					■					■					■				
Pennsylvania sedge					■					■					■					
Sunsedge					■					■					■					
Reflexed sedge																			■	■
Texas sedge																				■
Cedar sedge																			■	■
RUSHES																				
Spikerushes	■					■					■					■				
Flatstem spikerush						■	■											■		
Dark green bulrush						■														
Great bulrush	■					■					■					■				
Woolgrass								■								■				
Path rush	■			■		■	■									■				

GRASSES, SEDGES, AND RUSHES (cont'd)

Species	NORTHWEST — Northern Plains Shortgrass Region					NORTHEAST — Northern Tallgrass Prairie Region					SOUTHWEST — Southern Plains Shortgrass Region					SOUTHEAST — Southern Tallgrass Prairie Region				
	Lowland prairie	Mesic prairie	Upland prairie	Sand prairie	Aspen parkland	Lowland prairie	Mesic prairie	Upland prairie	Bur oak savanna	Black oak savanna	Lowland prairie	Mesic prairie	Upland prairie	Sand prairie	Ponderosa savanna	Lowland prairie	Mesic prairie	Upland prairie	Bur oak savanna	Post oak savanna
MOWABLE GRASSES, SEDGES, AND RUSHES																				
Path rush	■			■		■	■									■				
Western wheatgrass	■	■									■	■								
Scribner's panicgrass		■		■	■			■		■				■	■			■		■
Buffalograss		■	■								■	■	■					■		
Pennsylvania sedge					■					■					■					
Sunsedge					■					■					■					
Texas sedge																				■
Sideoats grama		■			■			■	■			■			■		■		■	■
Cedar sedge																			■	■
Blue grama			■								■									
Hairy grama				■			■			■			■					■		
Wilcox rosettegrass		■	■				■			■										

TO GAIN ACCESS TO YOUR PRAIRIE GARDEN, you can mow curving paths and lawnlike openings. Instead of using conventional, thirsty turf grasses, plant some of the same species of grasses, sedges, or rushes that you are planning to use in your prairie or savanna. In every prairie habitat, there is at least one common native grass or grasslike plant that thrives in paths or can be mowed often enough to make a lawn. This list is arranged from most wet-tolerant to most drought-tolerant.

Chapter 10

From the first greening of spring to the full ripening of autumn, the tall prairie is spangled by a vivid progression of flowers—

a rainbow host that first enamels the burned slopes of early spring and ends months later with great nodding blooms that rise

above a man's head. Sometimes as secret and solitary as jewels, but often in broad painted fields, the prairie flowers come on—

lavender, indigo, creamy white, pink, coral, gold, magenta, crimson, orange, and palest yellow and blue, their flowers tending

from ice to flame.

JOHN MADSON, Where the Sky Began

Cool Season Forbs

FORBS ARE FLOWERS, and they are more than just pretty. Their protein content often exceeds that of grasses. Their leaves, roots, and flowers contain medicinal substances. Their flowers provide nectar for bees, butterflies, and hummingbirds. Their small but nutritious seeds feed small birds and mammals, such as finches, moles, and shrews.

Choosing which forbs to use is lots of fun because forbs give prairie its variety and color. Here the forbs are arranged roughly by when they bloom, from spring to mid-summer. Occasionally, a fall-blooming species is included in a predominantly spring-blooming family.

The charts and maps will help you choose which forbs are native to your site. Native forbs are usually the healthiest and most rewarding forbs. But do not torture yourself trying to make "perfect" choices. As Neil Diboll of Prairie Nursery in Westfield, Wisconsin, said, "In ecology there is no right or wrong; there are merely consequences."

North American prairie forbs are so numerous that if every one were profiled, you could not have afforded this book. Or lifted it, for that matter. And, for the same reason, it was not possible to have a picture of each forb profiled. Therefore, the forbs whose photographs you see are primarily tallgrass flowers with an emphasis on the Missouri-Illinois-Wisconsin-Minnesota area, as that is where the greatest number of both current and potential prairie gardeners reside. In many locations, although no entries show on the charts, there exist a number of desirable related species that we simply had no room to include.

The bean, or legume, family (Fabaceae) includes trees, vines, perennials, and annuals. Seeds are usually in bean pods, which may be long or short, flattened or plump, and edible or poisonous. Most have flowers that resemble sweet peas, or if you prefer a more graphic description, they make you think of faces topped by old-fashioned sunbonnets.

The roots of these plants—or rather the microorganisms that live in their roots—know how to capture nitrogen and make it available in the soil. Both the number of legume species and the numbers of individual legume plants are greater in dry prairies and in nutrient-poor savannas like the post oak savannas.

SUNDIAL LUPINE (*Lupinus perennis* [loo-PINE-us puh-REN-iss]) grows on sandy prairies and savannas. After a burn, it appears in quantities, gradually disappearing by the fifth year. Lupines also love disturbed soil or bare, rocky ground. A lupine for the northern Great Plains is **Silvery lupine** (*Lupinus argenteus*),

and one for well-drained spots in the Blackland Prairie is **Texas bluebonnet** (*Lupinus texensis*).

Sundial lupine

Canadian milkvetch

CANADIAN MILKVETCH has creamy yellow spikes of flowers and long curving leaves composed of two rows of leaflets.

SILVERY LUPINE, with its silky leaves and purple flowers, is plentiful on hillside prairies in and around Calgary.

CANADIAN MILKVETCH (*Astragalus canadensis* [as-TRAG-a-lus kan-ah-DEN-sis]) grows with little bluestem in sandy eastern prairies and savannas and in moist northwestern prairies and woodlands. A long-lived rhizomatous perennial,

it makes a large bushy herb that is normally knee- to waist-high. The seed pods are not beanlike but form a cluster of capsules that rattle all winter.

GROUNDPLUM (*Astragalus crassicarpus* [as-TRAG-a-lus kras-ee-KAR-pus]) is native to well-drained prairies. The flowers are purple or two-toned purple and white. The egg-shaped fruits lie on the ground,

Groundplum

about as big as your thumb. They are juicy and sweet to eat while pale green. As they ripen, they turn a beautiful rosy color.

AMERICAN VETCH (*Vicia americana* [VEE-shee-ah ah-mer-ee-KAN-a]) is a viny plant with stems less than 3 feet long. The flowers are usually purple but are sometimes lavender, pink, or white. The short, slender bean pods turn rosy in midsummer. American vetch grows in mesic prairies and savannas and seems to prefer a half day of shade. On the drier parts of the Great Plains, there is a variety with thick leathery leaves called *Vicia americana* variety *minor*.

American vetch

INDIAN BREADROOT (*Pediomelum esculentum* [pea-dee-o-MAY-lum ess-ku-LEN-tum]) is sometimes called prairie turnip or prairie potato. The edible part is the rounded fist-sized portion at the top of the taproot. The hairy leaves and stems look silvery. The flowered spikes are blue, fading to yellow. Indian breadroot, tastiest when harvested just as the blooms fade, was an ancient and popular food with Native Americans. Native to dry prairies, limestone, and open woodlands, it is found most often in the northern part of its range. Similar edible *Pediomelums* are prevalent in Texas and the Southwest.

Indian breadroot

PRAIRIE GOLDENBEAN (*Thermopsis rhombifolia* [thur-MOP-sis rom-bee-FOLE-ee-ah]) carpets northern shortgrass prairies with golden yellow so early in the spring that the blooms sometimes get covered with snow. It blooms even before silvery lupine. Prairie goldenbean is a rhizomatous perennial, found on rocky hillsides, roadsides, the edges of buffalo wallows, and sandy prairies. The beans are poisonous.

INDIAN BREADROOT, woven into four arm's-length braids, was once considered valuable enough to be traded for a good-quality buffalo robe.

Prairie goldenbean

These bean family forbs bloom slightly later than the first group.

WHITE WILD INDIGO (*Baptisia alba* var. *macrophylla* [bap-TEE-zhah AL-bah variety mah-KROFF-uh-lah]) may be found in older books as *Baptisia leucantha* or *Baptisia lactea*. All names mean that the flowers are white. The flowering wands, which stick up over knee-high leaves, keep adding buds at the top, so bloom time can last for several weeks. The fat velvety pods turn black when ripe. This long-lived perennial thrives in sandy or rocky prairies and savannas from the Great Lakes to east Texas.

White wild indigo

WHITE WILD INDIGO blooms in June in northern oak savannas.

BLUE WILD INDIGO (*Baptisia australis* var. *minor* [bap-TEE-zhah aw-STRALL-iss variety MIE-nor]) blooms in May in the North and in April in the South. In height it is as tall as white wild indigo, but it is bushier and not so airy. It is native to well-drained rocky or sandy prairies and savannas primarily between Iowa and the Blackland Prairie, with scattered populations elsewhere. *Baptisia australis* var. *australis*, the blue wild indigo usually found in the nursery trade, is native east of the Mississippi River.

Blue wild indigo

CREAM WILD INDIGO (*Baptisia bracteata* var. *leucophaea* [bap-TEE-zhah brack-tee-A-tah variety loo-koe-FEE-ah]) is sometimes called *Baptisia leucophaea*. It is shorter than the other baptisias, and its pale yellow flowers are on fat spikes that droop downward. The whole plant turns black by midsummer. It likes mesic well-drained savannas. The western edge of its range includes southeastern Nebraska, all of Oklahoma except the extreme

Cream wild indigo

[SHRANK-ee-ah] *nuttallii*, is an ankle-high perennial with sprawling prickly stems—not a plant made for walking barefoot on. The leaves are sensitive to touch, closing up if you stroke them. The flowers are puffy balls of fragrant pink filaments tipped with golden yellow. Sensitive brier likes limestone uplands, dry sandy prairies, and sunny post oak savannas.

PURPLE LOCOWEED (*Oxytropis lambertii* [ox-ZIH-tro-pis lam-BUR-tee-eye]) has brilliant compact rosy purple flowers that are not only showy but scented like carnations. Cattle and horses can get addicted to this locoweed and poison themselves (sometimes fatally) if they eat large quantities for several days. Both the leaves and roots were used as medicine by Plains Indians. Locoweeds are very short, so they are found only in shortgrass prairies or on rocky outcrops where they are not shaded out by taller foliage. Other locoweeds, all extremely attractive, come in yellow, white, and pink.

west, and northeast Texas. It blooms at the same time as blue wild indigo.

SWEETBROOM (*Hedysarum alpinum* [hee-dee-SAR-um al-PIE-num]) is a northern legume that is native primarily to prairies and open woodlands in Canada, the northern Great Plains, and northern Europe, where it is both common and important for grazing and nectar. This is an attractive knee-high upright plant worthy of the perennial garden. The flowers are pink to purple.

Sensitive brier

GOAT'S RUE (*Tephrosia virginiana* [teh-FROE-zhuh ver-jin-ee-A-nah]) is often found in black oak or post oak savannas and in sandy prairies. The combination of pink and pale yellow flowers is unusual, and the clusters are large enough to be impressive. The leaves are velvety.

Purple locoweed

Sweetbroom

SENSITIVE BRIER (*Mimosa nuttallii* [my-MOE-sah nuh-TALL-ee-eye]), also known as *Schrankia*

Goat's rue

BLUE WILD INDIGO is found in southern tallgrass prairies.

Floyd Swink and Gerould Wilhelm write in *Plants of the Chicago Region* that showy ladyslipper (*Cypripedium reginae*) once "grew by the thousands in Lake County, Indiana, where downtown Gary now stands." Orchids (Orchidaceae) are still numerous and spectacular in old, high-quality prairies maintained by Native Americans. These long-lived perennials like a stable ecological niche. In our gardens where the soil is constantly disturbed, we create homes for weeds, not orchids. It is estimated that garden soil needs at least ten years of no artificial fertilizers and no herbicides before it can support enough mycorrhizal fungi to keep orchids alive.

Because native orchids are now rare, *never dig one* unless you are on a native plant society sponsored rescue. If you find orchids to buy, question the nursery owner closely to find out if they were dug in the wild and then "grown" on the premises. Scott Weber of Bluestem Farm in Baraboo, Wisconsin, is the only nurseryman we met who is growing native orchids from seed. From germination, it usually takes six years for the seedlings to gain enough maturity to flower.

LARGE YELLOW LADYSLIPPER (*Cypripedium parviflorum* var. *pubescens* [sye-pre-PID-ee-um par-vee-FLORE-um variety pew-BESS-ens]) grows in rich, mesic prairies or in light shade. In the southern Great Plains, it grows only in sand dunes in Texas. It differs from smaller yellow ladyslippers in that its hood and twisty wings are more green than dark red. The yellow ladyslippers, sometimes called *Cypripedium calceolus*, are pollinated by special tiny bees.

Large yellow ladyslipper

LARGE YELLOW LADYSLIPPER makes a spectacular show in late spring on wet, fall-burned prairies.

SMALL WHITE LADYSLIPPER (*Cypripedium candidum* [sye-pre-PID-ee-um kan-DEE-dum]) grows in sedge meadows, calcareous fens, and wet prairies with golden Alexanders. Before the prairies were plowed, it was present in the tens of thousands. Old plants develop fifty or more stems. The 1-inch slippers are pure white. Cream-colored

Small white ladyslipper

GRASSPINK blooms in the summer.

ladyslippers show hybridization with yellow ladyslippers.

GRASSPINK (*Calopogon tuberosus* [kal-low-POE-gon tu-ber-O-sus]) used to be called *Calopogon pulchellus*. It is native to prairie swales, peaty meadows, bogs, marshes, and fens. It has one grasslike leaf attached to the corm and one stem of two to twelve flowers.

Grasspink

Nodding ladies' tresses

NODDING LADIES' TRESSES (*Spiranthes cernua* [spy-RAN-theez sur-NEW-ah]) is the most common of the ladies' tresses in the North. Native to wet or dry prairies and open woodlands throughout the tallgrass region to central Texas, it is typically under a foot tall with narrow clasping leaves and white flowers arranged on a wand in a twisting spiral.

GREAT PLAINS LADIES' TRESSES (*Spiranthes magnicamporum* [spy-RAN-theez mag-nee-kam-PORE-um]) looks similar to nodding ladies' tresses, but it flowers later, after its narrow leaves have dried, and it is more frequently found farther south or west in dry prairies or on chert or gypsum soils.

Great Plains ladies' tresses

SLENDER LADIES' TRESSES (*Spiranthes lacera* [spy-RAN-theez lah-SER-ah]) is frequently found in sandy prairies, black oak savannas, and post oak savannas. It blooms earlier than nodding ladies' tresses and looks different, having rounded basal leaves.

Slender ladies' tresses

NODDING LADIES' TRESSES has fragrant blooms that can appear anytime between midsummer and frost.

Lilies, like orchids, are found in abundance in old, high-quality prairies. For the most part, lilies (Liliaceae) are perennial herbs with bulbs or corms that take several years to develop until they can store enough nutritional resources for the plant to bloom. Please follow all the same conservation rules that apply to orchids.

The lily family is large, varied, and ancient, with about 4,000 species worldwide. Some non-native lilies are domestic onions, leeks, and garlic, asparagus, Easter lilies, daylilies, and hostas.

WILD HYACINTH (*Camassia scilloides* [kuh-MAWS-ee-ah skill-LOY-deez]) has pale lavender flowers on a narrow spike. This lily is native to moist sandy or rocky prairies, swales, and savannas, primarily in the southern tallgrass areas. Where it grows on seemingly dry rocky hillsides, it indicates seep lines.

Wild hyacinth

Death camas

WILD HYACINTH in masses is not only gorgeous but wonderfully aromatic.

DEATH CAMAS (*Zigadenus venenosus* [zig-uh-DEE-nus ven-ee-NO-sus]) has thick spears of creamy flowers. The bulb is 2 to 6 inches deep. It is native to shortgrass swales and upland ponderosa savannas. The pale grasslike leaves are similar to those of wild hyacinth, except that the central vein is solid instead of hollow. It is definitely not recommended that you eat any *Zigadenus*, as they are extremely poisonous. Not that you would be able to swallow one—it tastes awful. **White**

WESTERN RED LILY is becoming rare from overpicking as well as loss of habitat.

camas (*Zigadenus elegans*), taller with loose wands of white flowers, is native to very moist northern prairies and ponderosa savannas.

WESTERN RED LILY (*Lilium philadelphicum* var. *andinum* [LIL-ee-um fill-uh-DELL-fee-kum variety an-DIE-num]) is native around the

Western red lily

SEGO LILY (*Calochortus gunnisonii* [kal-o-KOR-tus gun-nee-SONE-ee-eye]) is also called mariposa lily. This elegant lily abounds in high-quality shortgrass prairies, on rocky slopes, and in open woodlands. It is 4 to 12 inches high, and each flower is about 2 inches across. The three large fat petals vary from white to pale lavender. The center is yellow and pale green marked with red purple spots. The pollinator is a metallic green solitary bee.

NODDING ONION has flowers that nod.

Great Lakes and down the Rocky Mountain chain in ponderosa savannas. Each bulb produces one to three flowers on knee-high stems. The lower leaves are alternate, but the upper ones whorl.

MICHIGAN LILY (*Lilium michiganense* [LIL-ee-um mish-uh-gan-NENSE]) is most often found in northern mesic tallgrass prairies and savannas. It looks much like the eastern Turks cap lily (*Lilium supurbum*), with its several nodding upside-down flowers along a tall stem. The leaves are just the opposite of those of western red lily, because the whorled ones are on the bottom and the alternate ones are on top. Michigan lily blooms midsummer, two weeks later than western red lily.

Sego lily

NODDING ONION (*Allium cernuum* [AL-ee-um sur-NEW-um]) is native from Canada to Mexico. However, it is a common prairie forb only in northeastern tallgrass regions, where it is found in dry to mesic remnant prairies. In the West, it occasionally grows in ponderosa or aspen meadows. The delicate pink and white flowers appear in midsummer, unlike the more common wild onions, which bloom in early spring.

Nodding onion

Michigan lily

The iris family (Iridaceae) has long flat leaves that overlap in a fan design where they attach at the root. Swamp irises, or flags, possess rhizomes that can hold their own in a flood and can compete with marsh grasses and rushes. Their swordlike leaves are sometimes green almost all year.

Prairie celestial and blue-eyed grasses are spring ephemerals. They push up thin grassy leaves, bloom, set seed, and go dormant before the weather gets hot. Blue-eyed grass has fibrous roots and is often short-lived. Prairie celestial has a bulb and is a long-lived perennial. Both tend to grow in large colonies, and because they are among the first flowers to bloom in the spring when there is little competition or distraction, they put on a magnificent show.

BLUE-EYED GRASS (*Sisyrinchium angustifolium* [siss-eh-RINK-ee-um an-gus-tee-FOLE-ee-um]) is native to moist prairies and open woodland edges on the eastern side of the tallgrass range. All the blue-eyed grasses are generally only a foot tall or less, this being one of the taller ones. The flowers are held above a bouquet of stems. Although the light blue flowers are quite small, they bloom in such profusion that the effect is showy. On sunny days, that is. The flowers close up overnight and on rainy days, presumably when their pollinator stays home.

Mountain blue-eyed grass

BLUE-EYED GRASS comes in many species, all of them capable of turning a savanna or prairie into a sea of blue.

lands in the northern plains west of blue-eyed grass. In Texas, it is found only in river bottoms in the eastern Panhandle. **Southern blue-eyed grass** (*Sisyrinchium langloisii*) has recently had *S. pruinosum* lumped in with it. This is a short, drought-tolerant blue-eyed grass native to prairies and post oak woodlands in Arkansas, Kansas, Oklahoma, and central and coastal Texas. **White blue-eyed grass** (*Sisyrinchium albidum*) often has, as the name implies, white flowers, and it is common around Chicago.

Blue-eyed grass

MOUNTAIN BLUE-EYED GRASS (*Sisyrinchium montanum* [siss-eh-RINK-ee-um mon-TAN-um]), which very closely resembles blue-eyed grass, is native to prairies, plains, and open coniferous wood-

PRAIRIE CELESTIAL (*Nemastylis geminiflora* [nee-ma-STY-lis jim-uh-nee-FLORE-ah]) is as short and blue as blue-eyed grass, and while it has fewer flowers, they are much larger. On rocky, seemingly dry prairies, prairie celestial is often

Prairie celestial

growing where a fault in the rock channels extra groundwater to the surface.

BLUE FLAG (*Iris virginica* var. *shrevei* [EYE-ris ver-JIN-eh-kah variety SHREEVE-eye]) grows in marshes from southeastern Canada to eastern Nebraska and East Texas. It looks similar to a tall purple garden iris, except it has no beard.

Northern blue flag

Western blue flag

Blue flag

NORTHERN BLUE FLAG (*Iris versicolor* [EYE-ris ver-see-KULL-or]) is very like blue flag. It is native to marshes in far northeastern North America.

WESTERN BLUE FLAG (*Iris missouriensis* [EYE-ris missouri-EN-sis]) is native to the western Missouri

River territory but not to Missouri. This short clumping iris makes large cushions of leaves and flowers. The leaves are pale blue green, and the flowers are pale blue. It grows in wet prairies and marshes in the Great Plains and in wet meadows and ponderosa woodlands in the Rocky Mountains.

PRAIRIE CELESTIAL was described by early explorers as one of the "spectacular" spring wildflowers on southern prairies.

The primrose family (Primulaceae) is composed of about 1,000 species native to the Northern Hemisphere. While primroses (*Primula*) are a big deal in Europe, we have very few native ones here. Instead we have their first cousins, shooting stars and loosestrife. Although both genera are found as far south as Texas, they are infrequently seen in the southern prairies, and there is no record that they exist at all in Mexico.

WESTERN SHOOTING STAR

(*Dodecatheon pulchellum* [doe-duh-KAY-the-on pull-KELL-um]) is also called saline shooting star because it will grow in salty sloughs. It grows along creeks and in wet prairies, moist hillside prairies, and open woods. Western shooting star is normally about a foot tall, but it can get taller. The nodding flowers are usually magenta but can be a pale lavender, and they bloom in May to June, sometimes even July.

WESTERN SHOOTING STAR is still fairly common in wet to mesic prairies and savannas.

Western shooting star

EASTERN SHOOTING STAR

(*Dodecatheon meadia* [doe-duh-KAY-the-on MEAD-ee-ah]) is very similar in appearance, although the clusters can be larger and have more than twenty-five flowers. The blooms are usually magenta, but occasionally there are white ones.

Its habitat is both more southern and more drought-tolerant than that of western shooting star. It grows in mesic to dry prairies and savannas, tolerating thin rocky limestone soil, from southern Wisconsin and southeastern Minnesota to the northeastern third of Texas, including the Blackland Prairie, Grand Prairie, and cedar brakes. It blooms April to May.

Eastern shooting star

NARROWLEAF LOOSESTRIFE

(*Lysimachia quadriflora* [liz-ee-MOCK-ee-ah kwah-dree-FLORE-ah]) blooms in mesic to wet prairies and fens in early summer. The leaves are about a ¼ inch wide, and the flowers are about 1 inch across. Each flower stem can branch to form as many as four flowers (*flora*). Do not get this loosestrife confused with **whorled loosestrife** (*Lysimachia quadrifolia*), which grows in black oak savannas and has three to four leaves (*folia*) per whorl.

Narrowleaf loosestrife

FRINGED LOOSESTRIFE

(*Lysimachia ciliata* [liz-ee-MOCK-ee-ah sill-ee-A-tah]) has hairs (the fringe) on the leaf stalks. This herb was ranked by J. E. Weaver as the third most important forb of lowland prairies in Nebraska. Although no longer so numerous, it is still found in wet prairies, stream banks, marshes, and moist woods. It spreads by root to form colonies, which range from knee- to waist-high. Bloom time is in midsummer.

Fringed loosestrife

NARROWLEAF LOOSESTRIFE is dainty, especially in contrast to the large, broad leaves of prairie dock.

The evening primrose family (Onagraceae) has flowers that open at sunset, or less frequently at sunrise, and close the following morning. The evening primroses have huge showy flowers that are yellow, white, or pale pink, frequently turning deep pink as they wither. The stenosiphon, an oddball that is a genus all by itself, and the gauras have small butterfly-shaped flowers, and they are usually pink or white, often both at once.

MISSOURI EVENING PRIMROSE
(*Oenothera macrocarpa* [ee-no-THEER-ah mack-roe-KAR-pah]) is called *Oenothera missouriensis* in many books, and it has been lumped with *Oenothera fremontii*. There are four subspecies altogether. The plants have pale green leaves in a bunch close to the ground. The seed capsules are pale green but large enough to be ornamental. The complex as a whole is most likely to be found on limestone escarpments and dry hillside prairies from southeastern Nebraska to central Texas and the Texas Panhandle. This is a somewhat short-lived perennial that does not like a lot of competition or moisture.

Missouri evening primrose

PINK EVENING PRIMROSE
(*Oenothera speciosa* [ee-no-THEER-ah spee-see-O-sah]) is longer-lived and is found in dry or rocky prairies and disturbed areas like road embankments. It is believed that it was originally native from southeastern Nebraska and the eastern two-thirds of Kansas into Missouri, Oklahoma, Texas, and northeastern Mexico. A hillside with dozens of plants in every shade of pink from blush to rose is unforgettable. Northern populations tend to be whiter and open at night, while southern populations are pinker and tend to open in the morning, probably due to different pollinators. Pink evening primrose tolerates more moisture and competition than Missouri primrose. Both are so spectacular in the spring that they have been planted far outside of their native range.

FRAGRANT EVENING PRIMROSE
(*Oenothera caespitosa* [ee-no-THEER-ah seas-peh-TOE-sah]) is native to rocky or gravelly hillside prairies in the Great Plains and the southwestern deserts. The huge white flowers open in the evening and are pollinated by sphinx moths. While open, they smell like the best French floral perfume you can imagine.

Fragrant evening primrose

MISSOURI EVENING PRIMROSE, shown here in buffalograss, has 3-inch yellow flowers that turn orange or pink as they close up.

Pink evening primrose

PLAINS EVENING PRIMROSE

(*Calylophus serrulatus* [kal-ee-LOAF-us ser-roo-LOT-us]) is native to shortgrass prairies on the Great Plains, and to upland prairies, including the Wisconsin goat prairies, in tallgrass prairie areas. At a glance, a *Calylophus* looks almost identical to an *Oenothera*, and some botanists still lump them together. *Calylophus* has a knob on the end of its stigma (at the center of the flower), and *Oenothera* has a cross. *Calylophus* is more upright and bushy, and the flowers are always yellow and open during the day.

Plains evening primrose

STENOSIPHON (*Stenosiphon linifolius* [stee-no-SYE-fon len-ee-FOLE-ee-us]) is a biennial or short-lived perennial with a winter rosette. It seems to prefer alkaline soil and old high-quality remnant

Stenosiphon

STENOSIPHON has tufts of white flowers with pink stamens that seem to float atop this tallgrass prairie.

southern tallgrass or midgrass prairies, cliffs, stream valleys, and roadsides. It is an airy plant that dots itself here and there, sticking up over the prairie, as tall as big bluestem.

SCARLET GAURA (*Gaura coccinea* [GAW-rah cock-SIN-ee-ah]) is a short plant native to shortgrass prairies, upland prairies, and open woodlands from the western edges of tallgrass prairies throughout the Great Plains, preferring sandy, rocky, or well-drained soils. I find the gauras showy only in masses; an individual plant usually looks scraggly. Scarlet gaura spreads by under-

ground roots to cover large areas, and some of the early explorers wrote that it would create bright red fragrant carpets in the spring.

Scarlet gaura

You may be surprised to know that not all members of the rose family (Rosaceae) look like roses. Besides traditional roses, the family includes strawberry, plum, cherry, and blackberry. But this is a diverse family. Not all members produce rose hips or edible fruits. Some species, such as prairie smoke, package their seed in pink plumes. And queen of the prairie has its seed encased in small, dry tan capsules. Although most rose members have five petals with lots of long stamens in the center, there are exceptions, such as the burnets, which have four sepals and no petals.

PRAIRIE SMOKE (*Geum triflorum* var. *triflorum* [JEE-um try-FLORE-um variety try-FLORE-um]) covers northern shortgrass prairies with pink "smoke" in early summer after blooming in late spring. This long-lived, high-quality perennial stands less than a foot tall. Thick rhizomes create clumps as wide as the plant is tall. The leaves, mostly in a rosette, are quite fancy and attractive.

Prairie smoke

PRAIRIE CINQUEFOIL (*Potentilla arguta* [poe-ten-TILL-ah ar-GOO-tah]), a common component of high-quality northern prairies, is a slender, self-contained, upright plant, usually 2 to 3 feet tall. It associates with little bluestem and shooting stars. It can bloom until August, but we saw it only in early summer. A similar-looking bright yellow cinquefoil (*Potentilla recta*), an escapee from Europe, is seeding itself into remnant tallgrass prairies.

QUEEN OF THE PRAIRIE (*Filipendula rubra* [fill-uh-PEN-due-lah ROO-bra]) stands 4 to 8 feet tall and blooms just before the big gold climax of northeastern prairies. It has a very limited native range but has escaped from cultivation, so there is considerable disagreement among restorationists as to where it can be considered truly native. Some believe that it is probably native only from northeastern Illinois to Pennsylvania and south to North Carolina. Near Chicago it grows in calcareous fens with New England aster, spotted Joe-Pye weed, narrowleaf loosestrife, and rushes.

Queen of the prairie

AMERICAN BURNET (*Sanguisorba canadensis* [san-gwee-SOR-bah kan-ah-DEN-sis]) is a stately rhizomatous perennial native to cool, damp prairies and marshes. In Chicago, it was recently rediscovered growing in a prairie with big bluestem, cord-

Prairie cinquefoil

PRAIRIE SMOKE has deep pink flowers that turn into pale pink plumes, giving a prairie the appearance of being covered with a blanket of pink smoke.

grass, and prairie dock. Although the flowers have no petals, the thick white spikes are quite showy. This is a fall-blooming forb.

Indian physic

American burnet

INDIAN PHYSIC (*Porteranthus stipulatus* [pore-ter-AN-thus stip-u-LA-tus]) is also known as American ipecac (*Gillenia stipulata*). This attractive and airy savanna plant increases after a fire. It is normally 2 to 3 feet tall, and has 1-inch white starry flowers that appear after the trees are fully leafed out. Indian physic is native to rocky black oak and post oak savannas. The root was used to make an emetic.

Wild strawberry

PRAIRIE CINQUEFOIL, unlike other cinquefoils, is always white or creamy, never bright yellow.

WILD STRAWBERRY (*Fragaria virginiana* [fruh-GAR-ee-ah vur-jin-ee-A-nah]) is a ground cover in both tallgrass prairies and rich

QUEEN OF THE PRAIRIE has its five-petaled flowers in a large cone that looks like cotton candy.

or moist savannas. In the West, it is native only close to the Rocky Mountains, and in Texas it is native only east of the Blackland Prairie. The strawberries, smaller than hybrid commercial strawberries, range from ambrosial to tasteless.

Geraniums (Geraniaceae) are a small genus of about four hundred species found in temperate regions. The South African geraniums, which are so popular as house plants, are genus *Pelargonium*. The two divisions of the family in North America are called storksbill (*Erodium*) and cranesbill (*Geranium*), because the seed cases have birdlike beaks. The prettiest storksbill is *Erodium texanum*, a short magenta-colored annual that can be amazingly plentiful on rocky dry prairies in southwestern Oklahoma and central Texas, but only when it gets rain at the right time the previous year, an event that occurs sporadically.

Most of the cranesbills are annuals, small-flowered, and weedy—nothing to write home about—while sticky purple geranium and wild geranium are popular wildflowers.

STICKY PURPLE GERANIUM and its relative wild geranium grow in masses in savannas and sunny woodlands.

STICKY PURPLE GERANIUM (*Geranium viscosissimum* [jur-RANE-ee-um vis-koe-SISS-e-mum]) is native to mesic prairies in Alberta around Cardston and Calgary and also in scattered locations in open woodlands and along streams from Saskatchewan to British Columbia and south to the Black Hills of western South Dakota. Along the Rockies, it grows in meadows. The knee-high stems are sticky and hairy, and the magenta to pale lavender flowers are 1½ inches across. It blooms in the spring at the same time as silver lupine and balsamroot, and may bloom sporadically throughout the summer.

Sticky purple geranium

WILD GERANIUM (*Geranium maculatum* [jur-RANE-ee-um mack-u-LOT-um]) is similar in size and appearance. A quick, easy-to-grow savanna flower, it spreads by rhizomes to make handsome colonies that are a delight each spring. Wild geranium grows in either rich or poor soil under oaks from Canada into the Ozarks and Appalachians. It cannot tolerate poor drainage. It is often found growing with blue woodland phlox (*Phlox divaricata*).

Wild geranium

The madder family (Rubiaceae) is so named for the important Eurasian herb *Rubia tinctoria*, the root of which was used to make beautiful red dyes. Other members of the madder family are coffee and quinine. Bedstraw got its name from the European species *Galium verum*. This bedstraw has stems and leaves that are so soft and sweet smelling when dried that they were once used to stuff mattresses.

NORTHERN BEDSTRAW (*Galium boreale* [GAY-lee-um bore-ee-AL-ee]) is a circumpolar species that is native to cool, moist rocky hillsides, prairies, woodlands, and swales throughout northern or mountainous North America. About knee-high, northern bedstraw has creeping roots that allow it to spread in huge patches. It likes company, and numerous other flowers and grasses grow with it, so that it becomes a frilly white backdrop for the purples, pinks, and yellows of other forbs.

Northern bedstraw

NARROWLEAF BLUETS flower for months in dry rocky southern prairies.

NARROWLEAF BLUETS (*Hedyotis nigricans* [hee-dee-O-tis nih-gree-KANZ]) likes dry rocky hillsides, badlands, and other places where the soil is well drained and the vegetation is short and not too dense. It is native to the southern half of the Great Plains and to upland prairies in the southern tallgrass area. Only about 8 inches tall, it makes a well-shaped bouquet of dainty white from May to October. It is a perennial with a stout taproot that may live only about five years. In some books narrowleaf bluets is called *Houstonia nigricans*.

NORTHERN BEDSTRAW blooms like white lace for weeks in northern prairies.

Narrowleaf bluets

The crowfoot family (Ranunculaceae) was named because many of its species have distinctive leaves that must have reminded someone of a crow's foot. The flowers are unusual, varied, and popular with gardeners. In this family we find not only meadowrue, anemone, and delphinium, but also columbine, buttercup, monkshood, the red or white-fruited baneberry, rue anemone, false rue anemone, marsh marigold, and clematis.

TALL MEADOWRUE (*Thalictrum dasycarpum* [thuh-LICK-trum day-zee-KAR-pum]) is also called purple meadowrue because of its purplish stems. The plants are either male or female, and while the white, fringed male flowers are showier, the females are necessary if you want a continuing supply of seedlings. The stems are hollow, and Native American children used them to make toy flutes. Tall meadowrue is native to the full range of mesic tallgrass prairies from almost wet to almost dry. It is either not found or very rare in the southern Great Plains.

Tall meadowrue

PASQUE FLOWER (*Pulsatilla patens* ssp. *multifida* [pull-suh-TILL-ah PAY-tens subspecies mull-TIFF-uh-dah]) is called *Anemone patens* by many botanists, and the name has changed back and forth several times. This short, fuzzy, tap-rooted, perennial plant can occur in the hundreds, especially after a burn or in overgrazed pastures. Flowers vary in color from palest lavender to rich purple or blue. The shape of the flower is reminiscent of a crocus, which explains why it is sometimes called crocus anemone. The seeds

PASQUE FLOWER blooms at Easter in some parts of its range.

are almost as pretty as the flowers, being silvery plumes. Pasque flower is native to rocky soils, northern shortgrass prairies, and ponderosa pine savannas. In the Southwest it is found only at high elevations, not on the plains. Pasque flower is also native to Eurasia but is a different subspecies there.

MEADOW ANEMONE (*Anemone canadensis* [uh-NIM-o-nee kan-ah-DEN-sis]) has large white flowers, over an inch across, that are borne on hairy stems above a sea of green leaves. You never see just one

TALL MEADOWRUE is a staple in mesic tallgrass prairies, especially in the north. The shorter white flowers are of Indian hemp (*Apocynum sibiricum*).

Pasque flower

Meadow anemone

Prairie larkspur

PRAIRIE LARKSPUR (*Delphinium carolinianum* ssp. *virescens* [del-FIN-ee-um ker-o-lin-ee-A-num subspecies vuh-RESS-sins]) is a short-lived perennial that grows in sandy or rocky limestone soils in dry to mesic prairies. The flowers are usually greenish white, but on the eastern edges of its range, where this subspecies blends into the eastern larkspur (*Delphinium carolinianum* ssp. *carolinianum*), flower color can be pale blue, bright blue, or even dark blue with a hint of purple. *Delphinium wootonii* is currently split off and represents the southwest range of this variable species.

meadow anemone. It spreads by rhizomes to make a ground cover that is ankle- to knee-high. It is most prolific in moist to wet prairies with sweetgrass or iris. It can also tolerate a half day of shade. Meadow anemone is so easy to grow in its native habitat that its beauty and usefulness are often underestimated.

THIMBLEWEED (*Anemone cylindrica* [uh-NIM-o-nee suh-LINN-dree-kah]) is also called candle anemone or long-fruited anemone. This is a tall, slender, clump-forming perennial that grows in northern mesic prairies. The flowers are usually white to greenish white. Note the horizontal, deeply cut leaves clustered beneath the long flower stems.

Thimbleweed

THIMBLEWEED has flowers and fruits that form along a narrow cylinder shaped like an exaggerated thimble.

The parsley family (Apiaceae) is sometimes called the carrot family, and used to be called the Umbelliferae. I like the name Umbelliferae because it helps me remember that this is the family where the flowers are in umbels—*umbel* being the botanical term for a cluster of flowerets that radiate from one point on the stem like an upside-down umbrella. Queen Anne's lace, celery, coriander, fennel, carrot, and parsley are non-native parsleys we all know well.

GOLDEN ALEXANDERS (*Zizia aurea* [ZIZZ-ee-ah AW-ree-ah]) is plentiful in northern mesic to wet tallgrass prairies in early summer. It is also found in moist woods and dry upland savannas, but it hates southern summers. If you develop a healthy knee-high stand of golden Alexanders (a single plant is still called Alexanders), you probably have the right conditions to grow small white ladyslippers, shooting star, and alumroot.

Golden Alexanders

HEARTLEAF ALEXANDERS (*Zizia aptera* [ZIZZ-ee-ah AP-ter-ah]) is more drought-tolerant but otherwise very similar to golden Alexanders, except that the leaves close to the ground are heart-shaped. It grows best in western Canada. In the Great Plains, heartleaf Alexanders is found only in the Black Hills and in the mountains.

Heartleaf Alexanders

RATTLESNAKE MASTER (*Eryngium yuccifolium* [ee-RIN-jee-um yuck-ah-FOLE-ee-um]) is a long-lived perennial native to well-drained tallgrass prairies, rocky upland prairies, and post oak savannas. *Yuccifolium* means yucca-leaved, and the leaves do look like those of a yucca, their shape and pale blue color making a lovely addition to the texture of a prairie. The Mesquakies used the leaves and dried seed pods in their rattlesnake medicine dance, but it is not known if the plant is an antidote to rattlesnake venom or just sounds like a rattlesnake. The fiber in the leaves was evidently used to make fairly sophisticated shoes 8,300 years ago, as several sandals and slip-ons have been found in a cave on the Missouri River.

HEARTLEAF ALEXANDERS, unlike golden Alexanders, has heart-shaped leaves at its base.

Rattlesnake master

ERYNGO (*Eryngium leavenworthii* [ee-RIN-jee-um lev-en-WORTH-ee-eye]) is an annual with prickly leaves and prickly, bright purple, thistlelike heads studded with tiny electric blue flowers. On little bluestem and limestone prairies, it occurs in masses every fall.

Eryngo

BISCUITROOT (*Lomatium foeniculaceum* [lo-MAY-she-um foe-nick-u-LAY-see-um]) has a thick, starchy, edible taproot, which was ground into flour. Its parsley leaves were eaten raw in the spring. Biscuitroot is native to dry prairies in the northern Great Plains and to tall-grass prairies in north-central Texas. The yellow flowers look similar to those of the Alexanders, but the overall shape of the plant is shorter and lacier. There are several native *Lomatiums* that are desirable for western prairies.

Biscuitroot

PRAIRIE PARSLEY is more eye-catching in seed than in bright yellow flower.

PRAIRIE PARSLEY (*Polytaenia nuttallii* [polly-TEA-nee-ah nuh-TAWL-ee-eye]) is a knee- to waist-high biennial or short-lived perennial found in dry prairie remnants and open woodlands. It has smooth oval leaflets, yellow flowers, and strongly ribbed seeds. Endemic to the United States, this medicinal herb is becoming rare or extinct in much of its range. Its only relative is Texas prairie parsley (*Polytaenia texana*).

When RATTLESNAKE MASTER is not in bloom, it looks like a yucca, although the leaves are soft, not spiny.

Prairie parsley

The borage family (Boraginaceae) includes the familiar garden herb borage, forget-me-nots, and heliotrope. The family's basic characteristic is flower buds that are almost always on one side of a coil that unwinds as the flowers open. The seeds of both marbleseed and puccoon are as hard as stone, giving the name marbleseed (as hard and round as a marble) and the genus name *Lithospermum*, which literally means stone seed.

HOARY PUCCOON is a short perennial with egg-yolk yellow trumpet-shaped flowers and furry (hoary) leaves.

Hoary puccoon

HOARY PUCCOON (*Lithospermum canescens* [lith-o-SPUR-mum kuh-NESS-ens]) is a long-lived, tap-rooted perennial native to upland prairies in tallgrass prairie regions from Saskatchewan to northeastern Oklahoma. It prefers blacksoil prairies and limestone, while **hairy puccoon** (*Lithospermum caroliniense*), native from Ontario to Texas, prefers sand. Normally less than a foot tall, hoary puccoon's narrow stemless leaves and vivid deep yellow flowers appear while grasses are still short. The roots of hoary puccoon are said to make a beautiful red dye.

FRINGED PUCCOON (*Lithospermum incisum* [lith-o-SPUR-mum in-SIZE-um]) has a long-lived taproot that looks red but makes a purple dye. It gets its name from the fringed petals on its pale yellow spring flowers. Almost invisible self-pollinating fall flowers produce the seeds, which look like small white stones. Fringed puccoon, far more drought-tolerant than hoary puccoon, is native to dry upland short-grass prairies in Canada and the Great Plains. It grows throughout Texas and into northern Mexico.

Fringed puccoon

Marbleseed

MARBLESEED (*Onosmodium molle* [o-nus-MOE-dee-um molly]) has two main subspecies. The eastern variety, *Onosmodium hispidissimum*, is still often considered a separate species. It is native to upland prairies and savannas in the eastern tallgrass area. The western version, *O. molle* ssp. *occidentale*, is found most often from the Great Plains to central Texas. The white seeds, closer to the size of BBs than marbles, stay ornamental all winter.

The saxifrage family (Saxifragaceae) includes astilbe, grass-of-Parnassus, bishop's cap, and saxifrage. The family was larger until recently, when certain members were placed in the hydrangea family, the currant family, and others. Most of the members left in the saxifrage family are short perennial herbs that show a preference for moist rocky crevices, bogs, and damp woods. However, the two species profiled here—prairie rockstar and prairie alumroot—are northern prairie forbs.

PRAIRIE ALUMROOT (*Heuchera richardsonii* [HEW-kuh-rah richard-SONE-ee-eye]) is an exceptionally long-lived perennial that can sometimes hold on as the prairie around it gets degraded. The leaves are clustered at the base of bare stems, and each stem ends in a spike of small green flowers. The tiny green flowers may be tinged with yellow or rose but would never be considered showy. It is the leaves that are the main attraction. They range from heart-shaped to kidney-shaped with lobed edges. They are shiny and green above, and pale and fuzzy below. Alumroot is prized in gardens for its medicinal properties. A powder of the ground-up root can be sprinkled on painful rheumatic joints, while the leaves are used to make a rheumatism tea. Prairie alumroot is native to prairies, hillsides, and rocky open woods in both dry and mesic northern prairies.

Prairie alumroot

PRAIRIE ROCKSTAR (*Lithophragma parviflorum* [lith-o-FRAG-ma par-vee-FLORE-um]) is an uncommon perennial ranging from 4 to 16 inches tall, with showy white spikes and small, deeply lobed, silvery velvet basal leaves. It is native to grasslands from Nebraska and the Black Hills west to northern California.

PRAIRIE ALUMROOT has pretty leaves, tiny greenish flowers, and rosy brown round seed capsules.

Prairie rockstar

The bluebell family (Campanulaceae) has flowers that are bell-shaped and usually blue, although sometimes the flowers are white, lavender, or pink, or even as red as cardinal flower. The sap is white but as thin as milk, not at all like the thick and gooey sap of the milkweeds and euphorbias. Worldwide there are about two thousand species, including garden favorites such as bluebells, lobelias, platycodon, and Venus's looking glass.

HAREBELL (*Campanula rotundifolia* [kam-PAN-u-lah roe-tun-dee-FOLE-ee-ah]) is a well-loved short perennial that spreads by both rhizomes and stolons. It is native circumboreal and south down mountain chains. In Illinois and Wisconsin it is found on dry hill prairies and in black oak savannas, but in Montana and Colorado it is found only in woodlands and lowland prairies and along stream banks.

HAREBELLS are common across Canadian and northeastern prairies.

Harebell

TALL BELLFLOWER (*Campanulastrum americanum* [kam-pan-u-LAS-trum uh-mer-ee-KAN-um]) was called *Campanula* until very recently. It is included here for savanna gardens and wet prairies. An annual, it is prolific in the first few years after the garden is planted, crowding out less desirable weeds, and then it appears sporadically in successive years as the garden matures. Six feet tall, the flowers are blue with a white center. In tallgrass areas, its western native edge ranges from southern Ontario to western Nebraska to eastern Oklahoma.

Tall bellflower

Palespike lobelia

PALESPIKE LOBELIA (*Lobelia spicata* [loe-BEE-lee-ah spih-KAH-tah]) ranges in height from less than 1 foot to over 3 feet tall. On dry hill prairies in the northern tallgrass region, where it is principally found, it is short with several stems bearing spikes of pale blue flowers. In fens or mesic prairies it is more likely to be tall and slender. In its extreme northern and southern ranges, it shows a partiality for sand and a high water table. It starts blooming in the spring, long before great blue lobelia and cardinal flower, but can stay in flower as late as August.

GREAT BLUE LOBELIA (*Lobelia siphilitica* [loe-BEE-lee-ah siff-uh-LIT-a-kah]), like the great blue heron, likes to live near water. It has dark blue blooms in midsummer, and because it colonizes, it

forms giant masses that are spectacular. Great blue lobelia is native on its western edge from Manitoba to southwestern South Dakota, northeastern Colorado, south-central Kansas, and north-central Texas. It is more prevalent in the North than in the South.

CARDINAL FLOWER (*Lobelia cardinalis* [loe-BEE-lee-ah kar-duh-NAL-iss]) usually starts flowering about two weeks earlier than great blue lobelia. It grows natively in wet prairies and wet open woodlands. On the map, the Rocky Mountain cardinal flower (*Lobelia splendens*) is lumped in with *Lobelia cardinalis*. Cardinal flower is bright red and a great favorite with hummingbirds on their fall migration.

Cardinal flower

PALESPIKE LOBELIA blooms in the spring in a wide range of habitats from dry hill prairies to fens.

Great blue lobelia

The spiderwort family (Commelina-ceae) is also called the dayflower family. Spiderworts and dayflowers (*Commelina* species) have three petals and grasslike leaves with parallel veins. The flowers bloom only for a day or, more accurately, only for a morning. Then they close up. The fresh luminescent petals you enjoy in the morning become a tiny wad of dark wet tissue by lunchtime. However, the next morning the plants are gloriously covered with fresh flowers, and this goes on for several weeks.

The spiderworts all look pretty similar. They are 1 to 3 feet tall, depending on moisture, with grasslike leaves at the base and long green bracts that look as if narrow leaves are arranged horizontally just below the flowers. The flowers are bright blue, purple, or magenta (sometimes pink or white) and grow in clusters. A few flowers in each cluster open in the morning and close when the sun gets hot. They are short-lived and seed out in disturbed soil, making them a great addition to new prairie plantings.

OHIO SPIDERWORT is one of the most numerous and eye-catching forbs in mesic tallgrass prairies, but only in the morning.

OHIO SPIDERWORT (*Tradescantia ohiensis* [trad-ess-KAN-chuh o-hie-EN-sis]) is native to mesic prairies and dry woodlands throughout the eastern United States west to the Great Plains.

WESTERN SPIDERWORT (*Tradescantia occidentalis* [trad-ess-KAN-chuh ox-ee-den-TAL-iss]) is the chief spiderwort for the western half of the Great Plains.

BRACTED SPIDERWORT (*Tradescantia bracteata* [trad-ess-KAN-chuh brack-tee-A-ta]) is native in the eastern Great Plains and upper Midwest, between the ranges of Ohio spiderwort and Western spiderwort.

Ohio spiderwort

Western spiderwort

Bracted spiderwort

The dogbane family (Apocynaceae) includes the familiar non-native ground cover *Vinca minor* and the popular shrub oleander. The bulk of the family is found in tropical regions.

Both spreading and prairie dogbane, like their close cousins the milkweeds, have milky sap and long slender seed pods that expel seeds that float on tufts of silky hair.

The stems have long, tough but fine fibers that were used for sewing and fishing line. Coarser fibers were used to weave nets. A net drawstring bag five thousand years old was found in Danger Cave, Utah. Dogbane roots taste horrible, indicating the plant is poisonous, but they were used in small quantities for heart conditions, worms, and abortions and to treat syphilis. Modern research recognizes that the chemicals in dogbane act on the heart and fight tumors.

SPREADING DOGBANE

(*Apocynum androsaemifolium* [uh-POSS-ee-num an-droe-see-mee-FOLE-ee-um]) makes waist-high thickets that die to the ground each year. The flowers are fragrant clusters of pale pink and white bells that are easily visible above opposite drooping leaves. Adapted to moist northern prairies, spreading dogbane is rarely found in prairies south of central Nebraska.

Spreading dogbane

PRAIRIE DOGBANE (*Apocynum cannabinum* [uh-POSS-ee-num kuh-NAB-ee-num]) is more of a pioneer perennial, tolerating both wetter and drier conditions than spreading dogbane. Its height is knee- to chest-high, and its leaves stand erect around narrow bell-like white flowers.

TEXAS BLUESTAR (*Amsonia ciliata* var. *texana* [am-SO-nee-ah sill-ee-A-tah variety tex-A-nah]) has loose clusters of pale blue star-shaped flowers on short slender stems bristling with narrow leaves. It grows on rocky limestone and sandy well-drained prairies with grama grasses or little bluestem as far west as the Red Rolling Plains in Texas.

Texas bluestar

Prairie dogbane

SPREADING DOGBANE is often found growing with bracken fern under black oaks.

Scrophs (short for Scrophulariaceae) are usually tubular with a bottom lip and are attractive to hummingbirds. Non-native members of this family familiar to gardeners are snapdragon and foxglove.

Several scrophs, such as paintbrush and gerardia, are hemiparasitic. This means that they can make their own food, but they need to tap into the roots of a grass, oak, or another perennial to thrive in the long term. There is some evidence that hemiparasitism works both ways, and the host plant receives benefits also. This could explain why annual scrophs can be found in ancient prairies where other annuals cannot germinate.

The paintbrushes and penstemons profiled here are the more easterly species. As you go west, there are many more choices, and they come in brighter colors.

CULVER'S ROOT (*Veronicastrum virginicum* [ver-ron-ee-KASS-trum ver-JIN-uh-kum]) is almost always white, although it can be pink. About waist-high, it is native to moist oak savannas and mesic prairies from southern Ontario to forested northeast Texas. Prevalent in the northern part of its range, it is uncommon in the South.

Culver's root

SCARLET PAINTBRUSH (*Castilleja coccinea* [kas-tuh-LAY-ah kock-SIN-ee-ah]) is an annual or biennial native to moist sandy eastern prairies. Sometimes called **Indian paintbrush**, this name in wildflower catalogs usually refers to *Castilleja indivisa*, an annual paintbrush native to Texas, Louisiana, and southern Oklahoma.

Scarlet paintbrush

CULVER'S ROOT blooms in mid-summer in moist tallgrass prairies and oak savannas.

DOWNY PAINTBRUSH (*Castilleja sessiliflora* [kas-tuh-LAY-ah sess-uh-lee-FLORE-ah]) is called pink paintbrush in West Texas and downy yellow painted cup in Chicago. The flowers are pale, and the bracts are green, not colored. Downy paintbrush, native to well-drained prairies, is a long-lived perennial less than a foot tall. Its leaves and stems are downy with fine hairs.

Downy paintbrush

FOXGLOVE BEARDTONGUE (*Penstemon digitalis* [PEN-stuh-mun dih-juh-TAL-iss]) is the most moisture-tolerant of the penstemons. It sometimes hybridizes with even more easterly *Penstemon calycosus* and gets a pink tinge. Otherwise, it is pure white. Some botanists think these species should be treated as one plant and called *Penstemon laevigatus*. This many-stemmed clumping perennial, 1 to 3 feet tall and half as broad, grows in mesic and

LILAC BEARDTONGUE (*Penstemon gracilis* [PEN-stuh-mun grah-SILL-iss]) blooms in late spring in northern moist, sandy or gravelly shortgrass prairies. Although more drought-tolerant then foxglove beardtongue, it still requires moister soil than most penstemons. Its clustered spikes of lavender flowers are normally less than knee-high.

Lilac beardtongue

SCARLET PAINTBRUSH, usually red orange, can also come in pastels from cream to orange sherbet.

dry prairies and also on the edges of shade in the northern tallgrass region, where it shows a definite preference for sandy loam. In the southern tallgrass areas, it grows only in moist sandy prairies.

PURPLE GERARDIA (*Agalinis purpurea* [ah-juh-LINE-iss pur-PUR-ee-ah]) grows in wet prairies and sedge meadows from Minnesota to the Gulf Coast and eastward. **Rough gerardia** (*Agalinis aspera*) grows in dry prairies and savannas from Manitoba to north-central

FOXGLOVE BEARDTONGUE is the penstemon found most often in northeastern tallgrass prairies.

Texas. There are many species of *Agalinis*, often called gerardia (juh-RAR-dee-ah) or false foxglove, and there seems to be at least one species for every prairie and oak savanna. They make very attractive fall color because the 1-inch large pink or purple flowers are prominent on their slender bobbing stems. The leaves of most *Agalinis*, although not all, turn black when they dry, which gives you a little help with identification.

Foxglove beardtongue

Purple gerardia

The phlox family (Polemoniaceae) includes *Phlox*, *Gilia*, skyrocket (*Ipomopsis*), and Jacob's ladder (*Polemonium*). The flowers have five petals arranged at right angles at the end of a tube. The centers may have a ring of contrasting color.

DOWNY PHLOX (*Phlox pilosa* [FLOX pie-LOE-sah]) is also called prairie phlox because its myriad subspecies occur in both tallgrass and shortgrass prairies and in oak savannas throughout the tallgrass region. As a whole, downy phlox is a long-lived perennial with narrow fuzzy leaves and pink fragrant flowers. But there are differences. On limestone or clay, the stems tend to be very short, giving the phlox a creeping appearance, and on sand, the flowers will probably be in balls atop clumps of upright knee-high stems.

Downy phlox

MARSH PHLOX (*Phlox glaberrima* [FLOX glah-BARE-ee-mah]) is sometimes called smooth phlox because it looks like a hairless version of upright downy phlox. It grows in moist to wet tallgrass prairies. The large dense round heads of the flowers are hot pink in color and appear from June to early September.

Marsh phlox

BLUE GILIA (*Gilia rigidula* [JILL-ee-ah ruh-JID-u-lah]) is normally only about 6 inches tall. It forms almost woody clumps of stiff needle-like dark green leaves. The flowers, a little less than an inch across, are an amazing dark blue with golden centers. They open in late morning from March to July, and then again in the fall if it rains. Blue gilia is native to southern shortgrass prairies.

Blue gilia

DOWNY PHLOX blooms for weeks and is sweetly fragrant.

The flowers of the flax family (Linaceae) are made up of five overlapping satiny petals that open early in the morning and drop off by midday. Our native flaxes are prairie plants, although some take light shade, and they tend to be annuals or short-lived perennials. Growth habit is airy with many flowers widely spaced on slender, almost leafless stems.

Most species are golden yellow, but our only blue flax is such a vivid sky blue that it quickly captures everyone's attention. It is very closely related to the Eurasian *Linum perenne*, and to a casual observer, looks a lot like *Linum usitatissimum*, the common annual flax of Europe's linen crop. Both these Old World flaxes are widely naturalized in North America, and the annual flax especially is often mislabeled *Linum lewisii*. The non-native blue flaxes are short-lived, nonaggressive, and seem to do no harm, so the distinction is important only if you are working with remnant prairies or doing a restoration in areas where *Linum lewisii* is native.

The red flax (*Linum grandiflorum*) is native to North Africa.

Our native BLUE FLAX is greatly outnumbered by blue flaxes from Europe, especially in commercial seed mixes.

WILD BLUE FLAX (*Linum lewisii* [LIE-num loo-ISS-ee-eye]) was named for Meriwether Lewis of the Lewis and Clark Expedition. A western short-lived perennial, it is native principally to prairies and lightly wooded rocky hillsides in the western Great Plains from Calgary south to the Trans Pecos in Texas. In Kansas and Nebraska where it meets the naturalized Eurasian *Linum perenne*, hybrids are forming.

Stiffstem flax

Wild blue flax

STIFFSTEM FLAX (*Linum rigidum* [LIE-num RIDGE-ee-dum]) is an annual golden flax that usually grows less than 10 inches tall. The yellow petals are striped with orange, and the color becomes more intense at the center as the lines draw closer together. At the very center is a jade green dot. Bloom time is early summer. Stiffstem flax is native to sandy or rocky shortgrass prairies. There is considerable hybridization with *Linum berlandieri* and *Linum compactum*, sometimes considered to be varieties of *Linum rigidum*. Other yellow flaxes, of which there are many, are native to both wet and dry prairies from Massachusetts to Florida to southern California.

The mallow family (Malvaceae) includes hibiscus, Rose-of-Sharon, hollyhock, okra, cotton, and the original marshmallow (*Althaea officinalis*), whose roots were pounded and mixed with sugar to make marshmallows.

There are about one thousand species worldwide in tropical and temperate regions. The family characteristics are five satiny petals, which may be opened flat like a plate or almost closed like a cup, that encircle a fancy and prominent fused column of stamens.

The genera most important to prairies are poppy mallows and globe mallows. Both can germinate in bare ground and put on a big show for several years before they get squeezed down by grasses and other forbs to just a few flowering stems.

The poppy mallows have large cuplike flowers that come in magenta, pink, or white. The globemallows, more drought-tolerant, have smaller flowers in Chinese red, peach, or lavender. Their cupped petals are translucent and catch the light, so that their warm luscious colors glow like Tiffany lamps.

BUSH'S POPPY MALLOW

(*Callirhoe bushii* [kall-uh-ROE-ee BUSH-ee-eye]) is rarely seen and is native only to moist savannas or glades in Iowa, Missouri, southeastern Kansas, northwestern Arkansas, and possibly northeastern Oklahoma. The large magenta cup is held 2 feet high on a slender, almost leafless stem. It keeps its genetic information separate by blooming in midsummer, a week or so after the other poppy mallows have quit blooming and gone to seed.

Bush's poppy mallow

WINECUP (*Callirhoe involucrata*

var. *involucrata* [kall-uh-ROE-ee in-voe-loo-KRA-tah]) is the most commonly seen poppy mallow. Its stems lie along the ground, but do not root. Its root is a long-lived corm that can get as big as a turnip. Winecup, also called purple poppy mallow, is native to well-drained sandy or black-soiled prairies in the central prairie area, and elsewhere it is probably an escapee from gardens. It grows well with sideoats grama, buffalograss, and little bluestem. In Oklahoma it is known as cowboy rose.

Clustered poppy mallow

CLUSTERED POPPY MALLOW

(*Callirhoe triangulata* [kall-uh-ROE-ee try-ang-u-LA-tah]) has a cluster of smaller flowers on each stem rather than one large cup. It grows, or used to grow, in sandy prairies and black oak savannas.

BUSH'S POPPY MALLOW has tall slender stems and prefers a half day of shade.

Winecup

SCARLET GLOBEMALLOW, ankle-high, makes a sweet medicinal tea.

nal herb used for a number of major and minor illnesses. Today it is an ingredient in shampoos. But its most dramatic use was reported by Melvin Gilmore, who said that the Lakota would chew it to a paste and then rub the mucilaginous goo over their hands and arms before fishing a piece of meat out of a boiling stew.

GLADE MALLOW (*Napaea dioica* [nah-PEA-ah die-O-ee-kah]) is on the endangered species list. An alluvial prairie and bur oak savanna species accustomed to spring flooding, it has suffered widespread habitat destruction. Several native plant nurseries sell seed as part of a federal program. This head-high forb has pretty white flowers, large coarse leaves, and rhizomes. Individual plants are either male or female.

Glade mallow

SCARLET GLOBEMALLOW

(*Sphaeralcea coccinea* [sfuh-RAL-see-ah cock-SIN-ee-ah]) is native to dry shortgrass prairies, with its eastern boundaries in Manitoba and western Minnesota south to Texas west of the Blackland Prairie. This ankle-high perennial covers itself with small orange flowers from early summer to midsummer. The leaves are so hairy that they look gray green.

Scarlet globemallow is a medici-

Scarlet globemallow

The aster family (Asteraceae) so dominates prairie forbs that it is divided into many sections. Here are those species grown more for their beautiful silvery leaves than for their flowers.

Pussytoes are charming groundcover plants. The females have flower heads composed of small furry "toes." They prefer cool weather and are rarely seen in the South. Another name for pussytoes is ladies' tobacco, as Native American women used to smoke the leaves. Tea made from the leaves was drunk to prevent illness after childbirth.

Artemisias, called sage, sagebrush, or wormwood, are a highly visible component of our well-drained North American prairies. Those with the most eastern ranges are herbaceous. Those in the dry western steppes are shrubs. According to pollen records, artemisias started developing in the rain shadow of the Rockies about sixteen million years ago.

Tarragon is the dried leaf of an Old World artemisia. Root teas were used for menstrual regularity and childbirth in both America and Europe.

PLAINS PUSSYTOES (*Antennaria parvifolia* [ann-tuh-NARE-ee-ah par-vee-FOLE-ee-ah]) is native to dry shortgrass prairies. In Canada, it is called low everlasting, and the

Behind a bunch of bright green violet leaves, a patch of PUSSYTOES makes a ground cover of silver leaves above which are clusters of tiny white fuzzy flowers that are reminiscent of a pussy's toes.

Latin name is usually given as *Antennaria aprica*. The ½-inch wide leaves are equally furry both top and bottom. The flower heads may be nodding when they first start blooming but are upright by the time they go to seed. The stems are encased with clasping leaves.

LADIES' TOBACCO (*Antennaria parlinii* [ann-tuh-NARE-ee-ah par-LEE-nee-eye]) is the midwestern pussytoes and used to be lumped in with the eastern pussytoes (*Anten-*

Ladies' tobacco

naria plantaginifolia). It grows in dry or disturbed prairies in the tallgrass region but is more likely to be found in oak savannas. It has leaves that are often over an inch wide, are fuzzier underneath than on top, and are striped with three, five, or even seven parallel veins.

FIELD PUSSYTOES (*Antennaria neglecta* [ann-tuh-NARE-ee-ah neh-GLECK-tah]) grows in moist remnant prairies with big bluestem or in little bluestem savannas. In Canada it is called prairie everlasting (*Antennaria campestris*). Its leaves are almost smooth on top, and there is only one vein beneath. Also, the color can be yellow green instead of gray green.

Plains pussytoes

Field pussytoes

LOUISIANA SAGE (*Artemisia ludoviciana* [ar-tuh-ME-zee-ah loo-doe-vee-see-AN-ah]) is also called white sage or prairie sage. *Ludoviciana* refers to the Louisiana Territory, which is where it was first scientifically described. Although salvias are "true" sages, artemisias are also called sage, and both have strongly pungent foliage. Louisiana sage is native to upland prairies in its eastern range, and to lowland prairies and parklands in the West. Its leaves are fuzzy white both top and bottom throughout its range, but they are much whiter and broader in the Northwest.

Louisiana sage

PASTURE SAGE (*Artemisia frigida* [ar-tuh-ME-zee-ah FRIH-juh-da]) is a shrublet, meaning it is woody at the base, but most of the plant dies back each year at frost. The roots

Pasture sage

can colonize and form a mat. Its height is usually knee-high or shorter. The leaves, which are silvery on both sides, are small and lacy. When I was learning this plant, I would call it fringed sage to link the leaf shape and *frigida* in my mind. It is prevalent in mesic to dry prairies throughout the Canadian prairies and northern plains.

DWARF SAGEBRUSH (*Artemisia cana* [ar-tuh-ME-zee-ah KAY-nah]) is a shrub, not a forb, usually less than waist-high. The leaves, silvery white on both sides, are 1 to 3 inches long and narrow. This and other shrubby sages are an integral part of western shortgrass prairies. Usually each area has only one kind of shrubby sage native to it, and

Dwarf sagebrush

that sagebrush is a dominant component. The three most important shrubs, going north to south from Canada to Mexico, are dwarf sagebrush, big sagebrush (*Artemisia tridentata*), and sand sagebrush (*Artemisia filifolia*).

PASTURE SAGE, shown here in a garden, has aromatic silvery leaves.

The aster family is often called *Compositae* or the composite (kum-POZ-it) family. It is also called the sunflower family. Most people would recognize that both sunflowers and asters look like daisies, and all daisies are composites. What appears to you to be a single flower with a center encircled by petals is really a composite of many, many flowers. Each "petal," called a ray, has its own flower, and all the ray flowers together form a ring around the center. Then, smack in the middle of the center are oodles of different flowers called disk flowers, and they have very tiny tubular petals you might not even notice.

But just to confuse things, not all composites are daisies. Certainly, the artemisias and pussytoes are not daisies. Along with thistles, blazing stars, ironweeds, and bonesets, they have only disk flowers. And lettuce, chicory, and dandelions have only ray flowers.

Most members of the aster family bloom in late summer to fall, but a few members bloom in spring and early summer. This is a boon to early butterflies and bees, as composites as a whole seem to be nectar-rich.

Native American YARROW and yarrow native to Eurasia are found hybridized all over North America.

Yarrow

YARROW (*Achillea millefolium* [uh-KILL-ee-ah mill-ee-FOLE-ee-um]) is very easy to identify because nothing else looks quite like it. The leaves are ferny, and the flowers are plates of tiny white daisies. The roots colonize to form mats in bare ground but are quickly reduced to an occasional stem as your prairie garden matures.

The leaves have been used for thousands of years to stop bleeding, prevent infection, and hasten heal-ing. Coprolites found in southwestern pueblos dating to the 1300s verify that Native Americans used yarrow long before Europeans appeared.

Yarrow in North America has two appearances. The short version with a domed head and slightly curly woolly leaves is native to the northern Great Plains and the

Rocky Mountains. It used to be called *Achillea lanulosa* to distinguish it from the taller yarrow brought in from Europe that quickly naturalized throughout all of North America. Now, most botanists lump the two together and agree that they have no idea where yarrow grew in North America before 1492.

Because yarrow is probably not native to tallgrass prairie, it is not planted on purpose. But because it does not cause any problems, it is rarely weeded out.

PHILADELPHIA FLEABANE

(*Erigeron philadelphicus* [ee-RIDGE-er-on fill-uh-DELL-fee-kus]) is a biennial or short-lived perennial 1 to 2 feet tall, depending on moisture and how high the grasses are. Starting in May, it blooms for several weeks in recently disturbed moist prairies throughout North America. The fleabanes are not high-quality, long-lived white daisies, but they often have flushes of pink or lavender, they feed butterflies, and they fill in spaces in a fledgling prairie. Furthermore, they have a cheerful quality and are often numerous enough to brighten a prairie when other flowers are having a lull.

Philadelphia fleabane

TUFTED FLEABANE (*Erigeron caespitosus* [ee-RIDGE-er-on sess-pea-TO-sus]) is a handsome large-flowered compact perennial that is plentiful on dry hillsides and prairies in the Canadian prairie provinces and the northwestern Great Plains. This is not the only drought-tolerant fleabane. **Plains fleabane** (*Erigeron modestus*) is a showy fleabane for the southern Great Plains. Usually less than a foot high, it especially likes sandy soil. **Poor Robin's plantain** (*Erigeron pulchellus*) grows in both bur oak and black oak savannas. **Daisy fleabane** (*Erigeron strigosus*), usually an annual although occasionally

Tufted fleabane

a short-lived perennial, was found by Weaver to be prevalent in dry prairies. Daisy fleabane also grows in sandy savannas.

Fleabane daisies, like this PHILADELPHIA FLEABANE, usually appear on their own and are welcome airy spots of white.

A great many members of the aster family are yellow daisies. They are so numerous and so hard to tell apart that most of us simply do not try, and instead refer to them as DYCs—"damn yellow composites." (Although I know of one tender-hearted botanist who calls them "delightful yellow composites.")

Every habitat in North America has numerous desirable species of DYCs. The most important tallgrass DYCs are pretty well covered in this book. The important shortgrass DYCs extend into the desert regions and on west into California. Some I particularly like and could not include are greenthreads (*Thelesperma*), goldeneyes (*Viguiera* and *Heliomeris*), wingstems (*Verbesina*), and bitterweeds (*Tetraneuris* or *Hymenoxys*).

FALSE DANDELION (*Agoseris glauca* [ah-go-SEER-iss GLAW-kah]) is native to upland prairies in western Minnesota and Canada and to moist prairies through the northern Great Plains. It is a taprooted perennial about a foot tall with narrow basal leaves that may be toothed but are never deeply lobed like the lawn weed dandelion.

FALSE DANDELION is larger and showier than the weedy dandelion we all know, and you will be sorry it does not seed out better.

The flowers, one to each rosette, are on leafless stems. Like the other dandelions on this page, they have bright yellow flowers and fluffy seeds.

False dandelion

PRAIRIE DANDELION (*Nothocalais cuspidata* [no-tho-kah-LA-iss kus-pea-DA-tah]), also called *Agoseris cuspidata* and *Microseris cuspidata*, is frequent in the northern Great Plains. It also occurs in dry upland prairies in the northern

Prairie dandelion

tallgrass region. Like false dandelion, it requires excellent drainage and is nonaggressive.

DWARF DANDELION (*Krigia biflora* [KRIG-ee-ah bye-FLORE-ah]) grows with little bluestem and can also be found in black oak savannas. There are several species of *Krigia* native to well-drained prairies and sandy savannas, and all are desirable.

Dwarf dandelion

BLANKETFLOWER (*Gaillardia aristata* [guh-LARD-ee-ah air-RISS-tah-tah]) is frequently sold in wildflower seed mixes all over North America, but its native range is thought to be primarily in Canada and the northwestern mountains. It is a short-lived perennial that reseeds well in its native area where soils are loose and summers are cool.

Other showy gaillardias worthy of cultivation are southern. **Firewheel** or **Indian blanket** (*Gaillardia*

Blanketflower

pulchella) is also frequently sold in seed mixes. It is an annual believed to be originally native from south-central Kansas to Mexico and from southwestern Arkansas to eastern New Mexico. **Fragrant gaillardia** (*Gaillardia suavis*) consists of a reddish sphere of disk flowers on a straight leafless stem. Although not visually showy, it can perfume a prairie or a house with its intensely sweet scent. It is native from south-central Kansas through central Oklahoma and the western two-thirds of Texas to northeastern New Mexico.

PRAIRIE RAGWORT (*Packera plattensis* [pah-KARE-ah plah-TEN-sis]), previously (*Senecio plattensis* [suh-NEE-see-o]), is a short-lived cool season forb. Ragworts usually are characterized by a basal rosette

Prairie ragwort

of leaves, several slender stems, and a profusion of tiny yellow daisies that turn into white fluffy seeds. There are almost as many warm season ragworts as cool season ragworts. Most ragworts are short-lived perennials, but some are annuals and some are long-lived, and there seems to be one for every prairie and savanna habitat. Prairie ragwort is native to little bluestem prairies.

ENGELMANN DAISY (*Engelmannia peristenia* [ing-gull-MONN-ee-ah pear-iss-TEN-ee-ah]), known since 1840 as *Engelmannia pinnatifida*, is the only species in its genus. A long-lived perennial with a stout taproot, it is native to prairies in the southern Great Plains and to

the Blackland Prairie. The yellow ray flowers curl under during the heat of the day. This late-spring forb blooms dependably for several weeks every year, no matter what the weather.

Engelmann daisy

BLANKETFLOWER is now sold widely in wildflower seed mixes.

COOL SEASON FORBS

Species	NW Lowland prairie	NW Mesic prairie	NW Upland prairie	NW Sand prairie	NW Aspen parkland	NE Lowland prairie	NE Mesic prairie	NE Upland prairie	NE Bur oak savanna	NE Black oak savanna	SW Lowland prairie	SW Mesic prairie	SW Upland prairie	SW Sand prairie	SW Ponderosa savanna	SE Lowland prairie	SE Mesic prairie	SE Upland prairie	SE Bur oak savanna	SE Post oak savanna
BEAN FAMILY: SPRING																				
Sundial lupine							■			■										
Silvery lupine		■	■																	
Texas bluebonnet																	■			
Canadian milkvetch	■	■			■		■										■			■
Groundplum		■	■					■					■				■	■		■
American vetch		■	■					■		■	■	■								
Indian breadroot			■	■	■			■									■	■	■	
Prairie goldenbean		■	■	■	■															
BEAN FAMILY: EARLY SUMMER																				
White wild indigo						■	■	■								■	■			■
Blue wild indigo																	■		■	
Cream wild indigo						■	■	■								■	■			
Sweetbroom		■			■															
Sensitive brier												■	■			■	■	■		
Goat's rue							■	■									■			■
Purple locoweed				■	■						■	■		■			■			
ORCHID FAMILY																				
Large yellow ladyslipper	■					■	■				■					■				
Small white ladyslipper						■														
Grasspink						■										■				
Nodding ladies' tresses						■										■				
Great Plains ladies' tresses	■	■					■	■			■						■	■		
Slender ladies' tresses							■	■												■
LILY FAMILY																				
Wild hyacinth							■	■									■		■	
Death camas		■	■								■	■			■					
White camas	■	■		■		■														
Western red lily	■	■		■			■	■							■					
Michigan lily						■	■		■	■										
Sego lily		■		■											■					
Nodding onion				■			■	■							■					

Species	NORTHWEST Northern Plains Shortgrass Region					NORTHEAST Northern Tallgrass Prairie Region					SOUTHWEST Southern Plains Shortgrass Region					SOUTHEAST Southern Tallgrass Prairie Region				
	Lowland prairie	Mesic prairie	Upland prairie	Sand prairie	Aspen parkland	Lowland prairie	Mesic prairie	Upland prairie	Bur oak savanna	Black oak savanna	Lowland prairie	Mesic prairie	Upland prairie	Sand prairie	Ponderosa savanna	Lowland prairie	Mesic prairie	Upland prairie	Bur oak savanna	Post oak savanna
IRIS FAMILY																				
Blue-eyed grass	■					■		■												■
Mountain blue-eyed grass		■	■	■				■			■									
Southern blue-eyed grass																	■	■	■	■
White blue-eyed grass							■	■		■										■
Prairie celestial																	■	■	■	■
Blue flag						■										■				
Northern blue flag	■					■														
Western blue flag	■										■				■					
PRIMROSE FAMILY																				
Western shooting star	■			■		■					■				■					
Eastern shooting star							■	■	■	■							■	■	■	
Narrowleaf loosestrife							■	■												
Whorled loosestrife										■										
Fringed loosestrife	■					■										■				
EVENING PRIMROSE FAMILY																				
Missouri evening primrose																		■		
Pink evening primrose																	■			
Fragrant evening primrose			■									■			■					
Plains evening primrose		■		■				■				■						■		
Stenosiphon												■	■					■		
Scarlet gaura				■	■			■			■	■								
ROSE FAMILY																				
Prairie smoke		■	■					■												
Prairie cinquefoil	■	■						■	■	■										
Queen of the prairie						■														
American burnet						■	■													
Indian physic																				■
Wild strawberry	■			■		■	■		■	■					■		■		■	■
GERANIUM FAMILY																				
Sticky purple geranium		■		■											■					
Wild geranium									■	■										■

Species	NORTHWEST Northern Plains Shortgrass Region					NORTHEAST Northern Tallgrass Prairie Region					SOUTHWEST Southern Plains Shortgrass Region					SOUTHEAST Southern Tallgrass Prairie Region				
	Lowland prairie	Mesic prairie	Upland prairie	Sand prairie	Aspen parkland	Lowland prairie	Mesic prairie	Upland prairie	Bur oak savanna	Black oak savanna	Lowland prairie	Mesic prairie	Upland prairie	Sand prairie	Ponderosa savanna	Lowland prairie	Mesic prairie	Upland prairie	Bur oak savanna	Post oak savanna
MADDER FAMILY																				
Northern bedstraw	■	■				■	■	■												
Narrowleaf bluets												■		■			■			
CROWFOOT FAMILY																				
Tall meadowrue		■		■			■				■						■			
Pasque flower			■				■						■				■			
Meadow anemone	■					■					■							■		
Thimbleweed		■		■			■			■			■							
Prairie larkspur			■	■			■				■	■	■			■	■			■
PARSLEY FAMILY																				
Golden Alexanders						■	■		■	■						■				■
Heartleaf Alexanders	■	■		■																
Rattlesnake master							■	■									■			■
Eryngo																■	■			
Biscuitroot			■								■	■				■				
Prairie parsley							■					■					■	■	■	■
BORAGE FAMILY																				
Hoary puccoon			■			■	■	■									■			
Hairy puccoon										■										■
Fringed puccoon			■	■	■		■					■	■		■		■			
Marbleseed		■		■		■	■				■	■			■	■	■			
SAXIFRAGE FAMILY																				
Prairie alumroot		■	■			■	■	■												
Prairie rockstar		■		■																
BLUEBELL FAMILY																				
Harebell	■	■		■			■													
Tall bellflower	■			■			■	■												
Palespike lobelia		■				■	■	■	■						■			■		■
Great blue lobelia						■	■									■				
Cardinal flower						■					■					■				

COOL SEASON FORBS (cont'd)	NORTHWEST Northern Plains Shortgrass Region					NORTHEAST Northern Tallgrass Prairie Region					SOUTHWEST Southern Plains Shortgrass Region					SOUTHEAST Southern Tallgrass Prairie Region				
Species	Lowland prairie	Mesic prairie	Upland prairie	Sand prairie	Aspen parkland	Lowland prairie	Mesic prairie	Upland prairie	Bur oak savanna	Black oak savanna	Lowland prairie	Mesic prairie	Upland prairie	Sand prairie	Ponderosa savanna	Lowland prairie	Mesic prairie	Upland prairie	Bur oak savanna	Post oak savanna
SPIDERWORT FAMILY																				
Ohio spiderwort							■	■	■	■					■			■	■	
Western spiderwort			■	■								■	■	■					■	■
Bracted spiderwort							■	■												
DOGBANE FAMILY																				
Spreading dogbane				■				■	■						■					
Prairie dogbane	■	■				■	■	■				■				■	■			■
Texas bluestar												■	■					■		
FIGWORT FAMILY																				
Culver's root							■	■	■								■		■	■
Scarlet paintbrush																		■		
Indian paintbrush																		■		
Downy paintbrush			■					■					■							
Foxglove beardtongue								■												
Lilac beardtongue		■		■	■							■			■					
Purple gerardia						■										■				
Rough gerardia												■					■			
PHLOX FAMILY																				
Downy phlox							■	■	■	■							■	■	■	■
Marsh phlox						■	■									■				
Blue gilia												■	■							
FLAX FAMILY																				
Wild blue flax			■	■	■								■	■	■					
Stiffstem flax			■	■				■					■	■				■		
MALLOW FAMILY																				
Bush's poppy mallow																		■	■	■
Winecup		■	■					■				■	■					■		
Clustered poppy mallow								■		■										
Scarlet globemallow			■										■							
Glade mallow									■											

COOL SEASON FORBS (cont'd)

Species	NORTHWEST — Northern Plains Shortgrass Region					NORTHEAST — Northern Tallgrass Prairie Region					SOUTHWEST — Southern Plains Shortgrass Region					SOUTHEAST — Southern Tallgrass Prairie Region				
	Lowland prairie	Mesic prairie	Upland prairie	Sand prairie	Aspen parkland	Lowland prairie	Mesic prairie	Upland prairie	Bur oak savanna	Black oak savanna	Lowland prairie	Mesic prairie	Upland prairie	Sand prairie	Ponderosa savanna	Lowland prairie	Mesic prairie	Upland prairie	Bur oak savanna	Post oak savanna
ASTER FAMILY: SILVER LEAVES																				
Plains pussytoes			■									■			■					
Ladies' tobacco								■	■	■								■		■
Field pussytoes		■		■			■										■			
Louisiana sage		■		■			■						■				■	■		
Pasture sage		■	■	■										■						
Dwarf sagebrush			■	■							■				■					
ASTER FAMILY: SPRING WHITE COMPOSITES																				
Yarrow					■															
Philadelphia fleabane	■					■										■				
Tufted fleabane			■																	
Plains fleabane											■	■								
Poor Robin's plantain									■	■										
Daisy fleabane								■							■			■		■
ASTER FAMILY: SPRING DYCs																				
False dandelion		■									■		■							
Prairie dandelion			■					■				■								
Dwarf dandelion								■	■	■										■
Blanketflower			■																	
Firewheel												■		■			■	■		
Fragrant gaillardia												■					■			
Prairie ragwort		■						■			■	■			■	■	■	■	■	
Engelmann daisy											■	■	■			■	■			

Now the yellow and gold of the sunflower and the oxeye (false sunflower) intermingle with the purple of the button snakeroots and blazing stars. Many species of goldenrods occur, sometimes in great masses, and all add much beauty to the autumnal land-scape. Various rosinweeds dot the prairie where moisture is plentiful. Pleasing variety is added to the wealth of autumnal colors by the grayish-white flower of the false boneset, and the gray color of the sage, and the black fruiting heads of bush clover. Ironweed, gentians, tooth-leaved primrose, and many others are found. Numerous asters blossom from August until late fall, their colors varying from white or lavender to blue or purple.

J. E. WEAVER, North American Prairie

Warm Season Forbs

WARM SEASON FORBS bloom during that period after summer heats up and before the first frosts of autumn. Northern warm season forbs start flowering at midsummer, while southern ones start at the end of May or in early June. Some blossom for only a few days, but many are colorful for several weeks. For the most part, these flowers are taller than cool season forbs, as the grasses are high during this period, and the flowers must also grow tall to compete for sunlight.

In this chapter, the forbs are arranged according to bloom time, from summer to fall. So for a continuous display of color and nectar, choose at least one species from each group.

The mint family (Lamiaceae or Labiatae) is easy to identify. Look at a cross section of the stem, and you will see that it is four-sided, or square. Smell the leaves; they are aromatic. Plus, mints produce lots of nectar to attract butterflies, hummingbirds, hummingbird moths, and bees.

Rosemary, peppermint, and garden sage (*Salvia officinalis*) are European members of the mint family.

The variety of American mints is very rich. Besides the mints profiled in this chapter, you might want to experiment with native species of brazoria (*Brazoria*), savory (*Satureja*), skullcap (*Scutellaria*), betony (*Stachys*), germander (*Teucrium*), and giant hyssop (*Agastache*).

OHIO HORSEMINT (*Blephilia ciliata* [bluh-FEE-lee-ah sill-ee-A-tah]) is a knee-high perennial with fuzzy stems and lavender flowers. It grows on hill prairies or on shallow limestone soil from southeastern Kansas and eastern Oklahoma eastward. It can bloom under eastern red cedar (*Juniperus virginiana*).

Ohio horsemint

COMMON MOUNTAIN MINT (*Pycnanthemum virginianum* [pick-NAN-thuh-mum vur-jin-ee-A-num]) is a rhizomatous perennial that is aggressive at first and then settles down. Its narrow leaves are strongly aromatic. Waist-high, it is native to wet or mesic tallgrass prairies from southeastern North Dakota to central Oklahoma and eastward. In the north, it can also grow in dry prairies with little bluestem.

Common mountain mint

COMMON MOUNTAIN MINT has aromatic foliage and dainty snow white flowers that feed butterflies in midsummer.

WILD BERGAMOT (*Monarda fistulosa* [moe-NAR-dah fiss-tew-LOE-sah]) is a rhizomatous prairie and savanna perennial that grows with big bluestem. It has enormous regional variations. In the tallgrass region, it is likely to be waist-high

OHIO HORSEMINT lends a dash of vivid purple to prairies in that lull between spring and summer.

Wild bergamot

and lavender. In the Great Plains, it is downy, less than knee-high, and rosy purple. In the North, it is short-lived. In the South, it lives for decades. The Winnebago used bergamot tea to treat acne.

SPOTTED HORSEMINT (*Monarda punctata* [moe-NAR-dah punk-TAH-ta]) is an annual or short-lived perennial that grows in sand. Not showy at a distance, its combination of pastels in palest green, yellow, pink, and lavender with tiny purple spots is quite charming close up. In heavier soil, bright purple **lemon horsemint** (*Monarda citriodora*) grows on dry to mesic southern prairies with little bluestem or buffalograss.

Spotted horsemint

PITCHER SAGE (*Salvia azurea* var. *grandiflora* [SAL-vee-ah uh-ZUR-ee-ah variety gran-dee-FLORE-ah]) is a clump-forming perennial native to little bluestem prairies. It is believed by some botanists to be naturalized rather than native west of central Nebraska and east of central Illinois. Typically about 2 feet tall, it is a slender plant with bright sky blue flowers. From Konza Prairie southward, mealy blue sage (*Salvia farinacea*) becomes significant, and in Texas, most prairie gardeners will want to have at least two kinds of salvia in their prairie mix.

Pitcher sage

FALL OBEDIENT PLANT (*Physostegia virginiana* [fie-so-STEE-jee-ah vur-jin-ee-A-nah]) is a rhizomatous perennial found primarily in wet prairies and bur oak savannas in the tallgrass prairie region. Pink or lavender tubular flowers cluster stiffly up a chorus of straight stems. Other obedient plant species bloom in wet prairies from early to mid-spring.

WILD BERGAMOT has minty leaves and stems, and even its nectar—here visited by a hummingbird moth—smells and tastes like mint.

Fall obedient plant

The acanthus family (Acanthaceae) is large and centered in the tropics. Only a few members come north beyond Texas and the southwestern deserts, *Ruellia* being the only one important to our prairies and savannas. Most ruellias are lavender blue, although they tend to photograph pink, and occasionally white ones are found. The flowers are tubular and rich in nectar. These are short-lived perennials that can colonize slightly by roots but are more likely to seed out prolifically.

HAIRY RUELLIA (*Ruellia humilis* [roo-ELL-ee-ah HEW-mih-liss]) got its name from its fuzzy stems and leaves. Usually ankle-height, it can reach 2 feet, but when that happens, the stems tend to fall over unless they are held upright by grasses. The trumpetlike flowers open in the morning. After pollination and when the sun gets hot, the petals gently slide off, leaving the sexual parts intact. Hairy ruellia is native to little bluestem and shortgrass prairies throughout the southern tallgrass prairie region. It is endangered in Wisconsin and is native to only one county in eastern Minnesota. In the western and southern edges of its range, it is found as often in sunny woodlands as in prairies.

Hairy ruellia

LIMESTONE RUELLIA (*Ruellia strepens* [roo-ELL-ee-ah STRAY-pens]), similar in appearance to hairy ruellia, grows in bur oak savannas in tallgrass areas from Pennsylvania to southeastern Nebraska and southward to Texas.

VIOLET RUELLIA (*Ruellia nudiflora* [roo-ELL-ee-ah nu-dee-FLORE-ah]) far outnumbers hairy ruellia in the Blackland Prairie of Texas and southward into little bluestem savannas and buffalograss prairies.

HAIRY RUELLIA, also called wild petunia, blooms in shortgrass prairies through blazingly hot summers.

The verbena family (Verbenaceae), a southern family that includes vitex and lantana, attracts lots of bees and butterflies.

The verbenas themselves have been divided into *Verbena* and the nasty-sounding name *Glandularia*, which I have resisted using until now. The verbenas are the herbs with tall, skinny spikes of blue, purple, pink, or white flowers, and the glandularias are the spreading showy flowers that gardeners *know* as verbena. And if that is not enough to confuse you, botanists like to call all of them vervain. As a group, they tend to be short-lived perennials with hairy aromatic leaves and lavender, pink, or blue flowers.

Hoary vervain

HOARY VERVAIN (*Verbena stricta* [ver-BEE-nah STRICK-tah]) looks different from blue vervain in that its leaves are mostly attached to the stem without a stalk and never have two side lobes at the point of attachment. Also, the leaves are more likely to be so hairy that they look grayish, or "hoary." Hoary vervain is native primarily to dry prairies and disturbed areas. It blooms slightly later than blue vervain.

BLUE VERVAIN grows in wet tallgrass prairies and looks very similar to drought-tolerant hoary vervain.

Blue vervain

BLUE VERVAIN (*Verbena hastata* [ver-BEE-nah has-TAH-ta]) was called "medicine" by the Lakota, Omaha, and Ponca. Small amounts of the leaves, flowers, or roots were used for various illnesses, including stomachaches, colds, bladder infections, insomnia, and nosebleeds. It is native to cordgrass and cattail prairies over most of North America, but it is uncommon in the southern Great Plains and Texas.

Dakota vervain

DAKOTA VERVAIN (*Glandularia bipinnatifida* [glan-due-LAR-ee-ah bye-pin-uh-TIFF-uh-dah]) is also

known as prairie verbena. It greens up after Christmas if not covered by snow. The stems sprawl to make a showy mound of purple flowers. This is a shortgrass prairie forb that grows in scanty buffalograss or grama grass prairies, or in rocky places where it gets little competition and superb drainage.

Legumes, or bean family forbs (Fabaceae), are important because mycorrhizae on their roots enrich poor sandy or rocky soil, their flowers supply nectar, and their beans or peas provide food for birds and mammals.

Only the most widely used or commonly seen summer legumes have been chosen here. Once you learn to identify these plants, you can seek out related species native in your immediate area to add to your garden.

Watch out for non-native agricultural lespedezas that are escaping and becoming weedy, particularly Japanese lespedeza (*Kummerowia striata*) and Chinese bushclover (*Lespedeza cuneata*).

LEADPLANT (*Amorpha canescens* [ah-MOR-fah kah-NESS-sens]) has felty gray leaves that are so yummy that in pastures it is literally eaten to death. Although a small thicket shrub, it acts like a forb and is most often seen as a single plant dotted here and there across a prairie. Usually about 2 feet tall, it can reach twice that height if the prairie has not been burned or grazed for many years. Although leadplant looks like

LEADPLANT is a true shrub adapted to the fire cycles of dry and mesic tallgrass prairies.

a desert shrub, it requires a fair amount of moisture and is happiest in mesic prairies with big bluestem, Culver's root, and wild quinine. It is uncommon in Missouri and Oklahoma, and in the Great Plains it is found only at elevations high enough to support pinyons. At the southern end of its range in Texas, it has "peculiar disjunct distribution" in sandy prairies in the Red Rolling Plains and post oak savannas.

Leadplant was called buffalo bellow plant by the Omaha and Ponca because it blooms when the bison are rutting. The Lakota call it bird's wood because birds find it the handiest thing to perch on in a treeless prairie. A powder of the dried leaves blown on a wound · promotes scabbing.

Leadplant

INDIGOBUSH (*Amorpha fruticosa* [ah-MOR-fah froo-tee-KOE-sah]) is usually a tall thicket shrub in creek-side woodlands, but it can also be found in lowland prairies with cord-

grass and Canada wildrye. Unlike leadplant, its leaves are green and can be either smooth or fuzzy.

Indigobush

DWARF WILD INDIGO (*Amorpha nana* [ah-MOR-fah NAN-ah]) is the most drought-tolerant of the three shrubby prairie amorphas. Native to dry prairies, it stands knee-high and has stiff, smooth leaves and fragrant spiky purple flowers.

Dwarf wild indigo

SHOWY TICK TREFOIL (*Desmodium canadense* [dez-MOE-dee-um kan-ah-DEN-see]) is a pretty slender perennial forb with rosy pink flowers. *Trefoil* literally means three leaves, which is a botanist's way of saying that each leaf is composed of three leaflets. The seeds attach themselves to clothing, and an old-fashioned name for the trefoils is beggar's lice. You definitely do not want to walk through scads of seeds in the autumn. Individual plants are scattered in healthy prairies and sandy savannas, but when disturbance occurs, this Band-Aid plant appears in quantity to restore nitrogen to the soil. Showy tick trefoil is found mostly in sandy or rocky prairies and savannas in the tallgrass regions.

ROUNDHEAD BUSHCLOVER, with its pale lime green heads, is more eye-catching in fruit than in flower.

Showy tick trefoil

ROUNDHEAD BUSHCLOVER (*Lespedeza capitata* [lez-puh-DEEZ-ah kap-ee-TA-tah]) is a striking plant because of its dense round heads that are velvety luna moth green. This stout-rooted perennial grows with both big bluestem and little bluestem, most often in dry sandy prairies and savannas. Although it is native along the Red River in north Texas, it is uncommon there.

Roundhead bushclover

SHOWY TICK TREFOIL has triangular seeds that stick like a tick to clothing and fur.

The prairie clovers (not to be confused with bushclovers) belong to a large genus in the bean family called *Dalea*. Sometimes the prairie clovers are separated out from the rest of the daleas and are called *Petalostemum* (peh-tuh-LOSS-tuh-mum) because they look so different. The other daleas have traditional bean flowers and seed pods, but the prairie clovers have such tiny flowers and pods, arranged on a spike or ball, that they do not even look beanlike.

Legumes are third in importance in a prairie, behind grasses and species of the aster family. J. E. Weaver found prairie clovers to rank third in abundance among the most prevalent legumes and found them to be among the top ten forbs in the prairies he studied. They are found most abundantly on well-drained sites where their blooms can easily out-top the grasses in midsummer. They can be used to identify high-quality prairie because they are found only on pastures that have never been overgrazed. They are so nutritious and delicious, they are among the first plants that cattle eat to extinction.

PURPLE PRAIRIE CLOVER

(*Dalea purpurea* [DAY-lee-ah pur-pur-REE-ah]) is a perennial forb that is most often found on dry prairies in tallgrass prairie territory. Its range extends from Canada to north Texas.

The flowers start blooming at the base of a thick spike while tiny buds are forming at the top. At the end of the flowering season, flowers are at the top, and seed in various stages of ripening can be seen at the bottom. Colors range from hot pink to magenta to purple, so these flowers get noticed, even though they are not very large. The leaves are divided into very narrow segments. Stems are knee-high when upright but often sprawl, especially in Canada and the northern states.

The tough root system is orange brown and 6 feet deep, and eventually gets woody at the base of the stems. Sometimes lateral branches

PURPLE PRAIRIE CLOVER adds new flowers at the top of the bloom spike while it ripens seed at the bottom.

Purple prairie clover

develop, hosting new upright stems. Purple prairie clover is at its showiest when growing in masses.

WHITE PRAIRIE CLOVER (*Dalea candida* [DAY-lee-ah kan-DEE-dah]) looks like purple prairie clover except for three things: its white flowers are not as showy, the plant stands a little taller or, in the West, tends to sprawl, and the leaflets are slightly wider. It grows almost everywhere purple prairie clover does and has the added bonus of being more tolerant of clay and drought.

White prairie clover

Roundhead prairie clover

ROUNDHEAD PRAIRIE CLOVER has a dainty, perky quality.

ROUNDHEAD PRAIRIE CLOVER (*Dalea multiflora* [DAY-lee-ah mul-tee-FLORE-ah]) has small round heads of flowers and a bushy growth habit. It is usually only a foot tall with extremely narrow leaflets. Once abundant, it is native to dry rocky prairies, often where the limestone is exposed, in southeastern Nebraska, eastern Kansas, western Missouri, central Oklahoma, and central Texas. (The one herbarium specimen in Colorado came from some out-of-state seed.) It often grows with white prairie clover and is marginally less drought-tolerant and a lot less cold-tolerant.

By late summer, the dark dramatic seed heads of bean family members are as significant as flowers to the appearance of the prairie garden.

ILLINOIS BUNDLEFLOWER (*Desmanthus illinoensis* [dez-MAN-thus ill-ee-noe-EN-sis]) is native to big bluestem prairies. It is prevalent, however, only in southern tallgrass

Illinois bundleflower

prairies. A member of a tropical prairie genus, Illinois bundleflower is the only *Desmanthus* that grows north of Kansas. The leaves are ferny, and the genus is sometimes grouped with mimosas and acacias. The flowers are white fluffy balls, similar to but larger than those of roundhead prairie clover. A tall gangling perennial, this is an excellent pioneer plant because it grows readily from seed and does not mind disturbed soil. Commercial seed is available for range revegetation programs. As an herb, Illinois bundleflower contains antibacterial properties.

Wild licorice

WILD LICORICE (*Glycyrrhiza lepidota* [gly-sir-RYE-zah leh-pee-DOE-tah]) is the only species of licorice in North America. Although it blooms in the spring, it is not noticeable until fall when it forms its rich brown seeds that are spindle-shaped burs. This is a wet prairie plant readily found only on the Great Plains. The shoots are scattered, spaced a couple of feet apart, and although Weaver found that the roots go 16 feet deep, wild licorice does not invade dry prairie.

WILD LICORICE is more noticeable in seed than in flower.

The roots were a staple for Native Americans such as the Pawnee. Lewis and Clark reported that wild licorice tasted somewhat like sweet potatoes, but later naturalists have found them to be bitter. This plant spreads so quickly and vigorously by root that it seems a good idea to eat most of the crop each year.

PARTRIDGE PEA (*Chamaecrista fasciculata* [kam-ee-KRISS-ta fah-sick-u-LA-tah]) is an annual pioneer plant that comes in to mend the soil after disturbance. Like many other pioneer annuals, its seed can apparently lie dormant for decades or even centuries. It is common on bare sandy sites and sandy prairies,

ILLINOIS BUNDLEFLOWER has ram's horn seed pods that rattle in the wind from late fall until the following spring.

either very moist or dry. What partridge pea does not like is clay and competition. It is very showy with bright translucent yellow petals splashed with red. Through the hottest part of the summer, the flowers open every morning. In the afternoon the flowers wither, and the leaves close up to conserve moisture.

Partridge pea used to be a *Cassia*, but all the North American *Cassia* species have been split into either *Chamaecrista* or *Senna*.

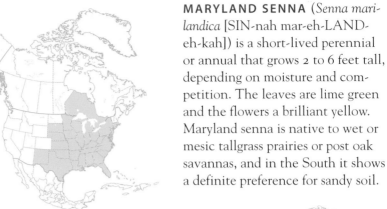

Partridge pea

MARYLAND SENNA (*Senna marilandica* [SIN-nah mar-eh-LAND-eh-kah]) is a short-lived perennial or annual that grows 2 to 6 feet tall, depending on moisture and competition. The leaves are lime green and the flowers a brilliant yellow. Maryland senna is native to wet or mesic tallgrass prairies or post oak savannas, and in the South it shows a definite preference for sandy soil.

Maryland senna

PARTRIDGE PEA is a pioneer annual that enriches disturbed soil so that long-term perennial prairie species can get a start.

The spurge family (Euphorbiaceae) includes several strange-looking plants, like doveweed (*Croton*), three-seeded mercury (*Acalypha*), and queen's delight (*Stillingia*), plus undesirables like bullnettle (*Cnidoscolus*) and noseburn (*Tragia*). Many members of the spurge family have sticky milky sap. One of the best known is the Christmas poinsettia, which is native to tropical Mexico. The sap of *Hevia brasiliensis*, native to the Amazon Basin, is tapped for latex.

The important genus for prairies is *Euphorbia*. Most of our native prairie euphorbias tend to be annuals or weedy, but a few are worth planting on purpose. Flowering spurge is our most conservative native prairie euphorbia.

Then there is the terrible leafy spurge (*Euphorbia esula*), which is native to Eurasia but is making a pest of itself in the northern Great Plains, spreading east and south, wrecking ranchland and prairies wherever it goes. Plus, there are a few other non-native euphorbias that are not adding to the quality of our roadsides and prairies.

FLOWERING SPURGE is one of the top ten most important forbs in many midwestern tallgrass prairies.

Flowering spurge

FLOWERING SPURGE (*Euphorbia corollata* [yew-FORE-bee-ah kor-o-LATE-ah]) has a deep perennial root and is native to mesic bluestem prairies and upland prairies—sometimes rocky ones—with prairie dropseed and porcupine grass. The bracts surrounding its tiny flowers look like five pure white petals. The flowers are arranged on five slender stalks that radiate from a circle of five leaves. Overall height is 2 to 3 feet.

Flowering spurge is native throughout almost the whole tallgrass region but is rare north of Iowa and southeastern Nebraska. In the South, it is scanty in the Blackland Prairie of Texas, where it goes no further south than Dallas County, and in the post oak woodlands of eastern Texas. If it becomes drought-stressed, it often jettisons its leaves to conserve enough moisture so it can flower.

SNOW-ON-THE-MOUNTAIN
(*Euphorbia marginata* [yew-FORE-bee-ah mar-juh-NA-tah]) is believed to be naturalized east of a line from southern Minnesota to northwestern Missouri to West Texas, and also naturalized west of Montana and New Mexico. This weedy annual does not get over 3 feet tall and seeks low ground and stock ponds in the Great Plains, although it is found on dry prairies to the north and east where there is more rainfall or less evaporation. The white and green striped leaves surrounding the tiny flowers are very pretty, and masses of this plant are extremely ornamental.

Fire-on-the-mountain

FIRE-ON-THE-MOUNTAIN
(*Euphorbia cyathophora* [yew-FORE-bee-ah sye-ath-o-FORE-ah]), also called painted euphorbia or wild poinsettia, has splashes of bright red orange on the long leafy bracts surrounding its flowers. It has charm, but is far less flashy than the Christmas poinsettia. Generally only 1 foot or so tall, it can reach 3 feet. It appears on its own in disturbed ground in sun or light shade. Its original native range may have been the southern tallgrass region. Swink and Wilhelm consider it to be non-native to the Chicago area.

Snow-on-the-mountain

SNOW-ON-THE MOUNTAIN holds its tiny white flowers above a ruff of ornamental white leaves.

The milkweeds (Asclepiadaceae) are numerous in prairies and savannas, most sites having at least one species and some two or three. Here are profiled a few of the green milkweeds, some of the white ones, and our only orange milkweed.

Milkweed flowers are in umbels or balls. Each flower has a stiff crown of five parts that stand upright and are called hoods. Below that are stiff lobes that curve downward like a skirt, except in antelope horns and spider milkweed (*Asclepias viridis*) where they curve upward.

When ripe, their seed pods split open to release the tightly packed seed. Each seed has a silky parachute of silvery fluff that wafts it on the wind to a new location far from the mother plant.

Milkweed leaves are entire, which means not divided into leaflets or lobes, but after that distinction, there is considerable variation. At one extreme is common milkweed, with its big fat leathery smooth leaves that go up the stem in twos facing each other. Very different is whorled milkweed, which has thready leaves that whorl around the stem in an ascending spiral like field horsetail.

ANTELOPE HORNS (*Asclepias asperula* [az-KLEE-pea-as as-puh-RULE-ah]) is the main milkweed for the southern Great Plains and is also found in dry prairies on the western edge of the southern tallgrass area. Usually closer to ankle-high than knee-high, it has large dense upright heads of pale green flowers marked with white and dark purple. The flowers bloom anytime from spring to fall, depending on when it rains. The "horns" are the seedpods.

Antelope horns

GREEN MILKWEED (*Asclepias viridiflora* [az-KLEE-pea-as vuh-rid-ee-FLORE-ah]), usually a foot tall, is the most important shortgrass prairie milkweed for the northern Great Plains and for upland prairies in the northern tallgrass region. The seedpods look like those of

GREEN MILKWEED has intricate green flowers that mature into slender hornlike pods packed with seed and milkweed fluff.

BUTTERFLY MILKWEED is a popular nectar plant for butterflies.

liant orange red to yellow flowers that attract scads of butterflies. A favorite in the nursery trade, it seems to prefer well-drained mesic prairies and sandy savannas from New Hampshire to Minnesota to north Texas. Its native range then pretty much skips over the Great Plains, except in Texas, and resumes (scantily) in the foothills of the southern Rocky Mountains.

Butterfly milkweed

DWARF MILKWEED (*Asclepias ovalifolia* [az-KLEE-pea-as o-vall-ee-FOLE-ee-ah]) is uncommon nowadays, but when found, it is usually in rich moist soil in partial shade. It seems likely that its main habitat used to be aspen or bur oak savanna. It grows only 8 to 20 inches tall, and its leaves are oval.

Dwarf milkweed

antelope horns, but the flowers of green milkweed look quite different. The flowers have on tight skirts, and they hang their heads, so that the whole cluster looks like a short thick tassel. The leaves are large and leathery with prominent netted veining and wavy edges.

Green milkweed

BUTTERFLY MILKWEED (*Asclepias tuberosa* [az-KLEE-pea-as tue-ber-ROSE-ah]) is a long-lived, low-growing, tidy plant with bril-

WHORLED MILKWEED (*Asclepias verticillata* [az-KLEE-pea-as ver-tiss-uh-LA-tah]), considered weedy in the Chicago area, is more appreciated to the west and south, where on little bluestem prairies it displays masses of delicate white flowers. It is rarely drought-tolerant enough for shortgrass prairies on the Great Plains. In Texas, it is native primarily to post oak savannas.

Whorled milkweed

POKE MILKWEED (*Asclepias exaltata* [az-KLEE-pea-as ex-all-TA-tah]) has white hoods and green skirts, and the flowers cascade down from the high center of the umbel on long pale peach stems. This milkweed is native to bur oak savannas. Swink and Wilhelm, in *Plants of the Chicago Region*, observe that some years it is not in evidence, only to show up in masses another year.

Poke milkweed

The nectar of most milkweeds is a favorite with butterflies, but only monarch butterflies use the milkweeds as a larval plant, as the white sap is poisonous to most other creatures. The mother butterfly lays her eggs on a milkweed so that the baby caterpillars will eat the foliage and milky sap. The sap makes them taste so awful that birds and other predators have been conditioned to give them a wide berth.

Despite the poisonous white sap, the purple milkweeds, especially common milkweed and showy milkweed, were eaten by Native Americans. They ate the young asparagus-like shoots, as well as the buds and blossoms and the young green seedpods. All were boiled before being eaten, and the water had to be changed two or three times to get rid of the bitter-tasting toxins. The roots, also toxic, were used to make medicinal teas, and modern research has shown them to have cardiac, antibiotic, and cancer-fighting benefits.

PURPLE MILKWEED (*Asclepias purpurascens* [az-KLEE-pea-as pur-pur-RASS-sins]) has big clusters of purple flowers and is found in moist tallgrass prairies with big bluestem, or in drier oak savannas or thickets. It accepts either sand or limestone soils. It is most prevalent in Illinois and Missouri. Its large firm leaves have a pink midvein, and its stems grow 2 to 3 feet tall.

Purple milkweed

SWAMP MILKWEED (*Asclepias incarnata* [az-KLEE-pea-as in-kar-NATE-ah]) is primarily a wet tallgrass prairie plant, and it can reach 6 feet tall. It looks similar to purple milkweed, except that the leaves are narrower. Although most botanists refer to its color as red, it always looks dark pink to me.

Native to marshes, it is more common north of the 39th parallel

PURPLE MILKWEED is both a host plant and a source of nectar for fritillaries and other butterflies.

Swamp milkweed

or at high elevations, such as along streams in ponderosa savanna. In the Chicago area, where it is abundant, it grows with common boneset as well as blue flag, blue vervain, bluejoint, and common cattail.

SHOWY MILKWEED (*Asclepias speciosa* [az-KLEE-pea-as spee-see-O-sah]), native to moist or wet prairies in the Great Plains, is the most western of the tall pink milkweeds. Ironically, it is the least showy. Like purple and swamp milkweeds, it has large balls of pinkish flowers, but they are too pale to be showy. However, they are fragrant. A. C. Budd reports in *Budd's Flora of the Canadian Prairie Provinces* that both he and the insects would feel sleepy after inhaling the nectar. The leaves are felty underneath, and the seedpods are densely woolly white.

Sullivant's milkweed

SULLIVANT'S MILKWEED (*Asclepias sullivantii* [az-KLEE-pea-as sul-lee-VAN-tee-eye]) is often called prairie milkweed, as it is native to high-quality northern tallgrass mesic prairies. It is also called smooth milkweed because of its smooth hairless leaves that are bright yellow green with a vibrant and broad red vein down the center. The flowers are purplish pink with touches of white or pale pink. Sullivant's milkweed is uncommon north of Iowa and east of Illinois.

COMMON MILKWEED (*Asclepias syriaca* [az-KLEE-pea-as sih-RYE-uh-kah]) is so common and weedy that you would not plant it on purpose. But if you live in its native range, it will most likely be the milkweed that introduces you to the genus. A coarse plant, it grows in disturbed areas on roadsides and in ditches, as well as in stable pastures. You would not call it unattractive, and the flowers *are* fragrant, so I would not weed it out unless you just have too many or it is outcompeting a more desirable plant. Despite its Latin name, it is not native to Syria.

Common milkweed

Showy milkweed

Three genera in the aster family (Asteraceae) are called coneflowers because the centers of these flowers form a cone (or column, or sphere, or just a rounded button). Instead of a yellow center, these coneflowers have a strong contrasting color, usually dark purplish brown. Basically, the petals (actually ray flowers) are colored pink or purple in the *Echinaceas*, and yellow in the *Ratibidas* and *Rudbeckias*. Of course, there are lots of confusing variations.

PURPLE CONEFLOWER (*Echinacea purpurea* [ek-uh-NAY-see-ah pur-PUR-ee-ah]) is in wildflower seed mixes and has cultivars in the nursery trade. It is rare in bur oak savannas in the Chicago area. In Missouri it is uncommon in mesic tallgrass prairies. It is naturalizing in moist sites around midwestern cities, but its native range is believed to have been east of the main prairie zone. This is the least drought-tolerant of our trio of purple coneflowers, and it has the broadest leaves.

Purple coneflower

PALE PURPLE CONEFLOWER (*Echinacea pallida* [ek-uh-NAY-see-ah PALL-eh-dah]) ranges from purplish pink to white and is usually paler in the South. Its long narrow ray flowers flutter downward like a hula skirt, and its pollen is creamy white, *not yellow*. Pale purple coneflower is native to mesic or semidry tallgrass prairies, oak savannas, and limestone glades.

BLACK SAMPSON (*Echinacea angustifolia* [ek-uh-NAY-see-ah an-gus-tee-FOLE-ee-ah]), the most drought-tolerant of the three purple coneflowers, is native to the Blackland Prairie and to mesic prairies on the Great Plains. Its thick black root is supposed to make the most efficacious medicine. The flowers are typically composed of pale pink horizontal rays. The narrow leaves range from green to woolly gray.

Black Sampson

GRAYHEAD CONEFLOWER (*Ratibida pinnata* [ruh-TIB-uh-dah pin-NAH-tah]) is very common in the dry prairies of the northeastern tallgrass region, especially in the early stages of a newly planted prairie. Four feet tall, it blooms along with

Pale purple coneflower

PALE PURPLE CONEFLOWER has narrow pale pink petals that droop beneath the round rosy cone.

GRAYHEAD CONEFLOWER has yellow petals at the bottom and ripening seeds at the top, and the two get progressively farther apart as the bloom time continues, until all the petals drop, and a very long skinny gray cone of ripe seed is left.

the silphiums, and the two together can turn a prairie garden bright yellow.

Grayhead coneflower

Mexican hat

MEXICAN HAT (*Ratibida columnifera* [ruh-TIB-uh-dah kollum-NIFF-er-ah]) is a knee-high short-lived perennial that sometimes behaves like an annual. Probably originally native to dry tallgrass and shortgrass prairies in the Great Plains, it is extremely drought-tolerant because its leaves are divided into skinny segments that allow very little moisture to evaporate. In western Canada, the flowers are normally all yellow, while in Texas and New Mexico, orange, red, or maroon markings predominate.

SWEET BLACKEYED SUSAN (*Rudbeckia subtomentosa* [rude-BECK-ee-ah sub-toe-men-TOE-sah]) is native where moist sandy prairies meet oak savannas. The common **blackeyed Susan** (*Rudbeckia hirta*) is a short-lived perennial pioneer species found in both degraded and high-quality mesic and dry prairies, as well as in bur oak and post oak savannas. Both provide nectar for butterflies.

Sweet blackeyed Susan

SWEET BLACKEYED SUSAN gets twice as tall as common blackeyed Susan, and some of its leaves are deeply divided into three lobes.

Summer yellow composites are in abundance everywhere. This chapter catches just the most important ones that are not profiled under cone-flowers, rosinweeds, sunflowers, and goldenrods.

FINGER COREOPSIS (*Coreopsis palmata* [koe-ree-OP-sis palm-A-tah]) has a leaf that looks like it has three skinny fingers. Two such leaves clasp either side of the stem at intervals but stop short of shadowing the pale yellow flowers with yellow centers. About knee-high, finger coreopsis, sometimes called prairie coreopsis, blooms in mid-summer in Wisconsin and earlier in Arkansas. This perennial forb is native to sandy prairies, rocky ridges, and sandy savannas in tall-grass regions.

FINGER COREOPSIS has green centers when the disc flowers are in bud.

with yellow centers, and the large toothed leaves bow out in a yoke shape opposite each other on the flower stalk.

Finger coreopsis

Oxeye sunflower

Sneezeweed

OXEYE SUNFLOWER (*Heliopsis helianthoides* [hee-lee-OP-sis hee-lee-an-THOY-deez]) is a boon to newly planted northern tallgrass prairies because it blooms all summer. In the western and southern parts of its range, that is, western Canada, the eastern Great Plains, the Sangre de Cristos, Oklahoma, and east Texas, it is pretty rare and likely to be found only in moist sand. The flowers are dark yellow

SNEEZEWEED (*Helenium autumnale* [heh-LYNN-ee-um aw-tum-NAWL-ee]) is a fall-blooming perennial forb native to wet prairies. It is uncommon in the western Great Plains, where other *Helenium* species are more prevalent. Despite the name, sneezeweed is unlikely to cause people to sneeze.

Like other gaudy flowers, it has heavy pollen that is not airborne but transported from flower to flower by insects.

HAIRY GOLDENASTER (*Heterotheca villosa* [heh-ter-o-THEE-kah vil-LOE-sah]) makes a low gray-leaved mound covered with quarter-sized bright yellow flowers that quickly turn to seed-laden puffballs. It is frequently lumped with *Heterotheca camporum* and *Heterotheca*

Hairy goldenaster

HAIRY GOLDENASTER, ankle-high, makes a mound of gold for six to eight weeks.

canescens under *Chrysopsis villosa.* These desirable forbs, all called hairy goldenaster, are perennial tap-rooted herbs that are native to dry or sandy prairies throughout the Great Plains and tallgrass regions.

SNEEZEWEED has spherical yellow centers and triangular yellow rays that do not overlap where they attach. Note the three scallops at the tip of each ray, which indicate that three petals are fused together.

Navajo tea

NAVAJO TEA (*Thelesperma mega-potamicum* [thell-iss-SPUR-mah meg-uh-poe-TAM-ee-kum]) has slender blue green stems, about 2 feet tall, that are sparsely covered with thready leaves. The stems and leaves make a delicious piney-tasting tea called cota. Atop each stem is a bright yellow flower that has no rays or petals. The flowers are larger and prettier than you might suppose, and there may be up to a hundred per plant. Navajo tea is believed to be native to dry prairies in the southern two-thirds of the Great Plains down into central Texas.

COWPEN DAISY (*Verbesina ence-lioides* [vur-bee-SINE-ah en-sill-ee-OY-deez]) is the equivalent to oxeye sunflower for dry southern prairies. This pioneer annual quickly covers bare disturbed ground and prepares the way for the long-lived perennial forbs and grasses. Native to the southern Great Plains and central Texas, it has naturalized elsewhere. About knee- to waist-high, the pale blue green leaves are triangular, and they alternate up the stout stems. The 2-inch flowers are in loose bouquets.

Cowpen daisy

The silphiums are the stars of northern tallgrass prairies. These giant forbs live for decades and hold their own with big bluestem, prairie dropseed, and switchgrass because they have thick swollen roots that penetrate to depths of 14 feet.

The easiest way to tell one silphium from another is by their leaves. Compass plant has stiff lacy leaves. Prairie dock has huge basal leaves. Rosinweed has stiff oval leaves that clasp the flower stalk in pairs. Cup plant has leaves that join so completely around the stem that they create little cups.

PRAIRIE DOCK (*Silphium terebinthinaceum* [SIL-fee-um tare-ree-bin-thuh-NAY-see-um]), unlike the other prairie silphiums, has a taproot and is not rhizomatous. Unlike the others, it has smooth, slender, almost leafless stems and a rosette of dramatically gigantic leaves. Native to deep loamy prairies, it can also grow in rocky sites. Prairie dock is most common in Illinois and Wisconsin.

Prairie dock

COMPASS PLANT (*Silphium laciniatum* [SIL-fee-um lah-sin-ee-A-tum]) is fairly ubiquitous in mesic tallgrass prairies. The rough, tough stem splits with the weight of the flowers and oozes a gummy sap that children use for chewing gum. The plant gets its name because its rigid sandpapery divided leaves are aligned on a north-south axis, so they are broadside to the sun morning and evening, and on edge at midday, maximizing photosynthesis and minimizing evaporation.

COMPASS PLANT is the silphium with stiff, deeply divided leaves that arrange themselves in relation to the sun.

PRAIRIE DOCK in bloom may stand well over 6 feet tall.

Compass plant

CUP PLANT (*Silphium perfoliatum* [SIL-fee-um pur-fole-ee-A-tum]) was called "weed that holds water" by the Winnebago, and the Omaha called it "weed with angled stem" because it has a square stem like the mint family. The roots were used by the Mesquakies for morning sickness and to reduce profuse menstruation. Cup plant is the most moisture-loving of the silphiums, native to lowland prairies and the edges of wet woodlands.

Cup plant

ROSINWEED (*Silphium integrifolium* [SIL-fee-um in-teg-ree-FOLE-ee-um]) has pale yellow flowers and oval leaves that feel like sandpaper, although occasionally some are velvety. Rosinweed is presently divided into five distinct varieties, and all of them interbreed with other rosinweed-like silphiums. The result is a rosinweed for nearly every tallgrass habitat and oak savanna. All rosinweeds are rhizomatous to some degree, and some are rampant until they are held in check by grasses.

Roughstem rosinweed

ROUGHSTEM ROSINWEED (*Silphium radula* [SIL-fee-um RAD-u-lah]) is probably just the southern version of rosinweed, as the difference seems to be that its stems and leaves are hairier. It is the chief rosinweed throughout tallgrass and mixed grass prairies in Oklahoma and Texas.

WHITE ROSINWEED (*Silphium albiflorum* [SIL-fee-um al-beh-FLORE-um]) looks like a compass plant with albino flowers. Both the ray flowers and the disc flowers are

Rosinweed

White rosinweed

white. This coarse but handsome forb is endemic to central Texas. Seldom over 3 feet tall, it grows in caliche or in deep black loam.

CUP PLANT can hold rainwater in the cups that are formed when its leaves join together around the flower stalk. It is a treat to see birds sipping from these caches.

By now you are probably thinking that every flower in the aster family is some kind of daisy, but that is not true. Remember pussytoes and artemisias? There are also curious-looking members of the aster family that are important and highly visible in summer prairies.

COMMON IRONWEED (*Vernonia fasciculata* [vur-NOE-nee-ah fas-sick-u-LA-tah]) is a long-lived perennial with radiant purply pink flowers. Native to wet mesic prairies, common ironweed is not at all common except in the center of its range. **Western ironweed** (*Vernonia baldwinii*) is the common ironweed of southern tallgrass prairies, and **plains ironweed** (*Vernonia marginata*) is the basic ironweed of the southern Great Plains. All the ironweeds grow in wet to mesic prairies and bloom in that lull after the midsummer climax. All the ironweeds have rhizomes as "tough as iron," and story has it that the noise they made as they were cut by a steel plow was deafening.

WILD QUININE has rough leaves and airy clusters of numerous small balls of snow white flowers.

COMMON IRONWEED has large heads composed of many fluffy purple puffs.

Common ironweed

WILD QUININE (*Parthenium integrifolium* [par-THIN-ee-um in-teg-ree-FOLE-ee-um]) is a long-lived perennial native to mesic or dry tallgrass prairies and oak savannas from southeastern Minnesota to the northeastern corner of Texas. It grows in sand or clay, and usually the stems fan out from a thick taproot to form a tidy clump about waist-high. Wild quinine was used as a substitute for tropical quinine during World War I, and its rela-

Wild quinine

range. On its western edges, it is found almost exclusively in savannas. It has firm pale green leaves that are white on the undersides. **Prairie Indian plantain** (*Arnoglossum plantagineum*) is native to wet or mesic prairies from South Dakota to central Texas to Kentucky. Referred to as *Cacalia* (kah-KALE-ee-ah) in most books, the Indian plantains are rated highly, by Swink and Wilhelm, as indicators of high-quality undisturbed prairie.

Pale Indian plantain

tives in the Chihuahuan desert were used to make rubber during World War II.

PALE INDIAN PLANTAIN

(*Arnoglossum atriplicifolium* [ar-no-GLOSS-um ah-truh-pliss-ee-FOLE-ee-um]) is a very tall perennial native to mesic or dry prairies and savannas in the eastern tallgrass

GLAUCOUS WHITE LETTUCE

(*Prenanthes racemosa* [pre-NAN-theez ray-see-MOE-sah]) is plainly not a very catchy name. *Glaucous* is a botanical term meaning a filmy white see-through covering that can be rubbed off. This stuff is often found on plums. In this case, it is the leaves that are glaucous, making them pale bluish green. At ground level they are further adorned with a bright purple midrib. The stems are red, smooth, and spotted and contain a milky juice. The pollinator seems to be a beautiful iridescent green solitary bee. Glaucous white lettuce is found only in the highest-quality mesic to wettish prairies.

GLAUCOUS WHITE LETTUCE has pale pink flowers, shown here fully open, and furry purple buds that look like kitty toes.

Glaucous white lettuce

PALE INDIAN PLANTAIN bears giant clusters of pale green bracts that overshadow tiny white flowers.

The sunflowers, another genus in the aster family, are aggressive but they are also important prairie forbs. Several of the perennial sunflowers have rambunctious roots. In a flower garden, for example, you could harvest enough Jerusalem artichokes to feed the entire neighborhood and still barely contain the plant to a suitable amount. Sawtooth sunflower (*Helianthus grosseserratus*) is just as vigorous, making huge robust colonies in damp weedy spots throughout the tallgrass region. The competition of big bluestem, however, eventually reduces these sunflowers to ordinary looking prairie forbs.

The sunflowers got their name because the common annual sunflower (*Helianthus annuus*) faces the sun from sunrise to sunset, doing a quick turnaround each dawn. It has been farmed at least since 5800 B.C. along the Missouri River. Native Americans ground the seeds to make bread.

WESTERN SUNFLOWER

(*Helianthus occidentalis* [hee-lee-AN-thus ox-see-den-TAL-iss]) grows no farther west than the easternmost edges of Minnesota and Texas; the early nineteenth-century botanists who named it thought Pennsylvania was "The West." It tolerates very little competition, so it prefers dry poor-soiled prairies. In the Chicago region, it grows with Indiangrass and porcupine grass in sandy prairies, and with little bluestem and prairie dropseed on hill prairies.

Maximilian sunflower

show. Overall height ranges from chest-high to almost 6 feet. Maximilian sunflower has a wide range of habitats, from moist ditches to rocky hillsides and sandy banks.

Western sunflower

MAXIMILIAN SUNFLOWER

(*Helianthus maximiliani* [hee-lee-AN-thus max-eh-mil-ee-AN-ee]) is very distinctive. The leaves look like peach leaves, folded upward and curving downward. The big yellow flowers have flat yellow green centers and alternate up 2 to 3 feet of stem, making quite a

Willowleaf sunflower

WILLOWLEAF SUNFLOWER

(*Helianthus salicifolius* [hee-lee-AN-thus suh-liss-ee-FOLE-ee-us]) is native to rocky limestone prairies in the southern tallgrass region.

WESTERN SUNFLOWER, in the foreground, is the waist-high flower with yellow centers and "naked" stems.

A rhizomatous perennial, it insists on perfect drainage and not too much drought. The disc flowers are dark red.

PRAIRIE SUNFLOWER (*Helianthus pauciflorus* [hee-lee-AN-thus paw-see-FLORE-us]) is described in many books as stiff sunflower (*Helianthus rigidus*). This vastly widespread and important sunflower is rhizomatous, and in old prairies it may have fifty to a hundred stems per square yard. The flowers have yellow rays and dark red centers.

Prairie sunflower

DOWNY SUNFLOWER (*Helianthus mollis* [hee-lee-AN-thus MOLL-iss]) has oval downy leaves attached directly to a downy stem. They may look downy soft, but they are actually rough to the touch. It is also called ashy sunflower because the fuzz on the leaves makes them look pale gray green, as though rubbed in ashes. The flowers have large yellow centers. Downy sunflower is native to sandy northern tallgrass prairies

Downy sunflower

and post oak savannas. **Paleleaf sunflower** (*Helianthus strumosus*), native to oak savannas, requires more moisture than downy sunflower but does not limit itself to sand. **Pale sunflower** (*Helianthus decapetalus*) grows in moist remnant savannas that have been cleaned by fire. It is rhizomatous and can form dense colonies with the slightly more drought-tolerant **woodland sunflower** (*Helianthus divaricatus*).

JERUSALEM ARTICHOKE (*Helianthus tuberosus* [hee-lee-AN-thus tu-ber-O-sus]) has large coarse rough leaves, rough leafy stems, and clusters of flowers with spherical yellow centers. It grows in wet tall-grass prairies and moist savannas from Manitoba to north-central

Texas. Its exact native range is uncertain, as it has been cultivated for centuries. An old stand of Jerusalem artichoke that is root-bound may be knee-high, but new plantings are sure to be taller than a man.

Jerusalem artichoke

SUNFLOWERS differ more in their leaves than in their flowers. The delicate texture in front is willowleaf sunflower, and the arched and folded leaves in back are those of Maximilian sunflower.

The gentian family (Gentianaceae), with their assortment of Latin names, are important in high-quality North American prairies. Gentian family flowers are four or five petaled and united at the base to make a shape resembling a bottle, vase, or bowl. Colors are often dark deep royal purple or rich blue.

The roots of all the gentians are considered to be good for digestion and to stimulate appetite after illness.

Downy gentian

DOWNY GENTIAN, unlike most warm season forbs, is short. Here it is seen hiding in the shade of taller forbs and grasses.

DOWNY GENTIAN (*Gentiana puberulenta* [jen-chee-AH-na pew-ber-you-LEN-tah]) is a short-lived perennial native to mesic and dry prairies and savannas. It blooms just as bluestems and prairie dropseed start to turn autumn colors. The downy sepals, which are fused to the outside of the petals, are colored an unusual combination of iridescent purple and tarnished brass.

Bottle gentian

BOTTLE GENTIAN (*Gentiana andrewsii* [jen-chee-AH-na an-DREW-zee-eye]), also called closed gentian, has a bottle-shaped flower that never opens. It takes a very determined bumblebee to force his way in. Of course, some clever insects just eat a hole in the side. This perennial gentian seems to be the one most likely to bloom every year. It is native to wet or wet-mesic northern tallgrass prairies. **Cream gentian** (*Gentiana alba*) is sometimes called *Gentiana flavida*. Now rare or extinct, it once was native to mesic prairies and savannas from southeastern Minnesota to north-eastern Oklahoma to the Great Lakes to North Carolina.

STIFF GENTIAN (*Gentianella quinquefolia* [jen-chun-NELL-ah kwin-kee-FOLE-ee-ah]) is an annual. Compared to the *Gentianas*, it has smaller flowers but more of them. Each almost-closed flower stands stiffly erect. Colors range from light purple to cream. Stiff gentian grows in mesic prairies and savannas, especially where limestone occurs.

Stiff gentian

Catchfly gentian

Similar looking **northern gentian** (*Gentianella amarella*) is fairly common in mesic Canadian prairies and savannas.

FRINGED GENTIAN (*Gentianopsis crinita* [jen-chun-OP-sis kruh-NEE-tah]) is an annual found in wet northern prairies. Colors range from pale lavender to dark purple blue. There are four petals instead of five. The lower halves of the petals wrap around each other to form a vase shape, and the upper halves swirl out to make a wide fringed lip.

Fringed gentian

CATCHFLY GENTIAN (*Eustoma exaltatum* [yew-STOE-mah ex-all-TA-tum]) has large flowers, usually colored royal purple or lavender blue but sometimes pink or white. Several knee-high stems carry two to six flowers each. These annuals,

or short-lived perennials, usually grow in moist alkaline prairies but occasionally are found on seemingly dry rocky slopes. Catchfly gentian is currently an amalgamation of *Eustoma grandiflorum*, *Eustoma russellianum*, and *Eustoma exaltatum*.

ROSE GENTIAN (*Sabatia campestris* [suh-BAY-shuh kam-PESS-triss]), an annual, is also called meadow pink. The flowers open flat and range in color from deep rose pink to pale pink to (rarely) pure white. Bloom time is early, while the grasses are still short and newly green. Rose gentian is native primarily to sandy prairies and post oak savannas.

Rose gentian

CREAM GENTIAN looks like bottle gentian except that it is the color of rich cream instead of royal purple.

Members of the genus *Liatris* are called blazing star in Chicago, gay-feather in Fort Worth, and button snakeroot in Lincoln. When I first heard the name blazing star, I tried to figure it out. Was the tip the star and the rest of the spike the tail on a falling star? This description fits for those pale blazing stars found in sandy eastern savannas. Gayfeather is easy if you consider purplish pink a cheerful color and look at those *Liatris* composed of a continuous feathery cluster of flowers. Button snakeroot is memorable after you have seen *Liatris aspera*, with its separate buttons of flowers. (Snakeroot seems to have been a common name for any slender plant with its flowers on a spike.)

Instead of rhizomes, each *Liatris* has a corm or tuber that can live three decades or so. To get a mass planting, leave the seed stalks uncut all winter to let them self-sow. Cold stratification seems to aid germination.

BUTTON SNAKEROOT has separate buttons of flowers dotted up the stalk. Note that new flowers are forming at the top of the spike.

Button Blazing Stars

BUTTON SNAKEROOT (*Liatris aspera* [lee-A-triss ASS-per-ah]), also called rough blazing star, grows in little bluestem prairies in the tall-grass region. The midwestern prairie forb called *Liatris scariosa* by J. E. Weaver is now *Liatris aspera*.

Meadow blazing star

MEADOW BLAZING STAR (*Liatris ligulistylis* [lee-A-triss lih-gue-lee-STY-liss]) looks similar to button snakeroot, but the terminal button is large and jagged, and the bright green leaves have a white midrib. Meadow blazing star is native to sloughs, sand hills, and moist parklands.

SAVANNA BLAZING STAR (*Liatris scariosa* var. *nieuwlandii* [lee-A-triss skare-ee-O-sah variety new-LAND-ee-eye]) looks different from button snakeroot in that its bracts are un-puckered and narrow. It grows in bur oak and white oak savannas.

Button snakeroot

Savanna blazing star

Dotted gayfeather

Feathery Blazing Stars

DOTTED GAYFEATHER
(*Liatris punctata* [lee-A-triss punk-TAH-tah]) has microscopic dots on the undersides of its leaves. Even easier to recognize are the narrow horizontal leaves in the flowering

In masses, PRAIRIE BLAZING STAR is quite a sight.

spike. Dotted gayfeather is the most drought-tolerant of the gayfeathers. Roots go down 7 feet in clay and 16 feet in sand.

PRAIRIE BLAZING STAR (*Liatris pycnostachya* [lee-A-triss pick-no-STAY-kee-ah]) is the main blazing star for dry-mesic to wet-mesic northern tallgrass prairies. Near the Gulf of Mexico, it is called cattail gayfeather because it grows with cattails. The upper leaves are narrow and stand out from the stem like ribs on a fish's spine. Prairie

blazing star can get as tall as 5 feet. Similar looking with more easterly distribution is marsh blazing star (*Liatris spicata*).

TEXAS GAYFEATHER (*Liatris mucronata* [lee-A-triss moo-kro-NAH-tah]) is closely related to dotted gayfeather but lacks the leafy spikes, looking generally more like prairie blazing star. It must have well-drained soil, and it loves limestone and caliche.

DOTTED GAYFEATHER has skinny stiff leaves interspersed between the flowers. From a distance, it looks as spectacular as prairie blazing star.

Prairie blazing star

Texas gayfeather

Bonesets, in case you were wondering, have nothing to do with mending broken tibias. But common boneset does have important medicinal uses. About 1790, a flu swept through the United States that caused such severe pain in the bones, it was called breakbone fever. Supposedly, *Eupatorium perfoliatum* proved effective at breaking this fever and alleviating this pain, but instead of calling it "feverbreak," people inexplicably named it boneset.

So, as a remedy for flu, common boneset was used by all the early settlers. A tea was made of the leaves, and the stronger the tea, the more effective it was at producing perspiration or "raising phlegm from the lungs." This concoction tasted so horrible and was used so universally that it may have given rise to the old pioneer saying: "If the medicine doesn't taste bad, it isn't good for you."

WHITE SNAKEROOT (*Ageratina altissima* [ah-jur-ah-TEE-nah all-TISS-uh-mah]) was known for years as *Eupatorium rugosum*. This somewhat weedy rhizomatous herb is normally only about knee-high with a profusion of pure white flowers that gleam in the dark shadows of a woodland edge.

FALSE BONESET (*Brickellia eupatorioides* [brih-KELL-ee-ah yew-pah-tore-ee-OY-deez]) is listed in many books as *Kuhnia eupatorioides*. This is a small, bushy, knee-high perennial with a taproot and no rhizomes. It grows in dry hill prairies and sandy or shallow-soiled limestone prairies, or in black oak or post oak savannas. Blooms appear as little bluestem starts developing fall color. The flowers may be dingy white and unimpressive, or they may be creamy white and quite pretty.

False boneset

White snakeroot

TALL BONESET has tiny individual tufts of flowers, but en masse is surprisingly exuberant.

TALL BONESET (*Eupatorium altissimum* [yew-pah-TORE-ee-um all-TISS-uh-mum]) is a head-high rhizomatous perennial. Although somewhat coarse and weedy, it provides lots of white fall flowers for little bluestem prairies.

Tall boneset

COMMON BONESET (*Eupatorium perfoliatum* [yew-pah-TORE-ee-um pur-fole-ee-A-tum]) has leaves that are fused around the stem, so it looks like the stem pierces the leaf. The very rough leaves taper to a pointed tip and have toothed edges and pale green undersides. The flowers are clusters of white fuzz. This waist-high perennial is commonly found in wet prairies with cattails and lowland switchgrass. It also grows in wet spots in post oak woodlands.

Common boneset

SPOTTED JOE-PYE WEED (*Eupatorium maculatum* [yew-pah-TORE-ee-um mack-you-LOT-um]) has flowers and stems that can be either deep ruby pink or rhubarb purple. This stately head-high perennial is native to wet prairies and moist woodlands primarily in the northern tallgrass region but with a Rocky Mountain branch running down to New Mexico. Because the Joe-Pye weeds look quite different from the bonesets, they are sometimes segregated into their own genus, *Eupatoriadelphus*.

Spotted Joe-Pye weed

PURPLE JOE-PYE WEED (*Eupatorium purpureum* [yew-pah-TORE-ee-um pur-PUR-ee-um]) is sometimes as bright as spotted Joe-Pye weed and sometimes far more

Purple Joe-Pye weed

SPOTTED JOE-PYE WEED has purple stems and purple flowers and even purple veins on the undersides of the leaves.

subtle with pale pink flowers and pale green stems spotted with purple. (How did they mess up the names like this? Spotted Joe-Pye weed has purple stems, and purple Joe-Pye weed has spotted stems.) It grows in woodlands, especially those that have been burned, and it was probably common in northern bur oak and white oak savannas. Its western boundary stretches from the eastern two-thirds of Minnesota to northeastern Oklahoma.

Goldenrods, despite enlivening autumn with bright yellow flowers, have a bad reputation. First, people think goldenrods cause hay fever. This is not true. Microscopic pollen floating in the air causes hay fever, and the pollen of goldenrods is too large and heavy to be airborne. It is ragweed, an omnipresent weed blooming at the same time, that causes hay fever.

Second, the goldenrods with big pyramidal heads that grow in every vacant lot and along every roadside are thugs. A whole field of Canada goldenrod might be just one plant. These goldenrods will invite themselves to your prairie, and some restorationists weed them out along with the non-native weeds. I have learned to be grateful for their color the first few autumns and to be patient as they shrink to become a minor part of the prairie.

But these pages are about clump-forming goldenrods you would plant on purpose.

STIFF GOLDENROD (*Oligoneuron rigidum* [o-lig-o-NEW-ron RIJ-uh-dum]), previously known as *Solidago rigida*, has several knee-high stiff stems per plant. The oval leaves are stalked where they attach to the lower stem but stalkless up near the flowers. Stiff goldenrod is native to little bluestem prairies. **Riddell's goldenrod** (*Oligoneuron riddellii*), much taller with smooth leaves folded longwise, grows in calcareous wet northern tallgrass prairies.

in big bluestem prairies or with little bluestem in sandy savannas. A western variety is found in ponderosa savannas along the Rockies. Unfortunately, showy goldenrod is common only in the northern tallgrass region.

Showy goldenrod

STIFF GOLDENROD stands knee-high with heads that are gently rounded on top, often broader than they are high.

Stiff goldenrod

SHOWY GOLDENROD (*Solidago speciosa* [sol-uh-DAY-go spee-see-O-sah]) makes a big thick plume of flowers that would be impressive by itself. But it often has a dozen plumes, so showy goldenrod is well named. About knee-high, it grows

ZIGZAG GOLDENROD (*Solidago flexicaulis* [sol-uh-DAY-go flex-ee-KAWL-iss]) is a knee-high, shade-loving goldenrod. It has a preference for limestone but does not require it. Because it is rhizomatous, it may need about four years to settle down and become well-mannered. It grows companionably with woodland sedges and savanna asters under bur oaks.

Zigzag goldenrod

MISSOURI BASIN GOLDENROD

(*Solidago missouriensis* [sol-uh-DAY-go muh-zur-ee-EN-sis]) is named for the Missouri River basin. Although only ankle- to knee-high in the West, its roots go 7 to 8 feet deep. It can be identified by its smooth, hairless reddish stems and matching leaves. A mature plant may have fifty to seventy-five stems. The flower head is erect in its western range and curved in the tallgrass regions. This is the first goldenrod to bloom each year, often starting in July. Missouri Basin goldenrod grows with little bluestem, needlegrasses, and grama grasses. In Texas, it is native only from the Red Rolling Plains eastward.

Missouri Basin goldenrod

VELVETY GOLDENROD (*Solidago mollis* [sol-uh-DAY-go MOLL-iss]) has pale velvety leaves and stems

Velvety goldenrod

ZIGZAG GOLDENROD has stems that twist, making them zig slightly one way and zag another, which arranges the flowers in a subtle but attractive spiral.

that are soft to the touch. The flower head is shaped like a narrow pyramid or cylinder. This knee-high goldenrod dominates the dry needlegrass prairies of western Canadian and the northern Great Plains; it is far less frequent in the South.

GRAY GOLDENROD (*Solidago nemoralis* [sol-uh-DAY-go nee-more-AL-iss]) has a narrow flower head that is bent over at the top. There is one head per stem, and several stems arise from each thick rootstock. The stems are covered with tiny fine hairs, as are the slender ashy gray green leaves, which give this goldenrod its name. Gray gold-

enrod, native to little bluestem and sideoats grama prairies, often in sand or rocky limestone, is plentiful from Canada south into central Texas.

Gray goldenrod

Every prairie has at least one aster. They are among the last prairie and savanna flowers to bloom in the fall, often withstanding several light frosts before going dormant.

Asters typically have narrow ray flowers that are colored white, blue, lavender, purple, lilac, rose, or pink. The yellow disk flowers turn red after pollination. All must be good nectar plants, judging by the number of bees and butterflies that feed on them.

To see photographs of a wide variety of asters and for nonscientific help in their identification, I especially like the book *Tallgrass Prairie Wildflowers* by Doug Ladd.

SKYBLUE ASTER (*Symphyotrichum oolentangiense* [sim-fee-AH-trih-kum oo-len-tang-ee-ENS]), also known as *Aster azureus*, is exceptionally pretty. The flowers are pale blue, and they seem to shine. The leaves, clustered at ground level, are long and rough, and heart-shaped where the stems attach. This is a very common species in mesic to dry northern prairies and savannas in the northern tallgrass region.

Skyblue aster

NEW ENGLAND ASTER (*Symphyotrichum novae-angliae* [sim-fee-AH-trih-kum noe-vee-ANG-lee-ee]) is native to wet or mesic tallgrass prairies and to ponderosa savannas. The New England aster found in the nursery trade, which has been selected and hybridized, is fine to use in a home garden but not in a real restoration. Another wet prairie aster is **willowleaf aster** (*Symphyotrichum praealtum*). Its

SKYBLUE ASTER has numerous small pale blue flowers that seem to float in midair on dark leafless stalks.

flowers are pale blue in huge loose clusters that float beside the tall turkey-foot flowers of big bluestem.

SMOOTH BLUE ASTER (*Symphyotrichum laeve* var. *laeve* [sim-fee-AH-trih-kum LAY-vee variety LAY-vee] is a waist-high, non-aggressive perennial with large blue to purple flowers and long, smooth pale blue green leaves. It is native to mesic and upland prairies, mainly in the northern tallgrass region. The western version of smooth blue aster *Symphyotrichum laeve* var. *geyeri* is found in the northern Great Plains and Rocky Mountains. In Texas, it grows only in the Trans Pecos. The two hybridize in the northeastern Great Plains.

Smooth blue aster

New England aster

NEW ENGLAND ASTERS display pink, lavender, and purple at Schaefer Prairie in south-central Minnesota.

Another companion aster for zigzag goldenrod in Illinois, Iowa, and Wisconsin is **Short's aster** (*Symphyotrichum shortii*). This waist-high, short-lived species has a preference for limestone slopes.

Heartleaf aster

FLAXLEAF ASTER (*Ionactis linariifolius* [eye-o-NACK-tis lih-nar-ee-ee-FOLE-ee-us]) has stiff stems and stiff brittle leaves. It grows ankle- to shin-high and has fairly large lavender blue flowers. It seems to prefer sandy or rocky soil near black oaks and post oaks, and it grows with nonaggressive grasses such as little bluestem and hairy grama. Although it requires excellent drainage, it is not all that drought-tolerant. In Oklahoma it is native only in the Ozarks, and in Texas it barely makes the extreme northeast corner.

AROMATIC ASTER (*Symphyotrichum oblongifolium* [sim-fee-AH-trih-kum ob-long-ee-FOLE-ee-um]) has vanilla-fragrant leaves, but only after they have dried. This rhizomatous perennial is the principal blue aster for southern tallgrass prairies and savannas, especially on limestone or alkaline soils.

HEARTLEAF ASTER (*Symphyotrichum cordifolium* [sim-fee-AH-trih-kum kar-dee-FOLE-ee-um]) is knee-high, sweet-smelling, and pale blue. The leaves at the base are heart-shaped. These asters can be seen in Minneapolis along River Road, where the parks department quit mowing regularly under the bur and red oaks and started mowing once a year after frost. The very first fall, long-frustrated heartleaf asters bloomed in profusion, along with zigzag goldenrod and wild sedge.

Aromatic aster

Flaxleaf aster

It is difficult, if not impossible, to separate some asters from others simply by looking at them. The latest attempt to divide asters into clear-cut species resulted in lots of different Latin names other than aster. The upshot is that most of our prairie asters are now *Symphyotrichum*, and only Europe, Asia, and Africa have true asters. Most botanists feel that this classification is temporary and that North America will soon be back to having asters too. Most current research on asters is being done by counting chromosomes.

Because the main body of white prairie asters interbreed, some botanists lump them together and call them the "*Multiflori* complex." Current terminology divides them into four main groups: (1) tiny-flowered and rhizomatous, (2) tiny-flowered and clumping, (3) larger-flowered and rhizomatous, and (4) larger-flowered and clumping. The tiny-flowered ones, called heath aster (*Symphyotrichum ericoides*), have a multitude of teensy yellow-centered white daisies, small, narrow heathlike leaves, and arching stems. The larger-flowered group, called white prairie aster (*Symphyotrichum falcatum*), has larger flowers than heath aster, about an inch across, but fewer of them, so the overall effect is not always as impressive.

Heath aster (*Symphyotrichum ericoides* var. *ericoides*)

HEATH ASTER is famous for its myriad of tiny white stars of flowers.

HEATH ASTER (*Symphyotrichum ericoides* var. *ericoides* [sim-fee-AH-trih-kum err-uh-KOY-deez variety err-uh-KOY-deez) is the one that is rhizomatous. It grows knee- to waist-high in dry to mesic prairies throughout the tallgrass prairie region. In Dallas, where it is some-what large, fast-growing, short-lived, and superbly adapted to black clay loam, it is likely to come in on its own without your having to plant it. In Chicago, it is hairy aster (*Symphyotrichum pilosum*) that is likely to seed itself into disturbed sites, and heath aster is found in old stable prairies in a variety of habi-tats ranging from hill prairies to moist sweetgrass prairies. In the southern Great Plains, heath aster is found in little bluestem prairies, juniper woodlands, and well-grazed pastures, where it covers the ground with fluffy mounds of white after abundant late-summer rains.

HEATH ASTER (*Symphyotrichum ericoides* var. *pansum* [sim-fee-AH-trih-kum err-uh-KOY-deez variety PAN-sum]) is tufted, not rhizomatous, and it seems to be ankle-high, demure, and long-lived. The tiny white flowers are, on rare occasions, flushed with pale pink. This heath aster grows with grama grasses and needlegrasses in western Canada and the northern Great Plains, and Native Americans boiled it to make a tea for washing wounds and soothing poison ivy.

WHITE PRAIRIE ASTER has larger flowers spaced further apart.

Heath aster (*Symphyotrichum ericoides* var. *pansum*)

WHITE PRAIRIE ASTER (*Symphyotrichum falcatum* var. *commutatum* [sim-fee-AH-trih-kum fall-KAH-tum variety com-mew-TA-tum]) is rhizomatous and grows about waist-high. It is an abundant aster in dry prairies and parklands throughout the Great Plains. In the South, it may be found in more mesic environments.

WHITE PRAIRIE ASTER (*Symphyotrichum falcatum* var. *falcatum* [sim-fee-AH-trih-kum fall-KAH-tum variety fall-KAH-tum]) is native primarily to mesic prairies in the cooler parts of the northern Great Plains. Well-mannered, it sends up a vase of stems from a woody corm.

White prairie aster (*Symphyotrichum falcatum* var. *falcatum*)

White prairie aster (*Symphyotrichum falcatum* var. *commutatum*)

Species	NORTHWEST Northern Plains Shortgrass Region					NORTHEAST Northern Tallgrass Prairie Region					SOUTHWEST Southern Plains Shortgrass Region					SOUTHEAST Southern Tallgrass Prairie Region				
	Lowland prairie	Mesic prairie	Upland prairie	Sand prairie	Aspen parkland	Lowland prairie	Mesic prairie	Upland prairie	Bur oak savanna	Black oak savanna	Lowland prairie	Mesic prairie	Upland prairie	Sand prairie	Ponderosa savanna	Lowland prairie	Mesic prairie	Upland prairie	Bur oak savanna	Post oak savanna
MINT FAMILY																				
Ohio horsemint																	■	■	■	
Common mountain mint						■	■									■				
Wild bergamot	■			■			■			■	■					■	■		■	■
Spotted horsemint														■						■
Lemon horsemint												■	■	■					■	
Pitcher sage																	■	■		
Fall obedient plant						■			■							■			■	
ACANTHUS FAMILY																				
Hairy ruellia								■									■	■		
Limestone ruellia									■										■	
Violet ruellia																	■	■		
VERBENA FAMILY																				
Blue vervain	■					■					■					■				
Hoary vervain			■					■					■	■						
Dakota vervain			■											■						
BEAN FAMILY: MIDSUMMER																				
Leadplant		■		■			■	■						■			■			■
Indigobush						■										■				
Dwarf wild indigo			■	■									■	■						
Showy tick trefoil							■		■	■							■			■
Roundhead bushclover								■		■				■					■	
BEAN FAMILY: PRAIRIE CLOVERS																				
Purple prairie clover		■					■					■		■			■	■		
White prairie clover		■	■					■	■		■	■	■				■	■		
Roundhead prairie clover																	■	■		
BEAN FAMILY: LATE SUMMER																				
Illinois bundleflower							■				■					■	■			
Wild licorice	■										■									
Partridge pea	■		■			■					■			■		■		■		
Maryland senna							■									■	■			■
SPURGE FAMILY																				
Flowering spurge							■	■									■	■		■
Snow-on-the-mountain			■	■							■	■		■						■
Fire-on-the-mountain																	■		■	
MILKWEED FAMILY: SHORT																				
Antelope horns												■	■						■	
Green milkweed			■	■				■												
Butterfly milkweed							■			■				■			■	■		■

WARM SEASON FORBS (cont'd)

Species	NORTHWEST — Northern Plains Shortgrass Region					NORTHEAST — Northern Tallgrass Prairie Region					SOUTHWEST — Southern Plains Shortgrass Region					SOUTHEAST — Southern Tallgrass Prairie Region				
	Lowland prairie	Mesic prairie	Upland prairie	Sand prairie	Aspen parkland	Lowland prairie	Mesic prairie	Upland prairie	Bur oak savanna	Black oak savanna	Lowland prairie	Mesic prairie	Upland prairie	Sand prairie	Ponderosa savanna	Lowland prairie	Mesic prairie	Upland prairie	Bur oak savanna	Post oak savanna
Whorled milkweed								■				■						■		■
Dwarf milkweed		■		■					■											
Poke milkweed									■											
MILKWEED FAMILY: TALL PURPLE																				
Purple milkweed							■		■	■							■		■	■
Swamp milkweed						■					■					■				
Showy milkweed	■	■		■							■	■								
Sullivant's milkweed							■													
Common milkweed						■														
ASTER FAMILY: CONEFLOWERS																				
Purple coneflower							■		■								■			
Pale purple coneflower								■									■	■		■
Black Sampson			■									■	■				■	■	■	
Grayhead coneflower								■												
Mexican hat			■	■								■	■	■	■			■		
Blackeyed Susan		■		■			■	■				■						■	■	
Sweet blackeyed Susan						■	■		■	■						■				
ASTER FAMILY: SUMMER DYCs																				
Finger coreopsis							■	■												
Oxeye sunflower							■	■	■						■					
Sneezeweed	■					■										■				
Hairy goldenaster			■	■			■					■	■							
Navajo tea		■	■								■	■	■	■				■		
Cowpen daisy												■	■					■		■
ASTER FAMILY: SILPHIUMS																				
Prairie dock							■	■												
Compass plant	■						■	■			■						■	■		
Cup plant						■										■				
Rosinweed		■				■	■	■	■	■							■			
Roughstem rosinweed																		■	■	■
White rosinweed																	■	■		
ASTER FAMILY: CURIOSITIES																				
Common ironweed	■					■	■													
Western ironweed																■	■		■	■
Plains ironweed											■	■								
Wild quinine							■	■	■	■							■	■		■
Pale Indian plantain							■		■											
Prairie Indian plantain						■	■											■		■
Glaucous white lettuce					■	■	■								■					

Species	NORTHWEST Northern Plains Shortgrass Region					NORTHEAST Northern Tallgrass Prairie Region					SOUTHWEST Southern Plains Shortgrass Region					SOUTHEAST Southern Tallgrass Prairie Region				
	Lowland prairie	Mesic prairie	Upland prairie	Sand prairie	Aspen parkland	Lowland prairie	Mesic prairie	Upland prairie	Bur oak savanna	Black oak savanna	Lowland prairie	Mesic prairie	Upland prairie	Sand prairie	Ponderosa savanna	Lowland prairie	Mesic prairie	Upland prairie	Bur oak savanna	Post oak savanna
ASTER FAMILY: SUNFLOWERS																				
Western sunflower							■	■		■								■		
Maximilian sunflower	■	■		■								■	■			■	■	■		
Willowleaf sunflower																■	■			
Prairie sunflower	■	■	■					■				■	■	■	■			■		
Downy sunflower								■				■					■			■
Paleleaf sunflower									■	■										■
Pale sunflower								■												
Woodland sunflower									■	■										
Jerusalem artichoke						■	■												■	
GENTIAN FAMILY																				
Downy gentian							■	■											■	
Bottle gentian						■	■													
Cream gentian							■		■	■										■
Stiff gentian							■	■	■											
Northern gentian		■		■											■					
Fringed gentian						■														
Catchfly gentian	■	■									■		■			■				
Rose gentian													■					■	■	■
ASTER FAMILY: BLAZING STARS																				
Button snakeroot							■		■									■		■
Meadow blazing star	■			■	■				■											
Savanna blazing star									■											
Dotted gayfeather		■	■								■	■	■	■						
Prairie blazing star						■	■									■				
Texas gayfeather												■							■	■
ASTER FAMILY: BONESETS																				
White snakeroot									■	■									■	■
False boneset		■	■					■		■	■	■	■					■		■
Tall boneset								■												
Common boneset	■					■					■							■		
Spotted Joe-Pye weed						■														
Purple Joe-Pye weed									■											
ASTER FAMILY: GOLDENRODS																				
Stiff goldenrod		■		■			■	■			■	■	■		■			■	■	
Riddell's goldenrod						■	■													
Showy goldenrod							■			■					■			■		■
Zigzag goldenrod									■											
Missouri Basin goldenrod			■					■				■	■		■				■	

WARM SEASON FORBS (cont'd)

Species	NORTHWEST Northern Plains Shortgrass Region					NORTHEAST Northern Tallgrass Prairie Region					SOUTHWEST Southern Plains Shortgrass Region					SOUTHEAST Southern Tallgrass Prairie Region				
	Lowland prairie	Mesic prairie	Upland prairie	Sand prairie	Aspen parkland	Lowland prairie	Mesic prairie	Upland prairie	Bur oak savanna	Black oak savanna	Lowland prairie	Mesic prairie	Upland prairie	Sand prairie	Ponderosa savanna	Lowland prairie	Mesic prairie	Upland prairie	Bur oak savanna	Post oak savanna
Velvety goldenrod		■	■									■	■							
Gray goldenrod			■				■			■		■						■		
ASTER FAMILY: BLUE ASTERS																				
Skyblue aster						■	■			■										
New England aster						■	■								■					
Smooth blue aster		■	■	■				■	■	■					■		■	■	■	■
Aromatic aster								■				■			■		■	■	■	■
Heartleaf aster									■											
Short's aster									■											
Flaxleaf aster										■										■
ASTER FAMILY: WHITE ASTERS																				
Heath aster		■	■	■			■	■			■	■	■	■			■	■		
White prairie aster		■	■		■						■	■	■		■					

It used to be that you couldn't give oak openings away, because they did not make good farm land. Now they're the most expensive

real estate. They're where everyone wants to live because of the interplay between the big old oaks and the prairie openings.

      DENISE GEHRING, Metroparks of the Toledo Area

Savanna Trees and Thicket Shrubs

WHERE PRAIRIE AND FOREST MEET, the prairie surrounds trees like ocean around islands. Individual trees seem to venture out into the grassland from the edges of the forest, and when they encounter creeks, they follow their meandering courses. This composition of tree and prairie is commonly called savanna, and to many eyes it is more exciting and attractive than either is by itself. In North America, savannas were once a bountiful supermarket of fruits, berries, nuts, grains, deer, elk, turkey, passenger pigeons, squirrels, and rabbits. Humans probably evolved in savannas, as that is the richest habitat for plants and animals.

A savanna garden around your home or office should include at least one tree, some shrubbery or thicket, and lots of prairie in place of lawn. The aim is to have no more than half of your garden in shade.

Which trees will work best for you depends on where you live. Trees are long-lived, so it is particularly important to have native trees that can withstand decades of winter storms and summer drought. You want trees that will need no watering once they are established, because watering the area around a tree throws off the height and balance of your prairie. If you plan to burn your prairie garden, choose a savanna tree that can take the fire. In other words, one that grows naturally alongside prairies.

The main savanna trees bordering tallgrass prairies are bur oak, black oak, post oak, northern pin oak, white oak, and escarpment live oak. Canadian and western mountain prairies are bordered by aspen, balsam poplar, and ponderosa pine.

The beech family (Fagaceae) (careful—the spelling is almost identical to the legume family, Fabaceae) includes chestnut, beech, and oak—all long-lived trees or large shrubs that bear edible nuts. Chestnut and beech are ancient species that have been winnowed down to only a handful of modern species, and our one native chestnut is virtually extinct because of a Eurasian chestnut blight. Oaks, on the other hand, are in a flurry of genetic growth, creating new species and hybrids at a botanically fast rate. Thought to have originated in Mexico, oaks have spread throughout the temperate northern hemisphere.

The pretty rosy round "fruits" often found on oaks are not fruits at all (the fruits are acorns) but galls, formed when a tiny wasp deposits her eggs into the tissue of an oak stem and secretes a chemical that causes the oak to grow a sphere around her eggs.

BUR OAK acorns are unusually large and capped with a cup that has a distinctive fringe (bur) around the edge. Bur oak is sometimes called mossy cup oak. Photo by Benny J. Simpson.

BUR OAK (*Quercus macrocarpa* [KWARE-kuss mack-roe-KARP-ah]) has thick dark bark, stubby horizontal branches, and large leaves with distinctive whitish undersides. Bur oaks are native primarily east of the 100th parallel from Canada to the Blackland Prairie and adjacent regions in Texas, and east on limestone to Alabama. In Minnesota, they grow with northern pin oak in acid, sandy oak savannas. In mid-western tallgrass areas, they border the prairies. In midgrass areas, they are found down along the creeks or in floodplains. They prefer rich, deep, loamy soil and do not mind silty or clay loam and brief periods of seasonal flooding.

The acorns tend to be even bigger in the South than in the North. Small crops mature each year, but large crops occur in cycles several years apart. Bur oaks typically live two to four centuries.

Bur oak is often spelled burr oak. *Burr* is the Middle English spelling of *bur*.

Companion plants found under bur oaks in both Chicago and Dallas include chinquapin oak (*Quercus muhlenbergii*), white ash (*Fraxinus americana*), American elm (*Ulmus americana*), the local species of red oak, gray dogwood in Chicago and roughleaf dogwood in Dallas, big bluestem, Virginia wild rye, a local woodland *Carex*, and a

Bur oak

BLACK OAKS, like other savanna oaks, have thick corky bark that protects the cambium layer from excessive heat during a fire.

BLACK OAK acorns take two seasons to mature. On the leaves, note the solitary bristle at the end of each lobe, a characteristic of black oaks and red oaks. Photo by Benny J. Simpson.

Black oak

woodland brome. Forbs may be local species of violet and spiderwort, as well as dogtooth violet (*Erythronium*), wild hyacinth, rosinweed, and fall obedient plant. Although this list of forbs helps give the flavor of bur oak savannas, more abundant local flowers may make a better show. For example, in Chicago plant lots of wild geranium, while in Dallas plant golden groundsel (*Packera obovata*, also known as *Senecio obovatus*). In Wisconsin and Minnesota, chinquapin oaks are replaced by **white oaks** (*Quercus alba*).

BLACK OAK (*Quercus velutina* [KWARE-kuss vuh-LOOT-in-ah]) is native as far west as southeastern Minnesota and Nebraska, and northeast Texas. It grows in nutrient-poor, oxygen-rich, coarse, acid soils that are characterized as dry because they drain rapidly, yet are moist enough to support bracken fern. The black oak savannas we saw in northern Indiana and southern Ontario were lush with ferns, grasses, and sedges dotted with brilliantly colored forbs such as butterflyweed, downy phlox, wild quinine, finger coreopsis, Ohio spiderwort, spreading dogbane, showy goldenrod, and orchids. The paths through these savannas were paved with pathrush. Beans and peas were

abundant, as they are good nitrogen fixers.

Companion species often found in black oak savannas are shagbark hickory (*Carya ovata*), hazelnut, Carolina rose, smooth sumac, big bluestem, little bluestem, Pennsylvania sedge, Junegrass, bracken fern, wild strawberry, starry false Solomon's seal (*Maianthemum stellatum*), wild lupine, goat's rue, leadplant, flaxleaf aster, false toadflax (*Comandra umbellata*), thimbleweed, and flowering spurge.

Black oaks are present but not dominant in both post oak and

northern pin oak savannas where conditions are moist enough. Black oak is distinguished from northern pin oak by its yellow orange inner bark and shaggy acorn caps. Also, its leaves tend to be glossier.

NORTHERN PIN OAK (*Quercus ellipsoidalis* [KWARE-kuss el-lip-SOYD-uh-lis]) is also called Hill's oak and is sometimes lumped in with scarlet oak (*Quercus coccinea*). Its deeply divided leaves look similar to those of black oak and scarlet oak, and together the three produce lots of hybrids. Northern pin oak is native to dry, acid uplands. The soil is sandy or gravelly and nutrient poor. As a result, northern pin oak savannas are generally less shady than black oak savannas, and more grasses are present.

Typical companion species include chokecherry, leadplant,

Northern pin oak

wild rose, porcupine grass, hairy grama, little bluestem, big bluestem, Junegrass, Scribner's panicgrass, Louisiana sage, birdfoot violet (*Viola pedata*), hairy puccoon, roundhead bushclover, rough or dotted blazing star, and purple prairie clover.

Wildlife you can expect to attract are lark sparrows, logger-head shrikes, and if you have lupins, Karner blue butterflies. Indigo buntings are common breeding birds.

POST OAK

POST OAK (*Quercus stellata* [KWARE-kuss stuh-LOT-ah]) is a burly, stubby-branched, lobed-leafed oak like bur oak. Post oaks are native primarily to sandy little bluestem prairies and savannas in the southern tallgrass region. They are found most often on coarse sands or on silty, sandy soils well laced with hunks of sandstone and ironstone—never limestone.

More drought- and heat-tolerant than black oak, post oak hates to be watered regularly. Well-shaded post oak understory is a thin covering of sedges, grasses, legumes, and other forbs, with rocks, lichens, and pussytoes covering the bare ground. The openings are thick with bluestem and Indiangrass. Fall is gorgeous with various species of aster, goldenrod, button snakeroot, and gerardia. Typical companion plants are blackjack oak (*Quercus marilandica*), black hickory (*Carya texana*), wild rose, grape vines (*Vitis*), greenbriar (*Smilax*), coralberry, ebony spleenwort (*Asplenium platyneuron*), mayapple (*Podophyllum peltatum*), little bluestem or split-beard bluestem, Virginia wild rye, blackeyed Susan, tick trefoil, and local species of woodland *Carex*, *Monarda*, and gerardia.

The post oaks themselves are at their most beautiful in early spring

Post oak

when they flower. The multitude of dangling catkins are brilliant yellow. Other oaks are lovely in flower also, but their catkins are a more subtle misty lime, pink, or peach.

ESCARPMENT LIVE OAK

(*Quercus fusiformis* [KWARE-kuss few-zee-FORE-mis]) is green all winter and changes its leaves in April, looking bare for about a week just as bluebonnets and pink evening primrose burst into bloom. It is native to thin limestone soil, slightly acid sandy soil, or dry alkaline prairie soil in Oklahoma, Texas, and Mexico, where conditions are too dry for bur oaks. Some botanists call it *Q. virginiana* var. *fusiformis*, making it a variety of the coastal live oak.

Understory varies considerably from Oklahoma to the Texas Hill Country. In Love County, Oklahoma, typical companion plants are shumard red oak (*Quercus shumardii*), elbowbush (*Forestiera pubescens*), rusty blackhaw viburnum, white limestone honeysuckle (*Lonicera albiflora*), plains yucca (*Yucca glauca*), little bluestem, sideoats grama, and a local woodland *Carex*.

In the Texas Hill Country, you will want to plant or preserve Texas red oak (*Quercus texana*), Texas persimmon (*Diospyros texana*),

POST OAK leaves typically resemble a rough cross. When the lower lobes are larger, as here, the leaves can be described as the silhouette of a person sitting cross-legged with outstretched elbows.

agarito (*Mahonia trifoliolata*), rusty blackhaw viburnum, twistleaf yucca (*Yucca rupicola*), baby blue eyes (*Nemophila phacelioides*), zexmenia (*Wedelia texana*), little bluestem, sideoats grama, the local woodland *Carex*, and frostweed (*Verbesina virginica*).

Escarpment live oak

Members of the pine family (Pinaceae) are conifers; their fruits are cones filled with seed, and they have needlelike leaves. On the western edges of the Great Plains, ponderosa pines are frequently surrounded by bluestem prairie, and pinyons by shortgrass prairie.

Junipers, in the cypress family (Cupressaceae), are also conifers. Not as fire-proof as ponderosa and pinyon, they still are amazingly impervious to quick cool fires. Junipers often grow in shortgrass or little bluestem prairies.

PONDEROSA PINE (*Pinus ponderosa* [PYE-nus pon-der-O-sah]) has thick fire-retardant bark that smells like vanilla. These large trees have tall straight trunks and medium-length needles in threes. South of Colorado, ponderosas are found only above 7,000 feet or on north-facing slopes.

Typical companion plants in New Mexico are tree-sized Gambel oak (*Quercus gambelii*), common juniper (*Juniperus communis*), wild rose, meadowrue, little bluestem, dotted gayfeather, and local species of snowberry, pussytoes, lupines, penstemons, and fleabane daisies.

Ponderosa pine

PINYON (*Pinus edulis* [PINE-us ED-u-lis]) grows in a habitat called pinyon-juniper scrub. This vegetational band is often the interface between shortgrass prairies and ponderosa savannas in the southern Great Plains.

Companion plants are likely to include shrubby Gambel oak, the local shrubby artemisia, blue grama, Indian ricegrass, needle-and-thread, pussytoes, reindeer lichen, dwarf prickly pear, plains yucca, and local species of juniper, lupine, buckwheat, phlox, evening primrose, fleabane, gaura, and globe mallow.

Pinyon

EASTERN RED CEDAR (*Juniperus virginiana* [joo-NIP-er-us ver-jin-ee-A-nah]) is considered a weed by prairie enthusiasts. Early accounts indicate, however, that it used to be a tall long-lived savanna tree for limestone barrens and cedar glades.

Companion plants include an interesting collection of endemics native to limestone, along with limestone-loving viburnums, aromatic sumac, little bluestem, sideoats grama, prairie dropseed, melicgrass, Short's or aromatic aster, blue wild indigo, and St. John's wort.

Only a month after a devastating crown fire, LUPINES are blooming and resprouts of snowberry and Gambel oak are greening up under the dead ponderosa pines.

Eastern red cedar

Aspens, cottonwoods, and willows, collectively called poplars, are found in the willow family (Salicaceae). All have fluffy airborne seed. Willows, whether trees or shrubs, are great for erosion control. They are common along waterways and in sloughs and wet prairies, where they tend to plant themselves.

Aspens and balsam poplars (*Populus balsamifera*) often grow in Canadian parklands north of the oaks and in Rocky Mountain meadows at elevations so high that most people live there only in the summer.

ASPEN (*Populus tremuloides* [POP-u-lus trim-u-LOY-deez]) is native where conditions are cool and moist enough. Individual aspen trunks tend to live only thirty years, but after fire or wind damage they regrow quickly from roots that can be over one thousand years old. Aspens sucker like bamboo, so a large grove is likely all one plant.

Native grass species that grow under aspens are big bluestem associates in Manitoba (frequently with balsam poplar); little bluestem, Hooker's oatgrass (*Helictotrichon hookeri*), and western porcupine grass (*Hesperostipa curtiseta*) in Saskatchewan; and needle-and-thread, fescue, and poverty oatgrass (*Danthonia spicata*) in Alberta. The same or similar species grow under Rocky Mountain aspens, depending on elevation. Other companion plants are sedges, ferns, horsetail, wild strawberry, pussytoes, wild rose, and local moist to wet prairie forbs.

ASPEN is a pioneer invader following forest fires.

Aspen

COTTONWOOD (*Populus deltoides* [POP-u-lus del-TOY-deez]), the shade tree of the Great Plains, needs water to germinate but is then drought-tolerant.

Cottonwood understory species are mesic rather than wet. Typical grasses and forbs are Canada wild-rye, woodland sedges, path rush, Canada anemone, coneflowers, Jerusalem artichoke, white snakeroot, common boneset, savanna asters, and goldenrods.

Cottonwood

The rose family (Rosaceae) includes not only roses but peaches, apricots, plums, and cherries. These fruit trees are in the genus *Prunus*. America was not blessed with peaches and apricots, but there is an abundance of plums and cherries. All grow in prairie thickets or in sufficiently sunny savannas. Our wild fruits are smaller than cultivated fruit, with thicker skin, less flesh, and varying degrees of sweetness, but they can survive without irrigation, pruning, smudge pots, and dormant oil.

Those that sucker too aggressively for a small garden are chokecherry, wild plum, Chickasaw plum, and creek plum. These thickets can withstand a prairie fire and bloom a couple of weeks later over still black ground.

Those that can be kept to a single trunk or low shrub are pin cherry, wild black cherry, Mexican plum, and sand cherry.

CHOKECHERRY (*Prunus virginiana* [PROO-nus ver-jin-ee-A-nah]) is a small tree that forms thickets. The tallgrass variety has tiny white flowers in fluffy tails, bright red to dark red fruit, thin oval leaves, shiny gray stems, and a maximum height of 30 feet.

The Great Plains variety is called black-fruited chokecherry (*Prunus virginiana* var. *melanocarpa*). It is 6 to 18 feet tall and has creamy flowers, black fruit, smooth thick leaves, and shiny reddish brown stems. Occasionally, the leaves are heart-shaped.

Chokecherry

CHOKECHERRY is a treat for birds and makes good wine, jelly, and pemmican.

PIN CHERRY (*Prunus pensylvanica* [PROO-nus pen-sill-VAN-uh-kah]) is a small tree with broad clusters of white flowers and tiny bright red cherries. It grows on hillsides with aspen, black oak, or bracken. It increases greatly after a fire.

Pin cherry

SAND CHERRY (*Prunus pumila* [PROO-nus PEW-mee-la]) is a small shrub with clusters of white flowers and purplish brown fruit. It normally makes knee-high thickets on dry prairies and sand hills.

Sand cherry

WILD BLACK CHERRY (*Prunus serotina* [PROO-nus suh-ROT-uh-nah]) is a small savanna tree with shiny red brown branches, shiny dark green leaves, white tails of flowers, and dark cherries. There

Wild black cherry

CHICKASAW PLUM (*Prunus angustifolia* [PROO-nus an-gus-tee-FOLE-ee-ah]), also called sandhill plum, looks similar to wild plum except that it is half as tall, and in loose sand, it makes thickets so big that early explorers wrote of having to detour several miles around to circle them. The zigzag branches are spiny, shiny red.

Chickasaw plum

Some THICKET PLUMS get too big but are gloriously sweet-smelling in early spring.

are two easy ways to distinguish well-mannered wild black cherry from rambunctious chokecherry: if the cherries still have the green calyx attached and if the leaves are at least twice as long as broad, you are looking at wild black cherry.

MEXICAN PLUM (*Prunus mexicana*), with fragrant clusters of white flowers, is the nicest wild tree *Prunus* for the South. Although native as far north as southeastern South Dakota, Mexican plum is prevalent only in the southern tallgrass region. The small, round plums are an inch across by late summer, and as they ripen, they color from pale green to yellow to mauve to purple.

WILD PLUM (*Prunus americana* [PROO-nus ah-mer-ee-KAHN-ah]) is eye-catching in the spring when its interlocking stems burst into fragrant white flowers. The tips of the small branches get hardened points like thorns, making a formidable thicket up to 24 feet tall.

Wild plum

CHICKASAW PLUM is ripe when it turns pink and yellow.

Other prairie-associated fruit trees in the rose family, besides plums and cherries, are serviceberries, hawthorns, and crabapples. All have nectar-rich white flowers that bloom in early spring, either before or just as their leaves are unfolding, and they all have small, tasty, red to black fruits that ripen in summer to feed fledgling birds or in fall to nourish migrating birds. Most have stupendous fall color.

Some of the species sucker so vigorously that they resemble shrubs more than trees.

LOW SHADBLOW, like other serviceberries, has unlobed leaves, no thorns, and fruits that ripen with the green calyx still attached.

JUNEBERRY (*Amelanchier arborea* [am-uh-LANK-ee-or ar-BORE-ee-ah]) is also called shadbush or downy serviceberry. A single-trunked small tree, Juneberry grows in black oak and bur oak savannas if there is good drainage and sufficient moisture. Early each spring before the canopy trees leaf out, it shines with narrow-petaled white blossoms. It is not often seen west of Wisconsin or south of Illinois. The fruits, which look like tiny apples, were used by Native Americans for stews and pemmican, and a tea brewed from the roots was used to prevent miscarriage.

Low shadblow

DOWNY HAWTHORN (*Crataegus mollis* [kruh-TEE-gus MOLL-iss]) is a single-trunked small tree with bright red haws. I suspect it was originally a component of bur oak savannas from southern Minnesota to north-central Texas. New stems and the undersides of leaves are downy at first but lose the fuzz by summer; sometimes the fruits are downy at one end. Thorns range from stout to almost nonexistent.

Juneberry

LOW SHADBLOW (*Amelanchier humilis* [am-uh-LANK-ee-or HEW-muh-liss]) usually forms low running thickets with trailing branches that root, but it can also get as tall as 15 feet. Native to savannas, open woodlands, and prairie ravines, it is very hard to differentiate from the eastern nonsuckering roundleaf serviceberry (*Amelanchier sanguinea*). On its western borders it is equally hard to distinguish it from the fiercely suckering **saskatoon** (*Amelanchier alnifolia*).

Downy hawthorn

Cockspur hawthorn

GREEN HAWTHORN (*Crataegus viridis* [kruh-TEE-gus VEER-uh-diss]) is likely to be less thorny than cockspur or downy hawthorn, and it is more heat- and drought-tolerant, venturing out into the eastern edge of the southern Great Plains but stopping short of the High Plains. Found in savannas and riparian woodlands with bur oak, post oak, and escarpment live oak, this ornamental tree has fruit that ripens to yellow, orange, or Chinese red—not green.

COCKSPUR HAWTHORN (*Crataegus crus-galli* [kruh-TEE-gus kroose-GOLL-ee]) has glossy leaves and huge thorns. Plant it in full sun, where the crown can get broad and the thorns will appear black against a winter sky. The haws are reddish brown or greenish. More drought-tolerant than downy hawthorn, cockspur hawthorn can grow on limestone bluffs with eastern red cedar or in the bottoms with white oaks and bur oaks.

Green hawthorn

Iowa crabapple

IOWA CRABAPPLE (*Malus ioensis* [MAL-uss eye-o-EN-sis]) may grow as a small single-trunked tree, or it may form thickets. The fragrant flowers have coral anthers and, often, a matching blush on the white petals. The ripe crabapples are waxy yellowish green. Iowa crabapple is native primarily to the northern tallgrass region. The variety in central Texas, called Blanco crabapple (*Malus ioensis* var. *texana*), grows on limestone bluffs with little bluestem and grama grasses. Crabapples waver botanically between pear (*Pyrus*) and apple (*Malus*).

DOWNY HAWTHORN blooms in midspring after its lobed leaves have half emerged.

Our native wild roses, unlike hybridized roses, do not have layers of petals. They have five pink or white petals and sexy golden centers that brazenly compete for pollination. The sweetly scented 2-to-3-inch flowers appear in late spring or early summer. The red somewhat mealy rose hips, rich in vitamin C, ripen in early fall for migrating birds and remain tasty through several freezes.

Long-lived and relatively disease-free, all but prairie rose are rhizomatous shrubs. Without competition they make a dense thicket, but in a mature prairie or savanna they are more likely to have single stems scattered a foot or so apart.

Unfortunately, there was no room to give details of common blackberry (*Rubus allegheniensis*), wild red raspberry (*Rubus idaeus*), black raspberry (*Rubus occidentalis*), and common dewberry (*Rubus flagellaris*), but these and other delicious *Rubus* are plentiful on prairie-woodland edges.

PASTURE ROSE (*Rosa carolina* [ROSE-ah ker-o-LINE-ah]), usually knee-high and pink-flowered, has three to seven smooth oval leaflets.

Pasture rose

The roots are up to 20 feet deep and very drought-tolerant and long-lived. Although it is the basic prairie rose in dry to mesic northern tall-grass prairies and sandy savannas, it is rarely seen as far south as East Texas.

SUNSHINE ROSE (*Rosa arkansana* var. *suffulta* [ROSE-ah ar-kan-SANE-ah variety suh-FULL-tah]), only shin-high, grows in prairies and sunny woodlands to the west of pasture rose. Where the two overlap, hybrids result. It is common in the northern half of its range and fairly uncommon in the southern half.

Sunshine rose

WESTERN WILD ROSE (*Rosa woodsii* [ROSE-ah WOODS-zee-eye]), native to ravines, sunny woodlands, and stream valleys, is found most frequently in the mountains or in the northern two-thirds of the Great Plains. The leaflets are dull green, not glossy, but at frost they turn colors that range from gold to all shades of red and purple. The winter stems are purplish pink.

Western wild rose

SUNSHINE ROSE is one of many short rhizomatous roses that appear in both prairies and savannas. Its nine to eleven glossy leaflets frame clusters of three flowers that, by fall, have ripened into round red hips.

WHITE PRAIRIE ROSE (*Rosa foliolosa* [ROSE-ah fole-ee-o-LO-sah]) is an almost spineless, ankle- to knee-high rose with widely spaced large white flowers. The leaves are dark green and glossy. Although it is not documented for New Mexico, I have seen it in ponderosa savanna near Mora.

White prairie rose

MEADOWSWEET is found on hummocks above cordgrass. A red-winged blackbird had her nest hidden among these spires of white flowers.

PRAIRIE ROSE has a cluster of a dozen flowers that, one by one, open deep pink and then fade to white. The leaves are usually divided into three leaflets with pale undersides.

PRAIRIE ROSE (*Rosa setigera* [ROSE-ah suh-TIJ-er-ah]) is, ironically, not native to prairies. Unlikely to sucker and form a thicket, instead it has long arching canes that can climb a tree to find sunlight.

Prairie rose

MEADOWSWEET (*Spiraea alba* [spy-REE-ah AL-bah]) is a moisture-loving shrub with flower heads that look similar to a white version of queen of the prairie but are usually half the size. In Canada it grows in aspen parklands and moist prairies. In Chicago it grows in wet prairies and marshes along with bluejoint and cordgrass.

Meadowsweet

■ HONEYSUCKLE FAMILY (*Viburnum, Symphoricarpos, Diervilla*)

The honeysuckle family (Caprifoliaceae) includes many horticultural favorites such as honeysuckle, abelia, weigela, and viburnum. Wayfaring tree (*Viburnum lantana*), from Eurasia, and European highbush cranberry (*Viburnum opulus*) are popular in the nursery trade. Both have escaped into the wild.

Our native viburnums have polite roots that either do not sucker or do so very slowly. They have platelike clusters of white flowers, leaves opposite each other, and fleshy red, purple, or black fruits—each containing a single large seed. They run a continuum from multistemmed shrubs to small single-trunked trees.

The genus *Symphoricarpos* consists of several knee- to waist-high thicket shrubs that have pale pink or white inconspicuous flowers and showy fruit. The snowberries have white fruit the size of porcelain marbles. Coralberry has much smaller fruit but lots of it, and the color is purply pink.

DOWNY ARROWWOOD (*Viburnum rafinesquianum* [vye-BURN-um rah-fin-es-kwee-A-num]) used to be lumped with the **southern arrowwood** (*Viburnum dentatum*). Both are large shrubs with straight stems, dark purple fruit, and leaves with toothed edges and prominent veins, and either a few or many downy

In August, ARROWWOOD displays drooping clusters of dark purply blue fruit.

hairs on the undersides. Downy arrowwood is native to bur oak and white oak savannas in the northern tallgrass region. Southern arrowwood is found in post oak savannas from Illinois to far east Texas.

NANNYBERRY (*Viburnum lentago* [vye-BURN-um lynn-TA-go]) is native to aspen and white oak savannas bordering moist northern prairies. The flowers are in clusters 5 inches across, and the blue black fruits are supposedly edible. Black-

Nannyberry

haw, *Viburnum prunifolium*, is the southern version of nannyberry.

Downy arrowwood

COMMON SNOWBERRY has round white fruits that ripen in late summer or early fall.

mildew there. Coralberry is native from the southeasternmost county in Minnesota to the eastern two-thirds of Oklahoma, and wherever post oaks grow in Texas.

Coralberry

WESTERN SNOWBERRY

(*Symphoricarpos occidentalis* [sim-fore-ee-KAR-pos ox-ee-den-TAL-iss]) is also called wolfberry. It makes large knee- to waist-high thickets in prairie ravines and savannas, primarily in the northern Great Plains. It has clusters of tiny white tubular flowers and oval leaves that frequently get over an inch long.

Common snowberry

savannas, it grows with bottlebrush grass and prairie dock. There are eastern and western varieties, and the western variety from the Pacific Northwest with its smooth (not downy) stems and leaves is the one more commonly grown for the nursery trade.

DIERVILLA (*Diervilla lonicera* [deer-VILL-ah low-NISS-er-ah]) grows in black oak savannas, especially those that have recently been burned. It also can be found with aspens in eastern Minnesota, Manitoba, and Saskatchewan. It is native to rocky slopes or sandy soil from eastern Canada down the eastern mountains. This attractive shrub has yellow honeysuckle-like flowers and large leaves. Uncommon in the wild, it is now being offered in the nursery trade.

Western snowberry

COMMON SNOWBERRY (*Symphoricarpos albus* [sim-fore-ee-KAR-pos AL-bus]) is found mostly in shade, is slow to make a thicket, and is much less frequently seen around prairies. When it is, it associates with big bluestem. In

CORALBERRY (*Symphoricarpos orbiculatus* [sim-fore-ee-KAR-pos or-bick-u-LA-tus]) takes far more heat and drought than the snowberries. It can form large colonies in sandy prairies and is a principal ground cover in western post oak savannas. It is common in southern bur oak savannas, although it tends to get

Diervilla

The dogwood family (Cornaceae) has only a few species in North America, but every state and province possesses at least one. Fossil remains of dogwood have been found in northwest Washington dating sixty-five to thirty-five million years ago. It was growing streamside with hawthorn, plum, sumac, cinquefoil, pine, fir, maple, elm, basswood, ginkgo, and metasequoia. The grasses first appeared in this time frame, about fifty-five million years ago.

Five of our dogwoods have showy white bracts surrounding a center of tiny flowers and bright red fruits. The best known of these are bunchberry (*Cornus canadensis*), which is a north woodland ground cover, and flowering dogwood (*Cornus florida*).

Flowering dogwood, long popular in the nursery trade, is now threatened by a disease that probably came in on Chinese dogwood. Flowering dogwood can grow in prairies from Pennsylvania northeastward, and it was undoubtedly a factor in white oak savannas.

The rest of North America's dogwoods are rhizomatous shrubs or small trees. They have flat-topped clusters of small white flowers and fruit that is dark blue, pale blue, or white. Dogwoods grow in both prairies and woodlands, but they fruit best in savannas or thickets where their flowers and fruits get full sun and their roots are shaded. Fall color is usually pink, mauve, or maroon, although some individuals may turn orange or yellow.

GRAY DOGWOOD (*Cornus racemosa* [KOR-nus ray-see-MO-sah]) is by far the most common dogwood in the northern tallgrass region. It has pale gray stems, and its roots are aggressive. The white fruits, borne on pretty red stalks, are prime bird food, so this shrub gets planted all over by birds; you need to learn what it looks like so you can weed it out where you get more than you want. In some reference books it is called *Cornus foemina* ssp. *racemosa*.

Gray dogwood

ROUGHLEAF DOGWOOD (*Cornus drummondii* [KOR-nus druh-MUN-dee-eye]) is the common dogwood in the southern tallgrass prairie region. It also has gray stems and white fruit on red stalks. It also

Unlike flowering dogwood, GRAY DOGWOOD has clusters of small white flowers that appear in late spring or early summer after the leaves are fully formed.

GRAY DOGWOOD, like roughleaf dogwood, has white fruits with red stems, which are favorites of birds on fall migration.

Roughleaf dogwood

has roots that are too vigorous for a small watered landscape. The leaves are even shaped like those of gray dogwood, but here is the difference: they are rough to the touch.

PALE DOGWOOD (*Cornus obliqua* [KOR-nus o-BLEE-kwah]) is also called swamp dogwood. It is native to wet prairies and wet woods from Ontario to eastern Oklahoma. The fruits are an amazing shade of sky blue.

Pale dogwood

RED OSIER DOGWOOD (*Cornus sericea* ssp. *sericea* [KOR-nus suh-RISS-ee-ah subspecies suh-RISS-ee-ah]) in some books is called *Cornus stolonifera*. Its chief beauty is its winter stems, which are deep to bright red—not maroon or rusty or chocolate like some of the other dogwoods. The fruits are white. Red osier dogwood grows in wet sunny or shady habitats with pale dogwood, Joe-Pye weed, or fowl mannagrass.

Red osier dogwood

The cashew family (Anacardiaceae) is largely centered in the tropics. This is the family that produces such edibles as cashew nuts, mangoes, and pistachios. Members of the family that are native to cooler temperate zones in North America are American smoketree, the sumacs, and poison ivy.

The American smoketree (*Cotinus obovatus*) is a gorgeous small tree that is native to prairie-covered limestone hillsides in the southern Smokies, the Ozarks, and the Texas Hill Country.

The sumacs (*Rhus*) are attractive shrubs or small trees that are native to savannas and prairies. They have brilliant fall color and good wildlife value. In the nineteenth century, sumac was often written as sumach and pronounced SOO-match instead of SOO-mack.

Poison ivy, poison oak, and poison sumac have recently been moved out of *Rhus* into *Toxidendron* to indicate that their fruits are toxic or poisonous to humans (birds adore them) and their sap can cause dermatitis. They are all native to prairies and savannas.

SMOOTH SUMAC has upright clusters of white summer flowers that quickly become chartreuse fruits that later turn orange and finally deep red. Note how the leaflets attach cleanly to the leaf stem with no leafy wings.

SMOOTH SUMAC (*Rhus glabra* [ROOSE GLA-brah]) has smooth shiny leaves and is often called shining sumac. It makes a large multistemmed thicket taller than a man. Found in well-drained prairies, sunny oak savanna edges, cedar glades, and rocky or sandy banks, it is found primarily from the northern tallgrass areas to the northern two-thirds of Texas. In the Southwest, it is almost always in sand, as it gets drought-stressed in clay. Staghorn sumac, *Rhus typhina*, a well-known nursery plant, is probably native on the eastern edge of the northern tallgrass region.

WINGED SUMAC (*Rhus copallinum* var. *latifolia* [ROOSE ko-pah-LIE-num variety la-teh-FOLE-ee-ah]) looks like smooth sumac, except that it has leafy wings running along either side of the leaf stem where the leaflets attach. Also, it can be more treelike, and its roots are less aggressive. It is native to black oak savannas and eastern post oak savannas. Those people living on well-drained limestone in central Texas should use prairie flameleaf sumac (*Rhus lanceolata*).

Winged sumac

Smooth sumac

AROMATIC SUMAC (*Rhus aromatica* [ROOSE err-o-MAT-uh-cah]) looks completely different from the tall sumacs. The leaflets are in threes. The stems form a waist-high shrub that may make a thicket in loose sand, but it is usually not aggressive. The tiny yellow flowers appear before the leaves do, in very early spring, and the orange red fruits ripen in midsummer. The aroma comes from the crushed leaves, and opinion as to its desirability varies considerably. Personally, I like its tangy sharpness.

Aromatic sumac is native to rocky black oak, bur oak, post oak, and live oak savannas as well as prairie ravines throughout the tallgrass regions. The aromatic sumac in the nursery trade that has large hairy leaflets over an inch long is

Aromatic sumac

SKUNKBUSH (*Rhus trilobata* [ROOSE try-lo-BA-tah]) is the western version of aromatic sumac.

Skunkbush

from northern stock, and it is not summer hardy in the south. **Dwarf aromatic sumac** (*Rhus aromatica* var. *arenaria*) is common on dunes around Lake Michigan and can also be found in black oak savannas in Illinois, Indiana, and Ohio.

AROMATIC SUMAC, shown here in fall color, is often visually indistinguishable from skunkbush in Texas and the Great Plains.

The citrus family (Rutaceae) has astringent oils in the leaves that give the members a distinctive and pleasant smell. Members of *Zanthoxylum* (occasionally spelled *Xanthoxylum* but pronounced the same) are often called toothache tree or tickle tongue because chewing the leaves causes the mouth to go numb. Most members of the citrus family are frost tender, but a few hardy species have adapted to winter. Wafer ash and prickly ash are not really ashes, although they do have vaguely ashlike leaves. They are frequently associated with prairies, thickets, and savannas, especially in limestone areas.

WAFER ASH has its seed encased in a large papery wafer.

WAFER ASH (*Ptelea trifoliata* [TEE-lee-ah try-foe-lee-A-tah]), like all species with an immense range, is divided into many subspecies and varieties. I have seen wafer ash in rich moist rocky woodland edges in the Appalachians, on dry sunny limestone riverbanks in central Texas, and along west-facing igneous rock faces of the Rio Grande gorge in northern New Mexico. The only common denominator seems to be that it likes seep-moist but well-drained rocky slopes. Wafer ash jumps from mountain to ravine to bluff to canyon on its march across the country. Those with leathery leaves or leaves that

are downy on the undersides are more drought-tolerant than those with thin, smooth leaves.

Prickly ash

PRICKLY ASH (*Zanthoxylum americanum* [zan-THOX-ee-lum ah-mer-eh-KA-num]) is a tall thicket shrub or small savanna tree that sometimes has small prickles between the leaflets. Indians powdered the inner bark of the tree to treat toothache and powdered the roots to treat gonorrhea. The small dry seed capsules are adored by birds. The seeds germinate wherever the land has been disturbed, and this

tree can be very weedy. Only female trees have seed.

HERCULES CLUB (*Zanthoxylum clava-herculis* [zan-THOX-ee-lum KLAV-ah HUR-kew-liss]) is a welcome tree in thickets, along sunny creek banks, or beneath bur oaks in Texas and Oklahoma. It has leathery leaflets with lots of spines between them and large spines on the trunk. Native west of Hercules club is **tickle tongue** (*Zanthoxylum hirsutum*), which prefers little bluestem prairies to savannas. It has glossy leaves that shine like mirrors in bright sunlight.

Wafer ash

Hercules club

The birch family (Betulaceae) has male and female flowers in catkins on the same tree, like oaks and hickories. The fruit is a nut, as in the hazelnut, or it is a winged nutlet, as in the alders and birches.

AMERICAN HAZELNUT (*Corylus americana* [KOE-ree-lus ah-mer-ee-KAN-ah]) was frequently mentioned in conjunction with bur oak and white oak savannas by early surveyors in the Chicago area. This understory shrub is native to northern tallgrass savannas and to savannas at high elevations in the Ozarks and the Appalachians.

American hazelnut

AMERICAN HAZELNUT has its brown edible nuts wrapped in a velvety leafy package.

BEAKED HAZELNUT (*Corylus cornuta* [KOE-ree-lus kore-NEW-tah]) is native to moist hillsides, acid-soil woodlands, and thickets, mostly west of American hazelnut. Its leaves are less hairy than those of American hazelnut, and the nuts look very different. Leafy bracts, that are loosely wrapped around the American hazelnut, unite to form a tight coating that sticks out beyond the nut as a long funnel-shaped "beak."

Beaked hazelnut

PAPER BIRCH (*Betula papyrifera* [BETCH-oo-lah pa-pea-RIFF-er-ah]), also called canoe birch, is an early-succession tree that paves the way for northern deciduous or conifer forests. Under an existing paper birch, you can grow prairie or savanna species such as rabbitberry, porcupine grass, Junegrass, purple prairie clover, and dwarf dandelion.

Paper birch

The oleaster family (Elaeagnaceae) includes the *Shepherdias* and a native *Elaeagnus*, as well as the exotic and highly invasive Russian olive (*Elaeagnus angustifolia*). Still being planted for ornament and to make wind breaks, Russian olive is taking over the watercourses of the West.

SILVERBERRY (*Elaeagnus commutata* [ee-lee-AG-nus kom-u-TA-tah]) is native to moist but well-drained sites, often in sand. Unlike Russian olive, it has no thorns, and its leaves, which are both fuzzy and shiny, are only twice as long as they are wide. On recently disturbed soil, silverberry may colonize to form a tall, wide thicket. Keep it contained manually until the competition of prairie forbs and grasses confines it to a comfortable amount.

Silverberry

BUFFALOBERRY (*Shepherdia argentea* [shep-HUR-dee-ah ar-jin-TEE-ah]) is a large thorny shrub or a small tree 18 feet tall. Its leaves are arranged in small bunches along the branches with thorns at the ends of the twigs. The fruit is bright red orange (a pretty contrast with the silver leaves) and very tart, making a good jelly. Buffaloberry is native to sloughs, ravines, and low prairies on sandy or fast-draining soils, and to pinyon-juniper scrub in New Mexico.

RABBITBERRY (*Shepherdia canadensis* [shep-HUR-dee-ah kan-ah-DEN-sis]) has no thorns, and its leaves are green above and silvery beneath. Unlike buffaloberry, the waist-high shrubs are either male or female, and only the females produce reddish fruit. Rabbitberry grows in the moist shade of aspens, limber pines, or paper birch.

Rabbitberry

SILVERBERRY has silver berries, firm silvery leaves, and tiny clusters of extremely fragrant yellow four-petaled flowers.

Buffaloberry

The buckthorn family (Rhamnaceae) includes buckthorns and *Ceanothus*. Two shrubs in the genus *Ceanothus* are an essential part of some of our prairies and savannas, but the buckthorns that are most likely to impinge on our prairies and savannas are non-native invasives, the worst being common buckthorn (*Rhamnus cathartica*).

Although NEW JERSEY TEA is a shrub, it grows in tallgrass prairies like a forb.

New Jersey Tea

REDROOT (*Ceanothus herbaceus* [see-a-NO-thus her-buh-SEE-us]) does have red roots, but so does New Jersey tea. Where their ranges overlap, redroot is found in the more alkaline and drought-tolerant habitats. No more herbaceous than New Jersey tea, redroot grows in little bluestem prairies, rocky open woodlands, or on limestone bluffs in the southern Great Plains and central Texas.

Redroot

NEW JERSEY TEA (*Ceanothus americanus* [see-a-NO-thus ah-mer-uh-KAN-us]) is native to mesic well-drained tallgrass prairies and oak savannas. Its woody stems eventually get waist-high, but after a fire, new nonwoody growth sprouts from its humongous woody root burl. The flowers attract butterflies, and the seeds are eaten by turkey and quail. The dried leaves, when steeped, taste somewhat like black tea and were drunk by Native Americans and colonists.

SAVANNA TREES AND THICKET SHRUBS

Species	NORTHWEST Northern Plains Shortgrass Region					NORTHEAST Northern Tallgrass Prairie Region					SOUTHWEST Southern Plains Shortgrass Region					SOUTHEAST Southern Tallgrass Prairie Region				
	Lowland prairie	Mesic prairie	Upland prairie	Sand prairie	Aspen parkland	Lowland prairie	Mesic prairie	Upland prairie	Bur oak savanna	Black oak savanna	Lowland prairie	Mesic prairie	Upland prairie	Sand prairie	Ponderosa savanna	Lowland prairie	Mesic prairie	Upland prairie	Bur oak savanna	Post oak savanna
BEECH FAMILY: OAKS																				
Bur oak	■						■	■	■								■		■	
White oak							■													
Black oak										■										
Northern pin oak								■												
Post oak																			■	■
Escarpment live oak																			■	
PINE FAMILY AND CYPRESS FAMILY																				
Ponderosa pine															■					
Pinyon													■							
Eastern red cedar							■											■		
WILLOW FAMILY																				
Aspen					■	■														
Cottonwood	■											■				■				
ROSE FAMILY: PLUMS AND CHERRIES																				
Chokecherry	■			■	■		■		■						■					■
Pin cherry							■			■										
Sand cherry			■	■				■												
Wild black cherry									■									■		■
Mexican plum																	■	■	■	■
Wild plum	■					■	■	■	■		■							■		
Chickasaw plum															■					
ROSE FAMILY: OTHER ROSE TREES																				
Juneberry								■	■										■	
Low shadblow	■				■				■											
Saskatoon	■	■																		
Downy hawthorn							■		■										■	■
Cockspur hawthorn							■	■	■										■	■
Green hawthorn											■					■			■	■
Iowa crabapple								■										■		
ROSE FAMILY: OTHER ROSE SHRUBS																				
Pasture rose							■	■	■											■
Sunshine rose			■	■													■			■
Western wild rose				■	■						■	■			■					
White prairie rose																		■		
Prairie rose									■										■	■
Meadowsweet	■			■		■														

SAVANNA TREES AND THICKET SHRUBS (cont'd)

Species	NW Lowland prairie	NW Mesic prairie	NW Upland prairie	NW Sand prairie	NW Aspen parkland	NE Lowland prairie	NE Mesic prairie	NE Upland prairie	NE Bur oak savanna	NE Black oak savanna	SW Lowland prairie	SW Mesic prairie	SW Upland prairie	SW Sand prairie	SW Ponderosa savanna	SE Lowland prairie	SE Mesic prairie	SE Upland prairie	SE Bur oak savanna	SE Post oak savanna
HONEYSUCKLE FAMILY																				
Downy arrowwood									■										■	
Southern arrowwood																				■
Nannyberry									■											
Western snowberry	■	■	■		■			■			■	■		■						
Common snowberry				■	■	■		■												
Coralberry																	■		■	■
Diervilla										■										
DOGWOOD FAMILY																				
Gray dogwood						■	■	■												
Roughleaf dogwood											■					■	■	■	■	■
Pale dogwood						■														
Red osier dogwood	■			■											■					
CASHEW FAMILY																				
Smooth sumac								■		■			■			■	■			■
Winged sumac								■		■						■	■			■
Aromatic sumac								■										■	■	■
Dwarf aromatic sumac										■										
Skunkbush		■	■								■		■	■						
CITRUS FAMILY																				
Wafer ash								■			■		■				■			
Prickly ash								■	■											
Hercules club																			■	■
Tickle tongue											■		■						■	
BIRCH FAMILY																				
American hazelnut								■	■										■	
Beaked hazelnut			■						■											
Paper birch	■			■				■												
OLEASTER FAMILY																				
Silverberry		■	■																	
Buffaloberry	■		■												■					
Rabbitberry			■	■																
BUCKTHORN FAMILY																				
New Jersey Tea						■	■	■	■								■			■
Redroot		■										■	■					■	■	

Glossary

annual   a forb or grass that lives one year only.

aspen parkland   savanna where the aspens of boreal forest meet northern prairies.

biennial   a forb that blooms the second year and dies after it sets seed.

black oak savanna   savanna dominated by black oaks growing in sandy soil with sand-loving grasses, forbs, and shrubs that tolerate a half day of shade.

bunchgrass   a grass with nonaggressive rhizomes; the stems and leaves are in a bunch.

bur oak savanna   savanna dominated by bur oaks, usually in rich heavy soil. In the southern tallgrass region, plants marked in the bur oak savanna can be used in escarpment live oak savannas in central Texas.

canopy trees   overstory trees.

conservative   noun or adjective describing a forb or grass that is found in old, undisturbed sites. Usually conservatives have the ability to live for decades if not centuries, but there are some annual conservatives, like fringed gentian and prairie agalinis.

cool season   when the active growth and bloom time of a grass or forb occurs sometime between winter and mid-summer. In southern prairies, cool season grasses and forbs usually set seed by the end of May.

dry prairie   prairie that is on land so sandy, rocky, thin-soiled, or steep that grasses and forbs cannot make a continuous cover. Because of damage from overgrazing, in the western and southern Great Plains dry prairie is the norm where there used to be mesic prairie. Under the pressure of continuous grazing, no nutrients are available to enrich the soil, and present-day rainfall is not sufficient to restore continuous cover.

family   a big group of related plants. For example, grasses are one family, called Poaceae.

forb   a herbaceous plant in a prairie or savanna that dies to the ground each year. Forbs are those plants in prairies that are not grasses, sedges, or rushes, and are not shrubs or trees.

genotype   the unique genetic makeup of any organism. When prairie restorationists urge gardeners to plant local genotypes, they mean the particular plant species that have evolved within a radius of 50 miles of where they will be planted.

genus   a smaller group, tightly related genetically, within a family. For example, grama grasses are a genus within the grass family. The plural of genus is genera.

hedgerow   a thicket arranged in a line by human intervention.

juniper grasslands savannas at low elevations in western mountains or in canyons where shortgrass prairie species mix with short scrubby junipers.

long-term aggressive a term that applies to conservative species that because of superior adaptations, gradually crowd out and outlive other species. Big bluestem is a long-term aggressive.

lowland prairie a swale or low-lying area that collects enough extra water from runoff or snowmelt to support species more moisture-loving than those found in the surrounding mesic prairie.

mesic prairie prairie that is not too wet and not too dry, except in monsoon or drought. The grasses and forbs form a continuous cover. The soil is rich with organic matter. Most level yards that used to be farmland are on soil that is right for a mesic prairie.

mountain parkland savannas on the eastern slopes of the Rockies where they merge with the prairies of the Great Plains. From lowest to highest in elevation are juniper grasslands, pinyon-juniper scrub, ponderosa savanna, and aspen meadows that are similar to those found in Minnesota.

mowable refers to grasses and forbs not harmed if mowed several times a year. Lawn grasses are mowable.

overstory an umbrella of grasses or trees that are taller than the grasses or trees growing underneath.

perennial a forb, grass, or woody plant that lives from several to hundreds of years.

pinyon-juniper scrub savannas at low to medium elevations in western mountains where dry to mesic prairie species mix with pinyon and several species of juniper.

pioneer noun or adjective describing a forb or grass that can handle the adverse conditions of bare or disturbed soil. A pioneer plant usually lives only a few years and then is replaced by conservatives.

ponderosa savanna savannas at medium to high elevations in the Rocky Mountains where mesic prairie species such as little bluestem mix with ponderosa pines.

post oak savanna savanna dominated by post oaks in sandy soil too hot and dry to accommodate black oak dominance.

prairie a grassland of native grasses, sedges, rushes, and forbs with woody plants affecting less than 10 percent of the space, maintained by fire, grazers, and drought, or one mowing a year.

replicated prairie a man-made replica of what the original prairie might have looked like on a specific site.

restored prairie a degraded virgin prairie that has been brought back, as closely as possible, to its original condition. Restoration tools are burning or haying, replanting local genotypes, and removing non-native invasive weeds.

rhizomes thickened horizontal underground stems that sprout aboveground stems and leaves at regular intervals.

sand prairie prairie composed of plants adapted to shifting dunes or deep coarse sand where rainfall washes out nutrients and organic matter. The only dependable moisture is several feet deep where evaporation does not occur.

savanna the transition from forest to prairie. When 10 to 25 percent of a prairie is shaded by trees, it can be called a savanna. Savannas used to be considered a mix of prairie and fire-resistant trees. Research in the mid-1980s by Stephen Packard and a group of volunteers called the North Branchers in the Chicago area discovered that there are special savanna species that exist in the semishade under the trees that are different from the prairie grasses and forbs that grow in full sun between the trees.

savanna tree a tree with thick bark that can survive prairie fires. A savanna tree can be deciduous, such as oak, aspen, and acacia, or coniferous, such as pine or juniper.

short-lived perennial a forb or grass that usually lives more than one year but rarely as long as four years.

short-term aggressive a term that applies to annuals or perennials that spread either by seeds or rhizomes prolifically the first few years after the soil is disturbed, and then dwindle to a small amount or disappear altogether.

shortgrass the signature component of shortgrass prairies, usually 6 to 24 inches in height.

sod grass a grass with rhizomes that travel outward to form a dense network of roots and stems.

species a specific plant within a genus. For example, species in the grama genus are blue grama, black grama, hairy grama, sideoats grama, and so on.

subspecies *see* **variety.**

tallgrass the signature component of tallgrass prairies, usually 3 to 6 feet tall when in flower, sometimes 12 feet in rich, moist conditions.

taproot a main thickened root that goes down like a carrot.

thicket a variety of shrubs growing together surrounded by prairie or wedged between prairie and woodland. Thickets provide nesting and bedrooms for birds and conceal burrows for mammals. Thicket shrubs often bear juicy fruits, like plums, cherries, and blackberries, as well as nuts and dry fruits that can withstand winter temperatures.

understory a collection of shorter grasses, forbs, or woody plants that can grow under the shade of taller grasses, forbs, or canopy trees. An understory cool season grass or forb becomes overtopped by warm season grasses in late summer.

unmowable refers to grasses and forbs that should be cut back or burned only once a year.

upland prairie prairies that are always well drained and are never covered with standing water, even for a minute.

variety a division within a species. Sometimes varieties are called subspecies. Some species have such a wide range with so many isolated pockets of evolution that there are marked genetic differences in leaf size or flower color or downiness or winter hardiness. Because they interbreed, most botanists agree they are not really enough different to be called a separate species, but this is a gray area, and many plants go back and forth between being called a separate species and a variety.

virgin prairie a prairie that has never been plowed.

warm season when the active growth and bloom time of a grass or forb occurs sometime between midsummer and frost. In the southern prairie states, midsummer heat and warm season plants tend to begin in late May.

wet prairie prairie growing in soil that is poorly drained but is not covered with water.

Gardeners' Resources

■ READING AND ORGANIZATIONS FOR EVERYONE

Periodicals

For the latest information on prairie plants, prairie ecology, prairie gardening, and prairie restoration, as well as other kinds of native plant gardening, these magazines are recommended reading for everyone, no matter where you live.

Native Plants is a quarterly publication of the Lady Bird Johnson Wildflower Center. The publication comes with membership in this national organization. Dues are on a sliding scale. Write to 4801 La Crosse Avenue, Austin, TX 78739; phone number: 512-292-4200; e-mail: bassett@wildflower.org.

Ecological Restoration is published three times a year by the Society for Ecological Restoration (SER), headquartered at the University of Wisconsin. To subscribe, write to Journal Division, University of Wisconsin Press, 2537 Daniels St., Madison, WI 53718-6772. This is SER's not-too-technical publication, and it contains the newest in experiments and results on restoring all types of North American habitats. Cost is $29 a year. Texas, Ohio, and Ontario have local chapters. The fax number

in Madison is 800-258-3632; e-mail: bajohnso@facstaff. wisc.edu.

The Prairie Reader is a quarterly newsletter devoted entirely to articles, news, book reviews, and symposia that have to do with preserving, restoring, and planting prairies and prairie gardens. To subscribe, write to PO Box 8227, St. Paul, MN 55108. Cost in 1999 was $18 for individuals and $25 for businesses, libraries, agencies, and institutions.

Wildflower is published quarterly. It covers all of North America's native flora from the Panama Canal to the North Pole. Read by professionals and amateurs alike, *Wildflower* is known for the high quality of its numerous and diverse articles, as well as for its sections on native plant news, book reviews, poetry, and graphic arts. To subscribe, write to Box 336, Postal Station F, Toronto, Ontario, Canada M4Y 2L7; fax: 416-466-6428; www.wildflowermag.com. Cost in 2000 was $35.

Wild Ones Journal is the newsletter for Wild Ones— Natural Landscapers, Ltd. The journal is published bimonthly with good information aimed at the upper Midwest. Chapters now exist in ten states from New York to Oklahoma, and the organization is still expanding. To subscribe, write to PO Box 1274, Appleton, WI

54912; fax: 920-730-8654; e-mail: Woresource@aol.com; www.for-wild.org. Cost in 2000 was $20.

Inspirational Books

A Sand County Almanac by Aldo Leopold, originally published in 1949 and recently reprinted by Oxford University Press, introduced the idea of restoring damaged habitats. This classic inspired a generation of Midwesterners to restore prairies and woodlands, start native plant nurseries, and plant prairie gardens.

Grassland: The History, Biology, Politics, and Promise of the American Prairie by Richard Manning talks about how bison and Native Americans used prairie, how Europeans and Euramericans misused prairie, and how it should be possible both to use and preserve prairie. Sobering and thought-provoking, this 1995 Viking Penguin book is readily available.

Siftings by Jens Jensen was originally published in 1939 and has been reprinted by Johns Hopkins University Press, Baltimore. This book was revolutionary in that it suggested landscaping not just with native plants but with native habitats. Although both the man and the book inspired Frank Lloyd Wright to build houses in natural habitats, the idea of landscaping with nature has not yet gained broad popular acceptance, so this book is still on the cutting edge.

Tallgrass Prairie is a 1993 coffee-table book with gorgeous photography by Frank Oberle and informative text by John Madson. The intent is to show how beautiful prairie can be and why it is worth saving for aesthetic reasons alone. Sponsored by The Nature Conservancy, the book gives phone numbers and directions to many of the best-preserved prairies in North America where the general public is allowed access. Falcon Press, PO Box 1718, Helena, MT 59624, or 800-582-2665.

Where the Sky Began: Land of the Tallgrass Prairie by John Madson is a beautifully written book that combines a very personal view of prairie with the historical impact it had on European settlers. First published in 1982 and reprinted by Iowa State University Press in 1995, this book is easy to find in bookstores.

Organizations

Joining a native plant or wildflower society devoted to preserving and educating the public about native plants will provide you with opportunities to meet people enthusiastic about prairies, prairie restoration, and gardening, to go on field trips with botanists and ecologists, and to get invited to go on plant rescues. The newsletters put out by these organizations are often quite informative. But please note: Because many of these grassroots organizations are run by volunteers, the addresses and phone numbers listed are usually those of the current presidents and can change each year. Instead of listing each organization with the latest address we have, I encourage you to consult the Lady Bird Johnson Wildflower Center or *Wildflower* magazine, both listed here, as they try to update this information annually.

Nature centers and natural history museums are also good places to go to find local experts who can answer questions and give guidance.

For northeastern tallgrass prairies, the Wild Ones, founded by Lorrie Otto, to whom we dedicated this book, is almost essential. See *Wild Ones Journal* above.

There are a number of annual conferences you might wish to attend. Two of the better known ones are the North American Prairie Conference, a four-to-six-day event each midsummer since 1983, and the North American Conference on Savannas and Barrens, an annual fall event since 1994. Since these are held at different sites (usually a university campus) each year and are often sponsored by different organizations, the best way to find out about them is by contacting any of the periodicals listed above.

■ REGIONAL RESOURCES

The best information for creating a prairie garden or doing a restoration is regional. For each region, I have listed one or two field guides I found helpful for identification, a botanical flora for serious keying out, and a few other sources or newsletters.

The nurseries listed here are also a very select group. There are many wonderful nurseries that carry a large number of native plants, and there are numerous landscape architects and designers that use native plants in combinations with non-natives. For a listing that includes these garden-oriented nurseries, consult with the Wild Ones or call the Lady Bird Johnson Wildflower Center. The few listed here are the most hard-core, purist prairie restorationists and nurseries that I happen to know.

Northeast Prairie Quadrant

FIELD GUIDES
Tallgrass Prairie Wildflowers by Douglas Ladd

Northland Wildflowers: The Comprehensive Guide to the Minnesota Region by John B. Moyle and Evelyn W. Moyle

Wildflowers and Weeds by Booth Courtenay and James H. Zimmerman

GRASS GUIDES
Grasses: An Identification Guide by Lauren Brown has line drawings not just of grasses but of sedges, rushes, horsetail, and other plants that might be mistaken for grasses. It also has invasive farm grasses and weedy grasses.

BOTANICAL FLORA
Manual of Vascular Plants of Northeastern United States and Adjacent Canada by Henry A. Gleason and Arthur Cronquist

HANDBOOKS
The Tallgrass Restoration Handbook edited by Stephen Packard and Cornelia F. Mutel

JOURNALS
Wild Ones Journal

The Prairie Reader

CURRICULUM
Prairie Restoration for Wisconsin Schools is put out by SER for teaching students K–12 how to restore a prairie habitat.

CULTURAL GUIDES
Prairie Moon Nursery Catalog has excellent charts for germination, sun, soil type, height, color, bloom time, and other necessary information for the myriad species of seed they carry. See nursery listing under Minnesota.

Restoring the Tallgrass Prairie by Shirley Shirley

HABITAT GUIDE
Plants of the Chicago Region by Floyd Swink and Gerould Wilhelm gives habitat and companion plants for all prairie plants in northeastern Illinois.

RESTORATIONISTS AND NURSERIES
Illinois
Enders Greenhouse
104 Enders Drive
Cherry Valley, IL 61016
815-332-5255 tel & fax

The Natural Garden, Inc.
38W443 Hwy. 64
St. Charles, IL 60175
630-584-0150 tel
630-584-0185 fax

Iowa
Ion Exchange
1878 Old Mission Drive
Harpers Ferry, IA 52146
800-291-2143 tel
319-535-7362 fax
www.ionxchange.com
hbright@means.net

Cindy Hildebrand
57439 250th Street
Ames, IA
515-232-3807

Carl Kurtz
1562 Binford Avenue
St. Anthony, IA 50239
515-477-8364

Southeastern Manitoba
Living Prairie Museum
2795 New Avenue
Winnipeg, Manitoba R3J 3S4
204-832-0167 tel
prairie@mbnet.mb.ca

Prairie Habitats
PO Box 1
Argyle, Manitoba R0C 0B0
John Morgan
204-467-9371 tel
204-467-5004 fax

Prairie Originals
17 Schreyer Crescent
St. Andrews, Manitoba R1A 3A6
Shirley Froehlich
204-338-7517

Michigan

Grow Wild Nursery
PO Box 401
Byron, MI 48418
Theresa Carter

The Native Plant Nursery
PO Box 7841
Ann Arbor, MI 48107
734-994-9592
www.nativeplant.com
plants@nativeplant.com

Nesta Prairie Perennials
1019 Miller Road
Kalamazoo, MI 49001
800-233-5025 tel
616-343-0768 fax

WILDTYPE Native Plants
900 Every Road
Mason, MI 48854
517-244-1140
wildtype@pilot.msu.edu

Minnesota

Prairie Moon Nursery – Route 3, Box 1633
Applied Ecology
4316 45th Avenue South
Minneapolis, MN 55406
Andy Sudbrock
612-724-8916 tel

Prairie Restorations
PO Box 327
Princeton, MN 55371
763-389-4342

Ontario

Native Plant Source
318 Misty Crescent
Kitchener, Ontario N2B 3V5
519-748-2298 tel
519-748-2788 fax

Sweet Grass Gardens
RR#6
Hagersville, Ontario N0A 1H0
519-445-4828 tel
519-445-4826 fax

Wisconsin

Applied Ecological Services, Inc.
(including stormwater systems)/
Taylor Creek Restoration Nurseries
17921 Smith Road
Brodhead, WI 53520
608-897-8641 tel
608-897-8486 fax
AppliedEco@brodnet.com

Bluestem Farm
S5920 Lehman Road
Baraboo, WI 53913
608-356-0179

Country Wetlands Nursery
577 W18549 Janesville Road
Muskego, WI 53150
262-679-8003

Kettle Moraine Natural Landscaping
W996 Birchwood Drive
Campbellsport, WI 53010
920-533-8939

Landscape Environmental Planners
N. 6143 Hilbert Road
Hilbert, WI 54129
Donald Vorpahl
920-853-3729

Little Valley Farm
Route E, Box 544
Snead Creek Road
Spring Green, WI 53588
608-935-3324

Prairie FUTURE Seed Company
PO Box 644
Menomonee Falls, WI 53052
Randy Powers
262-820-0221

Prairie Nursery
PO Box 306
Westfield, WI 53964
Neil Diboll
608-296-3679 tel
608-296-2741 fax
www.prairienursery.com

Prairie Ridge Nursery/CRM Ecosystems, Inc.
9738 Overland Road
Mt. Horeb, WI 53572-2832
Joyce Powers
608-437-5245 tel
608-437-8982 fax
crmprairie@inxpress.com

Prairie Seed Source
PO Box 83
North Lake, WI 53064-0083
Robert Ahrenhoerster
262-673-7166

Reeseville Ridge Nursery
309 South Main Street
Reeseville, WI 53579
920-927-3291

Retzer Nature Center, a service for Waukesha County
262-896-8007

Wehr Nature Center, a service for Franklin, Wisconsin
414-425-8550

Southeast Prairie Quadrant

FIELD GUIDES
Tallgrass Prairie Wildflowers by Douglas Ladd

Wildflowers of Arkansas by Carl G. Hunter

GRASS GUIDES
Common Texas Grasses: An Illustrated Guide by Frank W. Gould has line drawings and scientific descriptions of 523 native and naturalized grasses.

BOTANICAL FLORA
Manual of the Vascular Plants of Texas by Donovan Stewart Correll and Marshall Conring Johnston

Illustrated Flora of North Central Texas by George M. Diggs, Barney L. Lipscomb, and Robert J. O'Kennon

JOURNALS
The Missouri Prairie Journal publishes exclusively for Missouri, but the information is some of the best available for southern tallgrass prairies and post oak savannas. To subscribe, write to the Missouri Prairie Foundation, PO Box 200, Columbia, MO 65205.

CULTURAL GUIDES
Native Texas Plants by Sally Wasowski and Andy Wasowski

Growing Native Wildflowers by Dwight R. Platt and Lorna N. Harder

RESTORATIONISTS AND NURSERIES
Missouri
Missouri Wildflowers Nursery
9814 Pleasant Hill Road
Jefferson City, MO 65109
Merv Wallace
573-496-3492 tel
573-496-3003 fax
mowldflrs@sockets.net

Texas
Bluestem Nursery
4101 Curry Road
John Snowdon
Arlington, TX 76017
817-478-6202

Arnold Davis
6508 Welch
Fort Worth, TX
817-292-5588

Native American Seed
Mail Order Station 127
N. 16th Street
Junction, TX 76849
Bill and Jan Neiman
800-728-4043
www.seedsource.com

Southwest Prairie Quadrant

FIELD GUIDES
Wildflowers of Nebraska and the Great Plains by Jon Farrar

Wildflowers of the Western Plains by Zoe Merriman Kirkpatrick

Roadside Wildflowers of the Southern Great Plains by Craig C. Freeman and Eileen K. Schofield

GRASS GUIDES
A Field Guide to the Grasses of New Mexico, 2d ed., by Kelly W. Allred, has line drawings and scientific

descriptions of 461 grasses native and naturalized to New Mexico, which includes almost all grasses native to the southern Great Plains.

BOTANICAL FLORA
Manual of the Vascular Plants of Texas by Donovan Stewart Correll and Marshall Conring Johnston

Flora of the Great Plains by Great Plains Flora Association

CULTURAL GUIDES
Native Texas Plants by Sally Wasowski and Andy Wasowski

RESTORATIONISTS AND NURSERIES
Texas

    High Plains Natural Gardens
    5202 River Rd.
    Amarillo, TX 79108
    John and Melissa Ladd
    806-383-1705
    ladman@arn.net

    Native American Seed
    Mail Order Station 127
    N. 16th St.
    Junction, TX 76849
    Bill and Jan Neiman
    800-728-4043
    www.seedsource.com

Northwest Prairie Quadrant

FIELD GUIDES
Wildflowers of the Northern Great Plains, 3d ed., by F. R. Vance, J. R. Jowsey, J. S. McLean, and F. A. Switzer

Rocky Mountain Wildflowers, Peterson Field Guide, by John J. Craighead, Frank C. Craighead, and Ray J. Davis

BOTANICAL FLORA
Budd's Flora of the Canadian Prairie Provinces, updated and edited by J. Looman and K. F. Best

Flora of Alberta by E. H. Moss, revised by John G. Packer

CULTURAL GUIDES
Growing a Native Prairie Garden by Regina Prairie Garden Project

RESTORATIONISTS AND NURSERIES
Alberta

    ALCLA Native Plant Restoration Inc.
    3208 Bearspaw Drive N.W.
    Calgary, Alberta T2L 1T2
    Al and Pat Fedkenheuer
    403-282-6516

Saskatchewan

    Blazing Star Wildflower Seed Company
    PO Box 143
    St. Benedict, Saskatchewan S0K 3T0
    306-289-2046 tel & fax

    Miller's Native Plant Nursery
    426 Keeley Way
    Saskatoon, Saskatchewan S7J 4B2
    306-374-4785 tel & fax
    mlmiller@the.link.ca

    Prairie Mountain Roots
    Nora and Don Stewart
    Box 273
    Arcola, Saskatchewan S0C 0G0
    306-455-2513
    Prairiemt@sk.sympatico.ca

Colorado

    Western Native Seed
    PO Box 188
    Coaldale, CO 81222
    719-942-3935 tel
    719-942-3605 fax
    westseed@chaffee.net

South Dakota

    Seeds of the Plains
    HCR 76, Box 21
    Belvidere, SD 57521
    605-344-2265
    lehman@gwtc.net

Bibliography

Abbey, Ruth B. *From Montana's Mountains to Its Prairies*. Lewistown, Mont.: News-Argus Printing, 1997.

Abrams, Marc. "Fire and the Development of Oak Forests." *Wildflower* 12, no. 4 (autumn 1996).

Allred, Kelly W. *A Field Guide to the Grasses of New Mexico*. 2d. ed. Las Cruces: Agricultural Experiment Station, New Mexico State University, 1997.

Ambrose, Stephen E. *Undaunted Courage*. New York: Simon & Schuster, 1996.

Amos, Bonnie G., and Frederick R. Gehlback, eds. *Edwards Plateau Vegetation: Plant Ecological Studies in Central Texas*. Waco, Tex.: Baylor University Press, 1988.

Apfelbaum, Steven I., et al. *Prairie Crossing Project: Attaining Water Quality and Stormwater Management Goals in a Conservation Development*. Applied Ecological Services, Inc., 17921 Smith Rd., PO Box 256, Brodhead WI 53520.

———. "Prescribed Burning: What to Expect and Why" and "Prairie Restorations: What to Expect and Why." Applied Ecological Services, Inc., 17921 Smith Rd., PO Box 256, Brodhead WI 53520.

Arnett, Ross H., Jr., and Richard L. Jacques Jr. *Simon & Schuster's Guide to Insects*. New York: Simon & Schuster, 1981.

"Backyard Botanist." *Iridis*, Quarterly Newsletter of the Botanical Research Institute of Texas 9, no. 3 (1998).

Bailey, L. H. *Manual of Cultivated Plants*. Rev. ed. New York: Macmillan Publishing Company, 1949.

Barbour, Michael G., and William Dwight Billings, eds. *North American Terrestrial Vegetation*. New York: Cambridge University Press, 1988.

Barloga, Richard, "Preliminary Vegetation Inventories for Various Prairies in Walworth and Waukesha Counties, Wisconsin. Unpublished. May 1982 to October 1995.

Barr, Claude A. *Jewels of the Plains: Wildflowers of the Great Plains Grasslands and Hills*. Minneapolis: University of Minnesota Press, 1983.

Benson, Maxine, ed. *From Pittsburgh to the Rocky Mountains: Major Stephen Long's Expedition 1819–1820*. Golden, Colo.: Fulcrum, 1988.

Bones, Jim. "Seed Balls." *Light Writings*. http://qqq.seedballs.com. 1996.

Boon, Bill, and Harlan Groe. *Nature's Heartland: Native Plant Communities of the Great Plains*. Ames: Iowa State University Press, 1990.

Boyce, Mark S., and Alan Haney, eds. *Ecosystem Management: Applications for Sustainable Forest and Wildlife Resources*. New Haven: Yale University Press, 1997.

Britton, Nathaniel Lord, and Hon. Addison Brown. *An Illustrated Flora of the Northern United States and Canada*. Vols. 2 and 3. 1913. Reprint, New York: Dover Publications, 1970.

Brown, Lauren. *Grasses: An Identification Guide.* New York: Houghton Mifflin Company, 1979.

———. *Grasslands.* New York: Alfred A. Knopf, 1985.

Brown, Melvin L., and Russell G. Brown. *Herbaceous Plants of Maryland.* Baltimore: Port City Press, 1984.

Burrell, Colston. "Landscape Designer and Visionary— Nature, Art, Architecture: The Philosophy and Work of Jens Jensen." *Wildflower* 8, no. 3 (summer 1992).

———. "Redesigning the (North) American Front Yard." *Wildflower* 13, no. 2 (spring 1997).

Cheatham, Scooter, and Marshall C. Johnston. *The Useful Wild Plants of Texas, the Southeastern and Southwestern United States, the Southern Plains, and Northern Mexico.* Vol. 1. Useful Wild Plants, Inc., 2612 Sweeney Lane, Austin, Texas 78723. 1995.

Clancy, Paul. "Can Trees Put a Lid on Global Warming?" *Nature Conservancy Magazine,* Nov./Dec. 1998.

Clewell, Andre F. *Guide to the Vascular Plants of the Florida Panhandle.* Tallahassee: Florida State University Press, 1988.

Coffin, Barbara, and Lee Pfannmuller, eds. *Minnesota's Endangered Flora and Fauna.* Minneapolis: University of Minnesota Press, 1988.

Correll, Donovan Stewart, and Marshall Conring Johnston. *Manual of the Vascular Plants of Texas.* University of Texas at Dallas, Box 688, Richardson, TX 75080. 1979.

Courtenay, Booth, and James H. Zimmerman. *Wildflowers and Weeds: A Field Guide in Full Color.* New York: Simon & Schuster, 1992.

Craighead, John J., Frank C. Craighead Jr., and Ray J. Davis. *Rocky Mountain Wildflowers.* New York: Houghton Mifflin Company, 1963.

Curtis, John T. *The Vegetation of Wisconsin: An Ordination of Plant Communities.* Madison: University of Wisconsin Press, 1971.

Daniels, Stevie. *The Wild Lawn Handbook: Alternatives to the Traditional Front Lawn.* New York: Macmillan, 1995.

Darland, R. W., and J. E. Weaver. *Yields and Consumption of Forage in Three Pasture-types: An Ecological Analysis.* University of Nebraska Conservation and Survey Division, Nebraska Conservation Bulletin no. 27, Feb. 1945.

Davis, Linda W. *Weed Seeds of the Great Plains: A Handbook for Identification.* Lawrence: University Press of Kansas, 1993.

Denman, Norris. "A Sense of Prairies." *Wildflower* 12, no. 2 (spring 1996).

Diboll, Neil. "Ecotypic Variation and Genetic Diversity in Plants: Is There Right and Wrong?" Unpublished notes for conference, Prairie Nursery, PO Box 306, Westfield, WI 53964. 1997.

Diggs, George M., Barney L. Lipscomb, and Robert J. O'Kennon. *Shinner's & Mahler's Illustrated Flora of North Central Texas.* Fort Worth: Botanical Research Institute of Texas, 1999.

Duncan, Wilbur H., and Marion B. Duncan. *Trees of the Southeastern United States.* Athens: University of Georgia Press, 1988.

Engle, David M. "Oak Ecology." Abstract, Division of Agricultural Sciences and Natural Resources, Oklahoma State University, Stillwater, OK 74078. 1997.

Enquist, Marshall. *Wildflowers of the Texas Hill Country.* Austin, Tex.: Lone Star Botanical, 1987.

Farrar, Jon. *Wildflowers of Nebraska and the Great Plains.* NEBRASKAland Magazine, Nebraska Parks and Game Commission, PO Box 30370, Lincoln, NE 68503. 1990.

Fassett, Norman C. *Grasses of Wisconsin.* Madison: University of Wisconsin Press, 1951.

———. *Spring Flora of Wisconsin.* Rev. by Olive Thomsen. Madison: University of Wisconsin Press, 1976.

Flora of North America Editorial Committee. *Flora of North America North of Mexico.* Vol. 1, *Introduction.* New York: Oxford University Press, 1993.

Flores, Dan. *Caprock Canyonlands: Journeys into the Heart of the Southern Plains.* Austin: University of Texas Press, 1990.

Foote, Leonard E., and Samuel B. Jones Jr. *Native Shrubs and Woody Vines of the Southeast.* Portland, Oreg.: Timber Press, 1989.

Fralish, James S., et al., eds. *Proceedings of the North American Conference on Barrens and Savannas.* Illinois State University, Normal, Ill., 1994.

Freeman, Craig C., and Eileen K. Schofield. *Roadside Wildflowers of the Southern Great Plains.* Lawrence: University Press of Kansas, 1991.

Galatowitsch, Susan M., and Arnold G. Van der Valk. *Restoring Prairie Wetlands.* Ames: Iowa State University Press, 1994.

Gavine, Ken. *Natural Invaders: Invasive Plants in Ontario.* Federation of Ontario Naturalists. Don Mills, Ontario, Canada M3B 2W8.

Gilmore, Melvin R. *Uses of Plants by the Indians of the Missouri River Region.* 1914. Reprint, Lincoln: University of Nebraska Press, 1991.

Gleason, Henry A., and Arthur Cronquist. *Manual of Vascular Plants of Northeastern United States and Adjacent Canada,* 2d ed. Bronx, N.Y.: New York Botanical Garden, 1991.

Gordon, Robert B. *The Natural Vegetation of Ohio in Pioneer Days.* Columbus: Ohio State University, 1969.

Gould, Frank W. *Grass Systematics.* New York: McGraw-Hill Book Company, 1968.

———. *Grasses of the Southwestern United States.* Tucson: University of Arizona Press, 1993.

Gould, Frank W., and Thadis W. Box. *Grasses of the Texas Coastal Bend.* College Station: Texas A&M University Press, 1965.

Great Plains Flora Association. *Flora of the Great Plains.* Lawrence: University Press of Kansas, 1986.

Hatch, Stephan L., Kancheepuram N. Ghandi, and Larry E. Brow. *Checklist of the Vascular Plants of Texas.* College Station: Texas A&M University Press, 1990.

Hatch, Stephan L., and Jennifer Pluhar. *Texas Range Plants.* College Station: Texas A&M University Press, 1993.

Havinga, Donna, and Jean-Marc Daigle. *Restoring Nature's Place.* Ecological Outlook Consulting and the Ontario Parks Association, North York, Ontario, Canada M3C 3C6. 1996.

Henderson, Carrol L. *Landscaping for Wildlife.* St. Paul: Minnesota Department of Natural Resources, 1987.

Hickman, James C., ed. *The Jepson Manual: Higher Plants of California.* Los Angeles: University of California Press, 1993.

Hulten, Eric. *Flora of Alaska and Neighboring Territories.* Stanford, Calif.: Stanford University Press, 1968.

Hunter, Carl G. *Wildflowers of Arkansas.* 2d ed. The Ozark Society Foundation, PO Box 3503, Little Rock, AR 72203. 1988.

Iowa Prairie Network News, Iowa Prairie Network, spring edition, 1998.

Jensen, Jens. *Siftings.* 1939, Baltimore: Johns Hopkins University Press, 1990.

Jensen, Peter. "Dr. John Weaver—The Man." Unpublished, 5 pages, and personal conservation, September 12, 1997, Lincoln, Nebr.

Joern, Anthony, and Kathleen H. Keeler, eds. *The Changing Prairie: North American Grasslands.* New York: Oxford University Press, 1995.

Johnson, Lorraine. *Grow Wild: Low-Maintenance Sure-Success Distinctive Gardening with Native Plants.* Golden, Colo.: Fulcrum Publishing, 1998.

Johnson, Stephen. "The Towering Cordgrass of the Prairie." *Wildflower* 13, no. 4 (autumn 1997).

Kartesz, John T., and C. A. Meacham. *Digital Floristic Synthesis of North America North of Mexico.* Chapel Hill: Biota of North America Program of the North Carolina Botanical Garden, 1999.

Kearney, Thomas H., and Robert H. Peebles. *Arizona Flora.* Berkeley and Los Angeles, Calif.: University of California Press, 1960.

Kindscher, Kelly. *Edible Wild Plants of the Prairie.* Lawrence: University Press of Kansas, 1987.

———. *Medicinal Wild Plants of the Prairie.* Lawrence: University Press of Kansas, 1992.

Kirkpatrick, Zone Merriman. *Wildflowers of the Western Plains.* Austin: University of Texas Press, 1992.

Kleine, Adele. "Healing the Prairie: How Mycorrhizal Fungi Help Soil Restoration." *Wildflower* 14, no. 4 (autumn 1998).

Kurten, Bjorn. *Before the Indians.* New York: Columbia University Press, 1988.

Ladd, Douglas. "Reexamination of the Role of Fire in Missouri Oak Woodlands." Pages 67–80 in *Proceedings of the Oak Woods Management Workshop,* Eastern Illinois University, Charleston, Ill., 1991.

Ladd, Douglas. *Tallgrass Prairie Wildflowers.* Helena and Billings, Mont.: Falcon Press Publishing Co., 1995.

Lake, Stuart N. *Wyatt Earp, Frontier Marshal.* New York: Pocket Books, 1994.

Lamb, Larry. "Attracting Animal Life to Your Garden." Handout, University of Waterloo, Waterloo, Ontario, Canada. Revised 1995.

Lamb, Larry, and Gail Rhynard. *Plants of Carolinian Canada.* Federation of Ontario Naturalists, 355 Lesmill Road, Don Mills, Ontario M3B 2W8. 1994.

Lawyer, John. "Commercialization of Native Fruit Production." *Wildflower* 14, no. 3 (summer 1998).

Leach, Mark K., and Laurel Ross, eds. *Midwest Oak Ecosystem Recovery Plan: A Call to Action.* Midwest Oak Savanna and Woodland Ecosystems Conference, Springfield, Mo., Sept. 1995.

Leopold, Aldo. *A Sand County Almanac.* New York: Oxford University Press, 1960.

Lipscomb, Barney L., and George M. Diggs, "The Use of Animal-Dispersed Seeds and Fruits in Forensic Botany." Abstract in *SIDA* 18, no. 1 (Oct. 1998).

Living in the Edge. Proceedings of the North American Conference on Savannas and Barrens, Illinois State University, Normal, Ill., 1994.

Looman, J., and K. F. Best. *Budd's Flora of the Canadian Prairie Provinces.* Ottawa: Agriculture Canada, Canada Communication Group, 1987.

Lunn, Elizabeth T. *Plants of the Illinois Dunesland.* Illinois Dunesland Preservation Society, 1982.

Lyon, Thomas J., ed. *This Incomperable Lande: A Book of American Nature Writing.* Boston: Houghton Mifflin, 1989.

Madson, John. *Tallgrass Prairie.* Helena and Billings, Mont.: Falcon Press Publishing Co., 1993.

Madson, John, *Where the Sky Began: Land of the Tallgrass Prairie.* Ames: Iowa State University Press, 1995.

Mahler, William F. *Shinners' Manual of the North Central Texas Flora.* Dallas: Botanical Research Institute of Texas, 1988.

Manning, Richard. *Grassland: The History, Biology, Politics, and Promise of the American Prairie.* New York: Viking Penguin, 1995.

Marinelli, Janet, ed. *Going Native: Biodiversity in Our Own Backyards.* Brooklyn Botanic Garden Handbook no. 140, 1000 Washington Avenue, Brooklyn, NY 11225. 1994.

Marinelli, Janet, and John M. Randall. *Invasive Plants: Weeds of the Global Garden*. Brooklyn Botanic Garden Handbook no. 149, 1000 Washington Avenue, Brooklyn, NY 11225. 1996.

McArdle, Thomas, and Jedd Anderson. "St. Charles Wetland Mitigation Bank." *Land and Water Magazine* Jan./Feb. 1995.

McCarty, J. Kenneth. "The Ozarks of Henry Rowe Schoolcraft." *Ozarks Watch* (Southwest Missouri State University) 6, nos. 1 and 2 (1992).

McKelvey, Susan Delano. *Botanical Exploration of the Trans-Mississippi West 1790–1850*. Corvallis: Oregon State University Press, 1991.

McPherson, Guy R. *Ecology and Management of North American Savannas*. Tucson: University of Arizona Press, 1997.

Menon, Shanti. "Shoe Time." *Discover* 20, no. 1: 26–27 (Jan. 1999).

Missouri Prairie Foundation. "Prairie Natural Areas." *Missouri Prairie Journal* 18, no. 3 (summer 1997).

Mohlenbrock, Robert H. *Guide to the Vascular Flora of Illinois*. Carbondale: Southern Illinois University, 1986.

Morgan, John P., Douglas R. Collicutt, and Jacqueline D. Thompson. *Restoring Canada's Native Prairies*. Prairie Habitats, Argyle, Manitoba, Canada R0C 0B0. 1995.

Moyle, John B., and Evelyn W. Moyle. *Northland Wildflowers: The Comprehensive Guide to the Minnesota Region*. Rev. ed. Minneapolis: University of Minnesota Press, 2001.

Munz, Philip A. *A California Flora and Supplement*. Los Angeles: University of California Press, 1959.

National Audubon Society. *Field Guide to North American Insects and Spiders*. New York: Alfred A. Knopf, 1995.

———. *Field Guide to North American Reptiles and Amphibians*. New York: Alfred A. Knopf, 1974.

———. *Field Guide to North American Birds*. New York: Alfred A. Knopf, 1977.

Native Plant Society of Texas, "The Llano Estacado/Southern High Plains and Its Many Ecosystems." 1998 Symposium Proceedings, NPSOT, PO Box 891, Georgetown, TX 78627.

Nelson, Paul. "Quantum Leap: Back to a Hidden Paradise." *Missouri Resource Review* 9, no. 2 (fall 1992).

News from the Shack, Newsletter of the Aldo Leopold Foundation, spring 1997, E12919 Levee Rd., Baraboo, WI 53913.

Nigh, Tim. "The Forests Prior to European Settlement." Missouri Department of Conservation, PO Box 180, Jefferson City, MO 65102-0180.

Otto, Lorrie. "Growing with My Yard." *Wildflower* 10, no. 1 (winter 1994).

Owensby, Clenton E. *Kansas Prairie Wildflowers*. Ames: Iowa State University Press, 1980.

Ownbey, Gerald B., and Thomas Morley. *Vascular Plants of Minnesota*. Minneapolis: University of Minnesota Press, 1991.

Packard, Stephen, and Cornelia F. Mutel, eds. *The Tallgrass Restoration Handbook*. Washington D.C.: Island Press, 1997.

Parker, Ken. "1998 Native North American Plant and Reference Guide." Sweet Grass Gardens, Hagersville, Ontario, Canada N0A 1H0. 1998

Platt, Dwight R., and Lorna N. Harder. *Growing Native Wildflowers*. Newton, Kan.: Kansas Wildflower Society, c/o Kauffman Museum, 1991.

Prairie Reader, various articles from fall 1997, winter 1997, spring 1997, and spring 1998 issues. Word Rustlers/Liatris Productions, St. Paul, Minn.

Prater, Bayliss, and Kathleen McNeal. *Full Circle: Restoring Your Habitat to Wilderness*. Last Resort Press, 2359 Miller Road, Willard, Ohio 44890. 1993.

Radford, Albert E., Harry E. Ahles, and C. Ritchie Bell. *Manual of the Vascular Flora of the Carolinas*. Chapel Hill: University of North Carolina Press, 1987.

Rappaport, Bret. "To Mow or Grow?" *Wildflower* 12, no. 2 (spring 1996).

Regina Prairie Garden Project. *Growing a Native Prairie Garden*. Regina: Royal Saskatchewan Museum, 1996.

Roalson, Eric H., and Kelly W. Allred. *A Working Index of New Mexico Vascular Plant Names*. Ed. 1. Agricultural Experiment Station, Research Report 702, New Mexico State University, Las Cruces, N.Mex., 1995.

Robinson, Sara, "Prehistoric Footwear in Step with Style, New Study Shows," *Dallas Morning News*, July 3, 1998.

Rodger, Lindsay. "All Fired Up about Ontario's Tallgrass." *Wildflower* 14, no. 3 (summer 1998).

Runkel, Sylvan T., and Dean M. Roosa. *Wildflowers of the Tallgrass Prairie: The Upper Midwest*. Ames: Iowa State University Press, 1989.

Sachse, Nancy D. *A Thousand Ages*. University of Wisconsin Arboretum, 1974.

Sargent, Charles Sprague. *Manual of the Trees of North America*. 2d corrected ed., in 2 vols., 1922. Reprint, New York: Dover Publications, 1961.

Savory, Allan. *Holistic Resource Management*. Washington D.C.: Island Press, 1988.

Shirley, Shirley. *Restoring the Tallgrass Prairie*. Iowa City: University of Iowa Press, 1994.

Sierra Club Board of Directors. "Sierra Club Policy: Grazing on the Public Lands." Adopted 9-12-92, reprinted in *Rio Grande Sierran* Jan./Feb. 1998.

Simpson, Benny J. *A Field Guide to Texas Trees*. Houston, Tex.: Gulf Publishing, 1988.

Smith, Welby R. *Orchids of Minnesota*. Minneapolis: University of Minnesota Press, 1993.

Society for Ecological Restoration. "Sources for Native Ontario Plant Materials: 1997." Ontario, Canada.

Spencer, LeAnn. "Creating a Prairie Out of Arsenal Land." *Dallas Morning News*, Nov. 4, 1995, sec. C, p. 2.

Stevens, William K. *Miracle under the Oaks, The Revival of Nature in America*. New York: Pocket Books, 1995.

Stevens, William K. "Restored Wetlands Could Ease Threat of Mississippi Floods." *New York Times*, Aug. 8, 1995, Science Times.

Stubbendieck, James, Stephan L. Hatch, et al. *North American Range Plants*. 5th ed. Lincoln: University of Nebraska, 1997.

Stupka, Arthur. *Wildflowers in Color*. New York: Harper and Row, 1965.

Swink, Floyd, and Gerould Wilhelm. *Plants of the Chicago Region*, 4th ed. Lisle, Ill.: Indiana Academy of Science, Morton Arboretum, 1994.

Taylor, Constance E. S. *Keys to the Asteraceae of Oklahoma*. Durant: Southeastern Oklahoma State University Herbarium, 1997.

Taylor, John, and Constance E. S. Taylor. *An Annotated List of the Ferns, Fern Allies, Gymnosperms and Flowering Plants of Oklahoma*. Durant: Southeastern Oklahoma State University, 1994.

———. Notes on escarpment live oak, personal correspondence, Durant, Okla., Sept. 30, 1998.

Tester, John R. *Minnesota's Natural Heritage: An Ecological Perspective*. Minneapolis: University of Minnesota Press, 1995.

Thompson, Janette R. *Prairies, Forest, and Wetlands: The Restoration of Natural Landscape Communities in Iowa*. Iowa City: University of Iowa Press, 1992.

Towne, Gene. Personal communication and fax on bison and cattle comparative grazing studies. Kansas State University/Konza Prairie, egtowne@ksu.edu, Jan. 1999.

Tull, Delena. *A Practical Guide to Edible and Useful Plants*. Austin: Texas Monthly Press, 1987.

Tyrl, R. J., S. C. Barber, P. Buck, P. Folley, L. K. Magrath, C. E. S. Taylor, and R. A. Thompson. Oklahoma Flora Editorial Committee, 1999.

Ubelaker, John. Personal communication about hemiparasitism, Dallas, Southern Methodist University, October 2000.

U.S. Department of Agriculture. *Common Weeds of the United States*. New York: Dover Publications, 1971.

Vance, F. R., J. R. Jowsey, J. S. McLean, and F. A. Switzer. *Wildflowers of the Northern Great Plains*. 3d ed. Minneapolis: University of Minnesota Press, 1999.

Van Duch, Margaret. "Prairie Project Honors Pioneers, Helps Kids Learn." *Chicago Tribune*, Apr. 17, 1998.

Volkert, Bill. "The Flora and Fauna of Birchwood Lake." Report prepared for the State of Wisconsin Department of Natural Resources, Horicon Wis., and personal communication, autumn 1998.

Walton, Robert G. "Noxious Weeds: A Threat to Northern New Mexico 1998." Newspaper insert distributed throughout state of New Mexico.

Wasowski, Sally. "Where Have All the Grasses Gone." *Wildflower* 14, no. 1 (winter 1998).

Wasowski, Sally, and Andy Wasowski. *Native Texas Gardens*. Houston, Tex.: Gulf Publishing, 1997.

———. *Native Texas Plants: Landscaping Region by Region*. Houston, Tex.: Gulf Publishing, 1997.

Waters, Charles. *Weed Control without Poisons*. Metairie, La.: Acres USA, 1996.

Weaver, J. E. *North American Prairie*. Lincoln, Nebr.: Johnsen Publishing, 1954.

Weaver, J. E. *Prairie Plants and Their Environment: A Fifty-Year Study in the Midwest*. Lincoln: University of Nebraska Press, 1968.

Weaver, J. E., and F. W. Albertson. "Deterioration of Grassland from Stability to Denudation with Decrease in Soil Moisture." *Botanical Gazette* 101, no. 3 (Mar. 1940).

Weaver, J. E., and R. W. Darland. "Changes in Vegetation and Production of Forage Resulting from Grazing Lowland Prairie." *Ecology* 29, no. 1 (Jan. 1948).

Weaver, J. E., and W. W. Hansen. *Regeneration of Native Midwestern Pastures under Protection*. Nebraska Conservation Bulletin no. 23, June 1941.

Weaver, J. E., and John W. Voigt. *Monolith Method of Root-Sampling in Studies on Succession and Degeneration*. Reprinted for private circulation from the *Botanical Gazette* 111, no. 3 (Mar. 1950).

Weber, William A. *Colorado Flora: Eastern Slope*. Niwot, Colo.: University Press of Colorado, 1990.

Wild Ones Handbook: A Voice for the Natural Landscaping Movement. PO Box 23576, Milwaukee, WI 53223-0576. 1997.

Wild Ones Journal, various articles from Nov./Dec. 1997, Mar./Apr. 1998, and July/Aug. 1998 issues. Journal of The Wild Ones, Ltd., Milwaukee, Wis.

Wildflower 10, no. 4 (autumn 1994), entire issue devoted to oak savannas.

Wooten, E. O., and Paul C. Standley. *Flora of New Mexico*. 1915. Reprints of US-Floras, vol. 7, ed. J. Cramer. New York: Stechert-Hafner Service Agency, 1972.

Wovcha, Daniel S., Barbara C. Delaney, and Gerda E. Nordquist. *Minnesota's St. Croix River Valley and Anoka Sandplain*. Minneapolis: University of Minnesota Press, 1995.

Yanovsky, Elias. *Food Plants of the North American Indians*. Misc. Publication 237, U.S. Department of Agriculture, Washington, D.C.

Index

Kuhnia eupatorioides, 224
Kummerowia striata, 198

ladies' tobacco, 182, 192
ladies' tresses, Great Plains, 153, 188
  nodding, 153, **153,** 188
  slender, 153, 188
ladyslipper, 99
  large yellow, 152, **152,** 188
  showy, 152
  small white, 152, 188
Lamb, Larry, 3, 17, 22
  plan, **16**
Landscape Environmental Planners
    (Wisconsin), 17
larkspur, praire, 167, 190
larval plants, 88
Lasater, Mollie and Garland, 19
Latin names, 7
  pronouncing, 8
  why necessary, 8
  why they change, 8
Leach, Mark, 62
leadplant, 198, **198,** 232
Lehman, Rick, **29**
Leonard, Lula Schaefer, 45
Leopold, Aldo, 67, 93
lespedeza, Japanese, 198
Lespedeza capitata, 199
  cuneata, 198
lettuce, glaucous white, 217, **217,** 233
Leymus cinereus, 131
Liatris, 222
  aspera, 222
  ligulistylis, 222
  mucronata, 223
  punctata, 223
  pycnostachya, 223
  scariosa var. *nieuwlandii*, 222
  spicata, 223
Library at Hales Corners (Wisconsin),
    35
lichen, **70**
licorice, wild, 202, **202,** 232
Lilium michiganense, 155
  philadelphicum var. *andinum*, 154
  supurbum, 155
lily, mariposa, 155
  Michigan, 155, 188
  sego, 155, 188
  Turks cap, 155
  western red, 154–55, **154,** 188
lily family, 99
Lincoln Elementary School, 34, **97**
Linum berlandieri, 179
  compactum, 179
  grandiflorum, 179

lewisii, 179
  perenne, 179
  rigidum, 179
  usitatissimum, 179
Lithophragma parviflorum, 171
Lithospermum canescens, 170
  caroliniense, 170
  incisum, 170
Living Prairie Museum (Manitoba), 41
loam, clay, 99
  sandy, 99
lobelia, great blue, **44,** 173, 190
  palespike, 173, **173,** 190
Lobelia cardinalis, 173
  siphilitica, 173
  spicata, 173
  splendens, 173
locoweed, 70
  purple, 151, 188
Lomatium ambiguum, 57
  foeniculaceum, 169
Long Grove (Illinois), 27, **27**
Longbrake, Pete, 77
Lonicera albiflora, 239
loosestrife, fringed, 159, 189
  narrowleaf, 159, **159,** 189
  whorled, 159, 189
Lootens, Bob, 37
lousewort, swamp, 143
lovegrass, purple, 58
  sand, 58
lowland grasses, 138
lowland prairies, 41
lupine, 240
  silvery, **11,** 148, **148,** 188
  sundial, 148, 188
Lupinus argenteus, 148
  perennis, 148
  texensis, 148
Lygodesmia juncea, 56
Lysimachia ciliata, 159
  quadriflora, 159
  quadrifolia, 159

MacKinnon, Hensel, and Associates
    (Ontario), 35
Maddux, Roger, 97
Madson, John, 147
Mahonia trifoliolata, 239
Maianthemum racemosum ssp. *race-
    mosum,* **91**
  stellatum, 238
mallow, 180
  glade, 181, 191
Malus ioensis, 245
  ioensis var. *texana*, 245
mammals, grazing, 73, 76

mannagrass, fowl, 139, **139,** 145
maps, quadrant, 2
  range, explanation of, 117
marbleseed, 170, 190
marshmallow, 180
mayapple, 239
McKean, Helen, 18
  plan, **20**
meadowrue, purple, 166
  tall, 166, **166,** 190
meadowsweet, 247, **247,** 258
medicinal plants, 88
Melica bulbosa, 136
  nitens, 136
  porteri, 136
melicgrass, Porter's, 136, 145
  tall, 136, **136,** 145
Mequon Unitarian Church
    (Wisconsin), 35
mercury, three-seeded, 204
mesic prairie, 45, **46,** 47, **47,** 49, **50,** 66,
    261
Mexican hat, **61,** 211, 233
Microseris cuspidata, 186
midgrasses, 6
milkvetch, Canadian, 148, **148,** 188
milkweed, 99
  butterfly, 207, **207,** 232
  common, 209, 233
  dwarf, 207, 233
  green, 206, **206,** 232
  orange butterfly, **28**
  poke, 207, 233
  purple, 208, **208,** 233
  showy, 209, 233
  spider, 206
  Sullivant's, 209, 233
  swamp, **20, 44,** 208, 233
  whorled, 207, 233
Mima mounds, 77
Mimosa nuttallii, 151
Minnehaha Falls City Park
    (Minnesota), **59**
Minnesota Landscape Arboretum, 47,
    60
Minnesota Native Plant Society, **106**
Minnesota Valley National Wildlife
    Refuge, **106**
mint, 99, 194
  common mountain, **22,** 194, **194,**
    232
  lemon, **61**
Missouri Botanical Garden, 50, **50, 85**
Monarda, 239
  citriodora, 195
  fistulosa, 194
  punctata, 195

SALLY WASOWSKI is a nationally respected landscape designer and one of the country's leading authorities on landscaping with native plants. She was featured in *Southern Living* as one of the Top Ten Gardeners in the South and served as one of the experts for *Wild Garden*'s "Ask a Native Plant Expert." As a freelance writer, she has published most recently in *Wildflower*, *Perennials*, and *A Nature Company Guide: Natural Gardening*.

ANDY WASOWSKI is a freelance writer and photographer specializing in gardening and environmental issues. His work has appeared in *Sierra*, *The American Gardener*, *Country America*, *E Magazine*, *National Gardening*, the *Dallas Morning News*, Time-Life Books, and Brooklyn Botanic Gardens handbooks. He is a commentator for the National Public Radio programs "Living on Earth" and "The Cultivated Gardener."

The Wasowskis have coauthored eight books on native landscaping, including *Native Texas Plants*, *Gardening with Native Plants of the South*, *Native Landscaping from El Paso to L.A.*, *The Landscaping Revolution*, and *Building inside Nature's Envelope*.